The
Lumberjacks

The Lumberjacks

Donald MacKay

NATURAL HERITAGE/NATURAL HISTORY INC.

TORONTO

Published by Natural Heritage/Natural History Inc.
P.O. Box 95, Station O, Toronto, Ontario M4A 2M8

Third Printing, September 1998
Printed and bound in Canada by Hignell Printing Limited

Cover design by Blanche Hamill, Norton Hamill Design

Cover photo courtesy National Archives of Canada, PA12605
Frontispiece photo courtesy the publisher's personal collection.

Canadian Cataloguing in Publication Data

Mackay, Donald, 1925-
    The Lumberjacks

Includes bibliographical references and index.
ISBN 1-896219-46-2

1. Logging–Canada–History. 2. Loggers–Canada–Biography. I. Title.

SD538.3.C2M32 1998   634.9'8'0971   C98-931866-4

THE CANADA COUNCIL | LE CONSEIL DES ARTS
FOR THE ARTS | DU CANADA
SINCE 1957 | DEPUIS 1957

Natural Heritage/Natural History Inc. acknowledges the support received for its
publishing program from the Canada Council Block Grant Program. We also
acknowledge with gratitude the assistance of the Association for the Export of
Canadian Books, Ottawa.

To my family: Barbara, Dorothy, Marina, Karen, with love

ACKNOWLEDGEMENTS

An interest on the part of several organizations and many individuals in preserving the oral history of the lumberjacks has made this book possible.

I would like to acknowledge the special assistance of the Abitibi Paper Company Ltd., Consolidated-Bathurst Limited, the James Mac-laren Company Limited, The Price Company Limited, and the Reed Paper Group. For their interest and support, I am grateful to J. G. MacLeod and Donald Farrell of Montreal, Paul Masterson and K. D. Greaves of Toronto, and J. F. Maclaren of Buckingham, Quebec.

The Explorations Program of the Canada Council, Ottawa, provided a travel grant.

Many who contributed recollections and photographs are, by the nature of their contributions, mentioned in the narrative or in the source notes. There were many others who smoothed the way. I benefited from travelling the Ottawa Valley with Ewan Caldwell, whose roots go back to the square timber days, from exploring northwest Ontario with R. B. Loughlan of Toronto, and from the knowledge of A. D. Perley of Trois-Rivières and the Saguenay historian Monseigneur Victor Tremblay of Chicoutimi, Quebec. For their kindness in reading the manuscript I thank Herbert I. Winer, a Montreal-based director of the Forest History Society of Santa Cruz, California, and Terence Brennan of Montreal, whose contributions to the history of logging have been extensive.

Donald MacKay

INTRODUCTION

Along with red-coated Mounties and pictures of Niagara Falls, one of the abiding images of Canada around the world has been a shaggy, lonely figure swinging an axe amid the snow and evergreens of the north woods.

Fifty years ago the Ontario forestry journal *Sylva* published a somber memorial to that image: "Soon the old-time lumberjack will be forgotten. He has had his day. The rising generation will not know him. Canada owes much to the old time lumberjack who was one of the most fearless pioneers of our land. May his memory never die."

That was written shortly after World War II. Nearly thirty years later, however, when I began travelling the country to research *The Lumberjacks*, I found scores of white-haired veterans ready and willing to recall, with vivid detail, their labours in the woods with hand and horse. Some had gone into the camps as teen-age boys before the turn of the century.

The 19th century had spawned a breed of hard-working lumbermen with pride in their skills and rough codes of conduct. They called themselves lumberers, shantymen, timber beasts, les bucheron—and, more recently, lumberjacks in eastern Canada, loggers in British Columbia.

Of the three inter-woven ages of eastern Canadian logging, the first belonged to the bearded square timber men who hewed great baulks of white and red pine and drove them in huge rafts down the rivers to Quebec City, from where they were shipped to England in leaky sailing ships. Halfway through the 19th century the second age—the lumber industry—began to supply sawn timber to the growing towns of the United States as well as Canada. Then in the early 1900s the pulp and paper industry brought huge amounts of American and British capital into Canada and opened seemingly endless forests of spruce and balsam fir.

In British Columbia, where logging, like settlement, came late, migrant woodsmen, some from as far east as the Maritimes, founded a new phase of the industry in the late 1800s. Within a generation they replaced oxen and horses with steam power to handle the giant Douglas firs and cedars of the rain coast.

Across the country, farm boys had gone to the woods, that being the only winter work. Town boys had gone for adventure or to escape their troubles. Immigrants—Swedes and Finns more often than not—resumed the trades they had learned so well in the forests of northern Europe. They broke the cold, hard monotony of camp life far from home with songs, tall tales and card games. There was surprisingly little drinking in the camps, but when their work was done and their pay in their pocket they went on sprees in town.

Small boys in lumber towns looked up to them, especially the "white water men" who drove logs down wild rivers to market. In the Ottawa Valley town of Renfrew youngsters used to play "lumberjacks" in preference to the "cowboys and Indians" kids played elsewhere.

Like cowboys or sailors they developed their own lingo, some of which carried over into urban usage. "To get into a jam" derived from log jams in a river drive. "Skid row," some say, began as the west coast skid road on which logs were maneuvered into the water for transport to the mill. There are other words in common usage, such as Bull of the Woods, but who these days has heard of such common features of the lumber camps as the Crazy Wheel or the Go-devil or the Walking Boss?

Early lumbering, like farming, was a conservative business. Stoves had been used in town for a generation before they replaced the open fires in the center of lumber shanties. The crosscut saw, which permitted two men to produce twice the timber two axemen could cut, appeared in the camps long after it was introduced elsewhere.

In the early 20th century, modernization, beginning in coastal British Columbia, slowly crept east until, with the introduction of internal combustion engines, the horse gave way to tractors, bulldozers and trucks and a man with a chainsaw or his partner with a mechanical log skidder could earn in a day what his father earned in a month. In less than a century an apparently endless supply of low cost, high quality timber like the white pine, had disappeared and in many areas even the once ubiquitous prime spruce, balsam fir and jack pine were in short supply.

Today's lumberjack is a hard hatted "woods technician" snug in a weatherproof cabin atop a big, red mechanical tree harvester, articulated like a prehistoric monster. The rough old bunk houses have been replaced by camps with two men to a room, showers, game rooms, cafeterias and television. But this book is not about the new

9

ways. Rather it is about the axemen, sawyers, teamsters, river drivers and west coast rigging slingers, the men who cut and hauled square timber, saw logs and pulpwood from the birth of the industry to the 1950s. It is also about the foresters and timber cruisers who found the choice stands to harvest, and the temperamental camp cooks who fueled the men with huge meals.

When I wrote "The Lumberjacks" twenty years ago, books about Canadian lumberjacks were scarce. Travelling to lumber towns and searching archives from Halifax to Victoria I found contemporary reports in local newspapers and other publications, shantyman ballads, a few regional books published locally, and two or three volumes on the economic history of what was, along with beaver fur and wheat, one of Canada's three staple trades.

Much of "The Lumberjacks," the most enjoyable part for the author, is derived from interviews with men who were well past the age of retirement. They were kind and patient, generous with their memories. A few were in their nineties, others in their eighties and seventies when I saw them. Since the book first appeared, many, perhaps most, have passed away, along with the virgin forests they knew in their youth. They loomed large in the making of Canada. As the journal *Sylva* declared half a century ago: "Canada owes much to the old-time lumberjack."

Donald MacKay, 1998

CONTENTS

THE LOGGING FRONTIER 1

On an autumn day in 1799 a tall, lean Yankee rummaging around in search of farming land in the Indian country 120 miles west of Montreal beached his canoe where the Gatineau River meets the Ottawa.

"We climbed to the top of 100 or more trees," he wrote, "to view the situation of the country, which we accomplished in the following manner: We cut smaller trees in such a way as to fall slanting and lodge in the branches of larger ones, which we ascended until we reached the top. By this means we were enabled to view the country and also the timber, and by the timber we could judge the nature of the soil."[1]

In a wilderness known to Indians, fur traders, and few others, Philemon Wright had found tall pines and good alluvial soil. The area had been surveyed a few years earlier and named Hull Township but remained unsettled. The nearest settlers, and few of them at that, lived 70 miles to the east toward Montreal. Having found what he was looking for, Wright and two companions trekked back to Woburn, near Boston, Massachusetts, where he sold his farm and set about recruiting a small band of men and women to found a colony. For men like Philemon Wright, Massachusetts Bay had grown too crowded.

Early in February 1800, Wright's caravan of settlers started from

Woburn up the stagecoach road to Montreal on their 400-mile journey to Hull Township. Besides Wright, his wife Abigail, and their six children, there was his older brother Thomas and his family, the Choat and Allen families, and 10 single men. They had 14 horses to draw their seven sleighs, eight oxen, farm implements, and food which included barrels of pork "all destitute of bone."

Pausing at Montreal, a town of some 10 000, to swear allegiance to King George III, they set off up the Ottawa River, the Grand River, as it was called then. For the first three days they followed the trails cut by scattered settlers past the Lake of Two Mountains and on toward where Carillon now stands, but then they had to cut their own trails or travel on the ice of the river.

In the dead of winter they camped by night before bonfires, the men wrapped in blankets, the children and women sleeping in the covered sleighs. Two weeks from Montreal, 33 days after leaving Woburn, they reached the mouth of the Gatineau and each man took a ceremonial turn in chopping down the first tree on their campsite. Indians who had been tapping maple trees brought them gifts of syrup and deer meat. Wright gave the Indians rum, a little money, and convinced them that his arrival on their land was the will of their great father over the waters, King George, whereupon they made him an honorary chief.

A born patriarch, the "white chief of the Ottawa" could be kind or autocratic, generous or stingy, but all agreed he was more than a match for the wilderness he had come to tame. "His dark eyes were bright and observant," wrote one of his biographers. "His thoughtful face with its high forehead inspired confidence. He radiated kindness and vitality. He stood an impressive six feet tall. Wright did nothing without lengthy consideration but once he had thought out his projects and made his decision he completed his plans with a will."[2]

Wright and his men cleared the land; planted potatoes, peas, wheat, and hemp; built bake house, tannery, hemp, grist and sawmills; and called their settlement Wright's Village. It was well into the 1870s, long after Wright's death, before the settlement was formally named Hull, like the surrounding township. Since most of the food had to be hauled upriver from Montreal at considerable cost, within five years Wright had spent the $20 000 realized from the sale of his New England farm. "It was time for me," he wrote, "to look for an export market to cover my imports."

He had heard there was money to be made selling logs in Quebec City but he was a farmer, not a lumberman, and was reluctant to become the first to raft timber down the "dangerous rapids" between the head of the Long Sault and Lake of Two Mountains above Montreal. Although rafts of logs with deck loads of wheat, kegs of

Philemon Wright, father of the Ottawa Valley logging industry. His courage, ingenuity, and search for cash to pay off his debts combined to bring the first timber raft down the river. His friend John MacTaggart described Wright as a man with "a wonderfully strange, quick, reflective, wild eye. He is now about 70 years of age, but quite healthy and can undergo any fatigue; the most severe cold is nothing to him."

The Public Archives of Canada   C 11056

The Public Archives of Canada   C 2349

Flying the owner's flag and an array of "whites," or sails, to catch the west wind, a timber raft glides past Cap Santé on the St. Lawrence River in the 1840s en route to market at Quebec. The rafts, more common on the river than ships are now, swept down the river past Montreal all spring and summer.

potash for bleaching cloth, and cargoes of masts and barrel staves had been drifting down to Montreal and Quebec City from the upper St. Lawrence River for years, nothing had come down from the upper Ottawa except the canoes of the *voyageurs des pays en haut*. Nagged by his creditors, Wright negotiated a contract to deliver 6000 barrel staves, rough-hewn in his woods, to Quebec City by July 31, 1806.

"Accordingly I set out to examine the rapids quite down to the isle of Montreal. The *habitants*, who had been settled there nearly 200 years, told me that it was not possible ever to get timber to Quebec by that route on the north side of Montreal, as such a thing had never been done, nor was it possible that such a thing could ever be done. I said I would not believe it until I had tried it." Wright believed he could cut days off the 300-mile journey to Quebec City and avoid the Lachine Rapids south of Montreal by rafting across Lake of Two Mountains and north around the island through Rivière-des-Prairies.

On June 11 Wright and four men, including one of his sons, started down the river on a raft containing 700 logs, the barrel staves, and a deck cargo of boards. Halfway down the river his raft, which he christened "Colombo," broke up several times and he spent a month getting through the six miles of rapids at the Long Sault on the lower Ottawa. Wright had an awful journey but managed to navigate north around the island of Montreal as planned and, sorely battered, arrived at Quebec City two months after he set out. He was too late to honour his contract to deliver the barrel staves and it was November 12 before he had sold all his timber. He might have been somewhat less discouraged had he known that in that same month, November 1806, the fortunes of war in Europe would dictate a decision which was to have tremendous impact on the growth of the infant timber trade in British North America. Within a few years hundreds of rafts followed the path he had found down the rivers to Quebec City.

Up to that time timber exports had been small. Settlers, to be sure, had been cutting trees on the coves of Nova Scotia and Newfoundland and the shores of the St. Lawrence for as long as anyone could remember. The logs were mostly for their own use, to build their homes and small ships. France had forests of her own and sought little more than masts from her colony. England, her own forests destroyed, traditionally bought timber from the Baltic, and what she did not buy there, she imported from her colonies in New Hampshire and Massachusetts. Simeon Perkins, who cut timber on his land near Liverpool down the coast from Halifax and exported it to the West Indies, was one of the few to export square timber to England in the 1760s.

These old trade patterns began to change, however, when the American revolution disrupted England's supply of New England naval masts in the late 1770s and the English turned to their loyal colonies to the north.

The change could be seen in the fortunes of one man, William Davidson, a Scot who had settled on the Miramichi River in what is now New Brunswick. In 1777 Davidson had complained that the vagaries of the English market, such as it was, had left 660 tons of timber rotting in his yards. Two years later he was making money — and history — filling the first contract to cut Royal Navy masts on the upper Saint John River. Because of the difficulties in hauling tall, tapered pine trees out of the forest without smashing them, a naval mast of 90 feet or more, 35 inches at the butt, fetched as much as 130 pounds sterling. In 1782 Davidson's lumberjacks, still called "carpenters" in those days, cut 400.

Most of the construction timber from which England built ships and homes, both plain and stately, continued to come from the coasts of Prussia, Russia, and Scandinavia, but in the very month that Philemon Wright sold his wood to a slack market in Quebec, all that began to change. In November 1806, Napoleon Bonaparte ordered a blockade which kept British ships out of the Baltic. By 1808 England's timber imports from the Baltic had tumbled to practically nothing. The English turned to British North America for their wood and the great Baltic timber fleet was diverted to Quebec City. "I remember in May, 1809," said John Sewell, "the appearance round the point at Levis, of the first fleet of British ships coming in quest of our oak, pine, spars and masts for England's navies — royal and merchant."[3] The appearance of that fleet signalled the birth of Canada's timber trade. By 1810 wood had replaced fur as Canada's major export.

The British Admiralty turned to British North America not only for masts but for construction timber as well, as vital to the navy then as oil and steel are now. In one year, 1811 for example, the Atlantic provinces shipped 4000 masts and 200 000 loads of pine from ports like Saint John, New Brunswick, and Chatham on the Miramichi or Pictou, Nova Scotia. Five hundred ships set sail from Quebec City with 75 000 loads of pine and white oak and 23 000 masts.

A "load," which in medieval times had meant the amount of oak a horse could haul in a cart, had come to mean 50 cubic feet of timber, or about half the wood in one good white pine tree.

By the time Napoleon's blockade was raised in 1812 and the Baltic was reopened, the timber merchants in Quebec City and Saint John had established a foothold in the markets of Bristol, Cardiff, Liver-

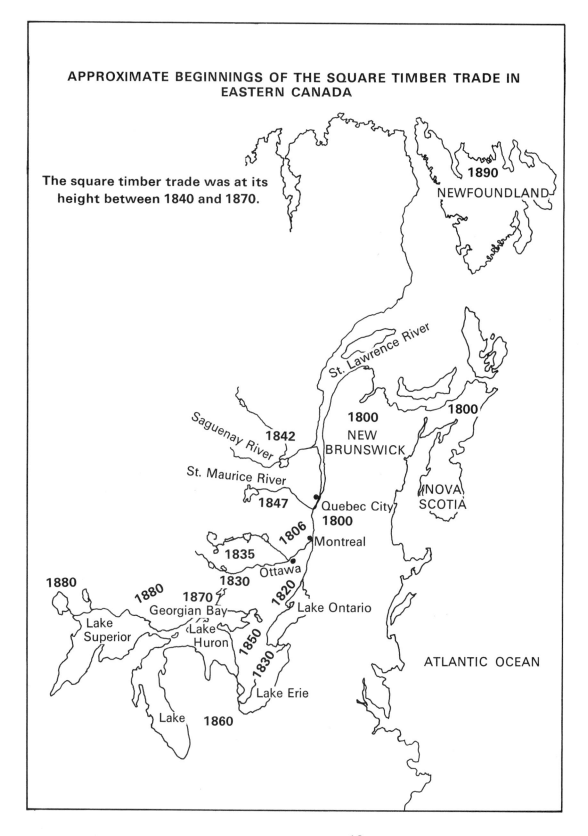

APPROXIMATE BEGINNINGS OF THE SQUARE TIMBER TRADE IN EASTERN CANADA

The square timber trade was at its height between 1840 and 1870.

1890
NEWFOUNDLAND

St. Lawrence River

Saguenay River

1842

1800
NEW BRUNSWICK

1800

St. Maurice River

1847

Quebec City

NOVA SCOTIA

1806

1800

Montreal

1835

1830
Ottawa

1880

1880

1870
Georgian Bay

1820
Lake Ontario

Lake Superior

Lake Huron

1850

1830

ATLANTIC OCEAN

Lake Erie

Lake

1860

pool, and London. They were aided by a heavy British duty on all timber except that shipped from the colonies, which compensated for the lower freight costs from the nearby Baltic.

In those early days, at least by law, logging was under Admiralty contract granted to middlemen such as the English firm of Scott, Idles and Company which maintained agents at Quebec City. Many of the contractors who actually cut the wood for them were Empire Loyalists who had settled in the Saint John River Valley or along the upper Saint Lawrence or the Bay of Quinte at the eastern corner of Lake Ontario in Upper Canada. Yankees such as Samuel Peabody, masting foreman for Hazen and White on the Saint John River, had brought in logging techniques which had taken root in 17th century New England where the very word "lumber," as applied to sawn timber, was coined.[4]

All that a timber crew needed was a team of oxen, a couple of felling axes, a broad-axe to square the fallen tree trunks, a few barrels of pork and flour, and perhaps a keg of rum. A five-man gang in New Brunswick in the 1820s would seek out a likely "vein," or clump of pine, like prospectors roaming for gold.

"Several of these people form what is termed a 'lumbering party' composed of persons who are all either hired by a master lumberer who pays the wages and finds them provisions, or of individuals, who enter into an understanding with each other to have a joint interest in the proceeds of their labours. The necessary supplies and provisions, clothing, etc., are generally obtained from the merchants on credit, in consideration of receiving the timber, which the lumberers are to bring down the river the following summer . . . They commence by clearing away a few of the surrounding trees and building a camp of round logs, the walls of which are seldom more than four or five feet high, the roof covered with birch bark . . . the fire either at the middle or the end, the smoke goes out the roof. Hay, straw or fir branches are spread across the whole length of the habitation, on which they all lie down together at night to sleep with their feet next to the fire. One person is hired to cook, whose duty it is to have breakfast ready before daylight, at which all the party arises, when each man takes his 'morning' or the indispensable dram of raw rum before breakfast. The meal consists of bread, or occasionally potatoes, with boiled beef, pork or fish, with tea sweetened with molasses. Dinner is usually the same with pea soup instead of tea, and supper resembles breakfast. These men are enormous eaters and they also drink great quantities of rum, which they seldom dilute."[5]

Farmers who could not make a living from hard-scrabble farms began to desert their land to cut timber, while boys were lured from the plodding labour of the plough by the cash and swagger of the new life. They acquired new names: "lumberer," and, later, "shanty-man," and one writer observed that their manner of living, "owing to the nature of the business they follow, is entirely different from that of other inhabitants of North America."[6] It was only when the British navy contractors sent gangs of axemen into the woods for months at a time in the early 1800s that logging became a separate occupation.

Townsmen viewed the new breed of woodsmen with some apprehension. They were, at the very least, a colourful bunch, ". . . shaggy of hair and beard, dressed out in red and blue and green jerseys, with knitted sashes about their waists, and red and blue and green tuques on their heads."[7] In Upper Canada they were a "light-hearted set of dare-devils and the greatest rascals and thieves that ever a peaceable country was tormented with . . . Hen roosts have quite disappeared from the river sides and lambs and little pigs have to be kept under lock and key."[8] On the Trent River near Peterborough, southwest of the Ottawa, they were "an incorrigible, though perhaps a useful, race of mortals, called lumberers, whom, however, I would name the Cossacks of Upper Canada."[9]

Those who knew them best defended them. Samuel Strickland, who farmed and logged near Peterborough, wrote, "Although large bodies of them have been lumbering close around me for the past four or five years, I have received nothing but civility at their hands; nor has a single application for a summons or a warrant against them been made to me in my magisterial capacity."[10] Decades later George Thompson, who logged on the Trent and the Ottawa, was to write, "Many of the people who so meanly refer to these brave fellows only see the poor shantyman perhaps once a year, at a time when he has money in his pocket and is enjoying himself with his companions after his winter's work . . . Take river drivers and shantymen when at their work and away from whiskey, a nobler or kindlier lot of men cannot be found."[11]

The King's Broad Arrow

In the beginning, first the French and then the British colonial governments tried to reserve prime timber for naval use. The British even blazed suitable trees with "the King's broad arrow," traditional mark of Crown property. But since both settlers and lumbermen often cut where they pleased and fought each other for the right to trespass, the government changed its policy and introduced licensed areas, "timber berths," or "limits," where a logger was supposed to cut to the limits of his lease and no farther.

By the 1820s British North America was supplying three-quarters of England's timber, most of it from the Miramichi and Saint John

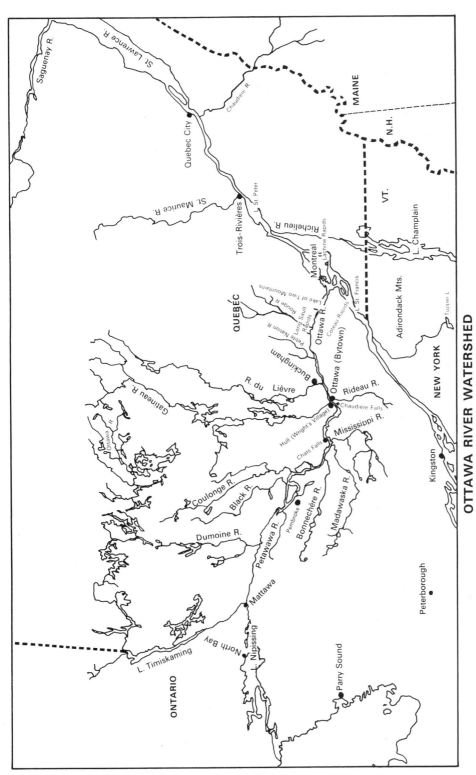

OTTAWA RIVER WATERSHED
MAJOR LOGGING RIVERS IN EASTERN CANADA

rivers in New Brunswick, the upper reaches of the St. Lawrence and the eastern shores of Lake Ontario, and, above all, from the Ottawa Valley. Logs hurtled down by the thousands from a dozen tributaries of the Ottawa, the Rouge, the Rivière du Lièvre, the Mississippi, the Madawaska, the Bonnechère, the Petawawa, and as far up the Ottawa as the Muskrat where Pembroke now stands, about 70 miles from Wright's Village.

There were years, when the market was good, when it seemed that everyone who could afford the price of a barrel of pork had gone into the pine woods. "What," asked an exuberant friend of the Wrights, "is the world made of? White pine!" Even the tavern keeper at Chats Falls, 40 miles above Chaudière Falls, could not resist the urge to turn lumberman and sent his sons rafting down to sell his logs to Philemon Wright.

Year after year, Wright logged the Gatineau and Rideau rivers and sent his cutters farther up the Ottawa. By 1814 he was employing more than 200 shantymen, and men were coming from as far east as Quebec City "to Hull (township) for the lumbering," as the saying went. Many set up on their own after working a while for the Wrights, for Philemon had been joined in the business by his three eldest sons. By 1824 the population of Wright's Village exceeded 1000, most of it New Englanders. Although Joseph Papineau had brought 20 French-Canadian axemen to cut on his timber limits on the Petite Nation tributary of the lower Ottawa as early as 1807, there were still few French in the Valley. For 20 years the Wrights were the biggest logging outfit on the Ottawa, often sending 20 rafts down to Quebec City in one summer.

Fortunes were made on the Ottawa, as on the Miramichi and the Saint John rivers, and it would be agreeable to be able to report that Philemon Wright had prospered financially. He was, according to a 19th century writer who knew him, "a man in constant motion, teaching and being taught — a true pioneer, an enthusiast in reclaiming and cultivating wild land . . . I felt I was in the presence of a considerable mind. . . ."[12] He had overcome great obstacles and acquired large tracts of land, but he was constantly short of cash. "The fact is," wrote his hard-headed grandson, Tiberius Junior, "he is out of money and would be if he had ever so much. He hires everything that comes along and pays them too much to do anything of any use." He was forever worrying about the square timber trade, tied as it was to a volatile British economy.

There was, for example, the bad year of 1813. Napoleon's Baltic blockade ended only to be followed by the War of 1812 with America which disrupted shipping. Wright lamented, "Not 1 single

The Public Archives of Canada   C 608

Philemon Wright's settlement, painted by his friend, Henry du Vernet, in 1823, when it boasted a church, a grist mill and sawmill at centre, and a "three-storey hotel" at right. Before Colonel By set up his construction camp to dig the Rideau Canal there was little on the Ottawa side of the river except the Sparks and Collins farms and a government store. After 30 years as Bytown it became Ottawa in the mid-1850s.

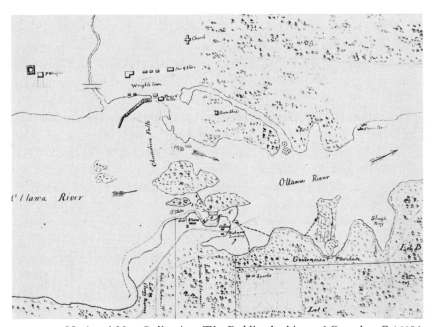

National Map Collection, The Public Archives of Canada   C 16156

23

Ship nor Vessell has arrived this year but has gone to the Boltick." There was another bad year in 1819 when recession prompted the *Quebec Gazette* of February 3, 1820, to declare, "Few make money by getting it (timber) out, and many who engage in the business ruin themselves." One of those who skidded toward bankruptcy was Philemon Wright.

When trustees were appointed to manage his affairs, Wright called his Montreal creditors "damned horse leeches" and retired in patriarchal dudgeon to his first love, farming and stockbreeding, and to his seat in the Lower Canada Legislative Assembly at Quebec City. He died at the age of 79, in 1839. There had been lumbermen in Canada long before Philemon Wright, and after he died there were greater lumbermen; but he had, almost single-handedly, pioneered the logging industry on the Ottawa, the greatest logging river of the country. Like Napoleon, he had assisted in the birth of the square timber trade.

Wright's sons carried on the business, determined to make timber pay. The year their father died, one of them declared in a letter, "I have got into a good grove of timber and intend to scoop all of the best of it out, previous to any other person having the pick of it." Competition was keen and prices had dropped so low that David Maclaren, agent for the Crown Lands Department at Quebec City, had written to his wife, "This is a trying season for the Lumberers. There is no doubt but ruin will be the lot of many of them."[13] But, as usual in the boom-and-bust square timber trade, prices were soon up again and the trade was booming.

New timber empires were opening up. The McConnel brothers had pushed north up the Ottawa unheard-of distances — 300 miles — to cut red pine on Lake Timiskaming in what had been Hudson's Bay Company fur trading country. It took them more than a month each autumn, in canoes and afoot, to reach their timber limits.

In 1831 a Quebec City merchant, Edward Grieves, built the first big shanty on the St. Maurice River, which shares headwaters with the Ottawa and drains a watershed as big as Belgium. Within 20 years eight companies were cutting on 6500 square miles of timber limits, the biggest company owned by George Baptist, a Scot who had once worked for Grieves. From Montreal eastward on the St. Lawrence watershed there had always been more spruce than pine and, once the pine had been cut off the St. Maurice, it became a spruce-logging area, as famous for its pulpwood as the Ottawa had been for its pine.

In Quebec William Price had founded his own company in 1816, six years after arriving from London as a 21-year-old agent for the

British naval contractors, Scott, Idles and Company. Price expanded from merely exporting timber to cutting and milling it as well. By 1827 he was exporting 50 cargoes each year and by 1833 he was exporting 100 cargoes. Eventually his timber empire extended from the Ottawa Valley to the Gaspé and he controlled more than 7700 square miles of timber, most of it up the Saguenay River.

Price's most notable expansion came in the early 1840s when the Hudson's Bay Company, which had controlled the Saguenay country for its fur trade, came to the end of its lease and the territory was opened to settlers. Many of the settlers who moved in were employed by Price and by the end of the 1850s 4000 depended on Price lumbering for their livelihood.

As well as exporting timber, Price, along with the Hamiltons at Hawkesbury on the lower Ottawa, was a pioneer in the trade of "deals," which were boards three inches thick designed for resawing in the saw pits of England. When Price died at the age of 78 in 1867 his gravestone at Chicoutimi, overlooking the fiords of the river, was inscribed *"le père du Saguenay."* At the time of his death the greatest days of the timber trade had passed, but within 30 years his grandson, the second William Price, created a new pulpwood industry which flourishes to this day.

By the 1840s the mean hovels of the early years were giving way, particularly on the Ottawa, to big "cambuse," or "camboose," shanty camps of a size previously unknown. John Egan, an Irish immigrant from Galway, arrived on the Ottawa in the early 1830s and progressed in 10 years from merely supplying provisions to lumber camps to owning them. He thought nothing of hiring 3800 men to cut wood and 400 teams of horses to haul in supplies — 6000 barrels of pork and 10 000 barrels of flour each winter. Egan, who sent 55 rafts down to Quebec City each summer in the mid-1840s, succeeded Philemon Wright as "King of the Ottawa."

When men spoke of a "shanty" they meant not only a log structure, perhaps 40 feet by 35, but also the men, oxen, horses, and provisions that went with it. The term cambuse shanty apparently evolved from both the Dutch *kaban huis*, which was the deck-house on sailing ships, and the French *chantier*, or workshop. The hallmark of the cambuse shanty was the log fire always burning in the centre of the floor.

At the end of the century, Charles Macnamara of Arnprior on the Ottawa wrote, "The sole entrance to the shanty was a rather small door in one end of the building, about six feet high and three feet wide ... and all the light and ventilation (not much light but lots of ventilation) came through a large hole in the roof, 12 feet

Ont. Ministry of Natural Resources

Cambuse shanty, 1888. A camp such as this cost about $300 to build, the most expensive item being the "scoop" roofs which became common in the 1870s. Scoop roofs were made by fitting hollowed halves of logs over each other, topped off with a log smokestack for the open cambuse fire.

The home of the shantymen, with cambuse fire in the centre of the floor providing a kitchen for the cook and light and heat for the men. As late as May 1903 the *Canada Lumberman* reported there were still a few such shanties on the Ottawa River although they had largely been replaced by "stove shanties." "This old style has been abandoned on almost all other streams for the American style — the cooking range and box stove, which is considered more up-to-date and economical but there are still concerns who prefer to keep up the old style on account of its being more cheerful for the men and because they think it more cleanly and healthful."

The first of the pine forest shanties in New Brunswick were hardly more than two or three logs high and even in the Ottawa Valley, where the biggest shanties were built, there were some not much higher than a man's head.

The Public Archives of Canada   C 48663

Notman Photographic Archives, McCord Museum

square, surrounded by a square chimney of flatted timber five or six feet high and tapered to about eight feet square at the top. Besides letting in light and air the opening carried off the smoke of the camboose . . . The floor was of flatted timber not very closely fitted, and the spaces between the pieces soon filled up with rubbish. To the right of the door as you came in was a pile of four-foot firewood. The hardworking choreboy had to provide about a cord and a half every 24 hours, as well as six large 'back logs.' In front of the door, between it and the (fire), was the place of the grindstone, usually two, which in the evening were in constant use sharpening axes. To the left of the door were two barrels of wash water for the men and a stand for a couple of wash basins. It often froze up in winter and the ice had to be forcibly punched out. Along the left wall came the cook's shelf for meat and other stores, the cook's work table and the bread shelf. Farther along this the clerk had his desk and beside it the van chest which held the tobacco, moccasins, clothing and sundries for sale to the men. The right side of the building was all taken up by two tiers of bunks, six or seven in each tier, and across the end fartherest from the door were two more tiers of seven bunks each in which the men slept with their feet to the fire . . . the bunks were floored with flatted poles and the bedding was usually balsam boughs, sometimes hay. Each man was supplied with a pair of heavy grey wool blankets, and two men slept together. A properly made balsam bed is quite comfortable, and as the men took off no more than their moccasins on retiring, when covered with two pairs of blankets they were warm enough, despite the large opening in the roof. At night the camboose fire supplied the only light."[14]

To the regret of George Thompson stoves did not become common until late in the 1800s. Thompson did not like the cambuse. "The chances are one will be half-blinded with smoke the greater part of the time . . . It is said the smoky odour of one's clothes can be detected by a good 'smeller' nearly half a mile distant. When the fire gets low during the cold winter nights the large opening in the roof lets in the cold and the crew are half frozen to death."[15]

By the 1850s, 10 000 men were living in such shanties, some so far up the southern tributaries of the Ottawa, such as the Madawaska River, they swore they could hear the ringing axes of loggers from Peterborough cutting toward them over the height of land which was later to become Algonquin Park.

Brigades of tough, healthy men cooped up all winter in such remote camps could make roaring nuisances of themselves when they came down on the spring log drives and fought with rival gangs. Bytown, little more than trees and cranberry bog before

1825, had become the wildest logging town west of Bangor, Maine, and no spring went by without pitched battles between the shantymen from the woods and the Irish navvies imported to build Colonel By's Rideau Canal. Until the 1820s loggers on the Ottawa had been mostly Yankees, English, Scots, and Irish but around that time Philemon Wright's payrolls began to show an increasing number of French names until seven out of 10 shantymen were Québécois. The Irish were also increasing in number.

Over the years the Irish of Mount St. Patrick and Barry's Bay have produced some of the Ottawa Valley's best loggers, but in 1832 a less favoured group of Irish found themselves jobless when Colonel By finished the canal to Kingston. Some were hard veterans of the Erie canal and others had come direct from Limerick or Wicklow in Ireland. They were called "Shiners," possibly because they had been cutters of oak, or *chêne*, on the Rideau and *chêneurs* had been anglicized to Shiners. When Martin Hennessy, or Bobby Boyle, or the seven Slavin brothers tried, by fair means or foul, to take jobs away from the French, the men from Quebec fought back, their champion being Joseph Montferrand from Montreal. Unlike the fictional Paul Bunyan — the superman of the pine camp tales — Joe Montferrand was real, a shantyman and raft foreman working out of Wright's Village.

The Shiners were wicked opponents. From their mud hovels and shacks in Corktown and from Mother McGinty's notorious tavern, the Shiners terrorized lower Bytown, waylaid rafts, and ousted the French crews taking the rafts as their own. They threw their enemies into the boiling Chaudière Falls between Bytown and Wright's Village, threatened opponents with "Limerick whips," long switches topped with sharp wood chisels, and sliced the ears and tails off the horses of magistrates who offended them. The *Brockville Recorder* called them "demons in human shape," their riots were the "Shiners' War," and their "King" was the high-handed Peter Aylen, a wealthy lumberman who got his start working for the Wrights. He befriended the Shiners for dubious reasons of his own. During the early 1830s fifty deaths were attributed to the riots until the citizens of Bytown had had enough and formed a vigilante committee. The riots petered out but there was feuding for years, even into the 1900s. "Did the French and the Irish fight on the Ottawa River? Gentle! Gentle! Like a cat and a dog."[16]

Less bloody was "The Lumberman's War," an international incident also known as the Aroostook War between New Brunswick and the State of Maine. In the days before there was a clear international boundary, the proud lumberman of Bangor, Maine, laid claim to the white pine on the Aroostook River which flows into the Saint John River. When they heard that 50 New Brunswick lumberers were cutting pine up the Aroostook in February 1839, they marched out in patriotic wrath. The New Brunswick men, forewarned, armed themselves and not only faced down the Bangor Tigers, as the men of the Penobscot liked to call themselves, but took a few prisoners as well. That brought out the Maine militia to guard the river with a couple of comic opera brass cannons in an ox cart. Fortunately the encounters that followed resulted in only a few bloody noses, one broken arm, and the Webster-Ashburton international boundary of 1842.

The lumbermen went right on invading each other's territory. "Main John" Glasier once fought his way up the Allagash in Maine heading a gang armed with axes to stop the Americans from building a dam which threatened to lower the level of the Saint John River in New Brunswick. Glasier, who wore a stove-pipe hat and a black wig to disguise baldness caused by typhoid, belonged to a family that employed 600 men but he always insisted that "I am the *main* man." "Main John" became a lumberjack name for The Boss throughout New Brunswick long after Glasier was gone.

That easterners were fighting over timber rights was not surprising. The growth of the towns, particularly in the United States, had opened up a new market — the lumber market — as a welcome alternative to the unstable, boom-and-bust square timber trade to Britain. The two trades complemented each other since the square timber makers sought only the best and tallest pine — perhaps only a tenth of the trees in a given stand — while the men who cut the shorter sawlogs for the mills were happy enough with the timber maker's rejects. Philemon Wright's sons turned to sawlog cutting in the 1840s and so did the Gillies Brothers Limited of Braeside, on the Ontario shore of the Ottawa, which lumbered for more than 100 years before becoming part of Consolidated-Bathurst.

New men appeared, with capital for sawmills that had been unnecessary in the simpler days of the square timber makers — Americans such as Captain Levi Young from Maine or H. F. Bronson from New York. Another American, E. B. Eddy, arrived with only $40 in his pocket and got his start selling matches made from pine butts, door to door. Local lumbermen like Daniel McLaughlin of Arnprior founded great companies. James Maclaren, whose father, David, had despaired of the timber trade in 1837 when he was government agent at Quebec City, not only logged at Buckingham on the Lièvre River and on the Gatineau, but expanded into Vermont, Massachusetts, and eventually British Columbia where he opened mills near Vancouver. After his death in 1892 at the age of 73, the Maclaren lumber business was carried on by his sons at Buckingham.

John Rudolphus Booth, described by the *American Lumberman* in 1904 as one of North America's two greatest lumber kings, the other being H. Frederick Weyerhaeuser in the United States. The journal estimated that Booth's 4250 square miles of timber limits on the Ottawa watershed were "sufficient timber land to make a strip a mile wide reaching across Canada from the Atlantic to the Pacific."

Ont. Ministry of Natural Resources

William Price came to Quebec City from England in 1810 as a young employee of a British company of naval contractors. He established his own business seven years later with timber limits and mills all the way from the Ottawa to the Gaspé and up the Saguenay River where he was known affectionately as "*le père du Saguenay*."

The Price Company Ltd.

In 1858, a 25-year-old carpenter, John Rudolphus Booth, arrived at Hull from his father's farm near Waterloo in the Quebec Eastern Townships. With $9 in his pocket he rented a small shingle mill from the Wright family and hired as his apprentice young Robert Dollar. Dollar himself became a lumber baron in Michigan, founded Dollarton in British Columbia, and built a west coast shipping line to freight his lumber to Asia. In the 1860s, with Bytown now renamed Ottawa, Booth won a contract to supply lumber for the new parliament buildings. He talked the banks into lending him money to secure the Egan timber limits on the Madawaska after Egan had gone bankrupt and died, and in due time had 4000 shantymen working an area larger than Prince Edward Island. To transport his wood, Booth built a railway south from Ottawa to the American border and then pushed rails westward through his forests to Parry Sound on Lake Huron. By the time he sold his railway, the Canada Atlantic, it had cost him $18 million, ran for 500 miles, and was the largest railway ever built by one man. Booth died at the age of 99 in 1925. Old-timers still remember him: small, white-haired, bearded, slightly stooped, and puttering around one of his camps picking up horseshoes so they would not be wasted, his bright blue eyes missing nothing.

In New Brunswick, with its logging dynasties of Snowballs, Glasiers, and Frasers, Booth's counterpart was Alexander "Boss" Gibson who began as an axeman and rose to own a sawmill business near Fredericton, employ 2000 woodsmen, and run his own railway. His Canada Eastern between Fredericton and Chatham, which had been shared by his rival, Jabez Snowball, before Gibson bought him out, linked lumber camps and towns in the Nashwaak and Miramichi valleys in that province of river valleys. Gibson died at the age of 94 in 1913.

By the time Canada became a nation in 1867, lumber exports to the United States had surpassed square timber sales to England. More than 150 steam sawmills were operating in Ontario, as well as scores of old water-driven mills, and a layout like Charlie Parry's new mill near Peterborough cut 90 000 board feet every day — enough to build five houses in Chicago. Toronto, Oakville, and Hamilton were all shipping lumber across Lake Ontario to the United States. Blue and white barges hauled lumber down the lower Ottawa; the blue ones headed for Montreal, the white for the United States by way of the canals, Lake Champlain, and the Hudson River.

In New Brunswick, on the Saint John, the Miramichi, and the Restigouche, logging was in its glory days. In Quebec and Ontario 25 000 shantymen were working on the Saguenay, the St. Maurice, the Ottawa, and the Trent, as far west as Lake Simcoe. But at least until the turn of the century, logging generally meant white pine in the east and the eastern pineries were running thin, especially along the rivers where loggers could get at them. In the 1870s the virgin forests east of Georgian Bay, an area as big as some European countries, was opened for auction and began to rival the Ottawa Valley. Axemen fed whining mills at Midland, Penetanguishene, Victoria Harbour, and Parry Sound and then moved north to the top of Georgian Bay to do the same at Blind River, Sprague, and Thessalon. They moved west into the pine forests between Thunder Bay and the Manitoba border and cut around Lake of the Woods and Rat Portage, which became Kenora. A few went to British Columbia where the lumber industry had started only in the 1860s.

In the east the old square timber trade, which had peaked around 1865, declined during the depression of the 1870s and practically disappeared after 1900. The lumber trade, on the other hand, continued to flourish but turned to spruce to take the place of the diminishing pine. The peak years of the eastern Canadian lumber industry are generally reckoned as having been 1870 to 1900. Spruce was also ideal for the new industry which was to dominate the eastern forests — the pulpwood industry.

Until the construction of two mills which made paper from wood in southwestern Quebec in 1866, paper had been made from straw or rags. Rags had become so hard to get that one American paper maker imported a shipload of Egyptian mummy wrappings.

By 1870, Alexander Buntin's mill at Valleyfield, Quebec, was turning out a ton of groundwood pulp a day, grinding wood to fibre by a technique recently developed in France. But it was many years before the pulp-and-paper industry came of age. By the 1890s there were 24 pulp mills in Canada, most of them in Quebec where the Laurentide Paper Company mill at Grand'Mère ushered in the era of Canada's great newsprint trade. Trois-Rivières, at the mouth of the St. Maurice, was later to claim the title of newsprint capital of the world.

On the Ottawa, E. B. Eddy opened a pulp mill near the Chaudière Falls where Philemon Wright had settled a century earlier. The Maclarens started a mill on the Lièvre in 1901, and on the Saguenay the heirs of William Price complemented their dozen sawmills with a pulp mill. When that king of pine, J. R. Booth, turned to pulp and paper and opened a mill on the Ottawa in 1904, the old pine woods shantymen realized it was time to quit or move — west to Chapleau, and the Blind River country in the rugged country north of Lake Huron, or on to Lake of the Woods where there was still pine along the rivers. Some went to British Columbia where the lumber trade was starting to boom. By the late 1920s British Columbia would produce half of Canada's annual cut of lumber.

It became clear that the grinders and cookers which reduced solid wood to fibre would gobble spruce and balsam fir at such a rate that the forests of the settled river valleys would last no longer than the pine, for it took a cord of wood, as well as electricity and hundreds of tons of water, to make a ton of pulp.

The new industry began to seek its wood and water up on the Canadian Shield in Quebec and Ontario and in the Boreal Forest which lay, almost unexplored, across the height of land which drains north to Hudson Bay. A restless entrepreneur from the United States, Francis H. Clergue, opened the Sault Ste. Marie Pulp and Sulphite Company, and mills were built at Sturgeon Falls west of North Bay and Espanola west of Sudbury. In the empty black spruce country near Lake Abitibi, which straddles the Quebec-Ontario border, Frank Anson from Montreal built one of the biggest pulp-and-paper mills in the world at Iroquois Falls. The Bathurst Lumber Company began producing pulp on the Bay of Chaleur in New Brunswick and pulp mills appeared in British Columbia. The mills consumed nearly three million cords of wood each year.

Like the sawn lumber trade, the pulpwood industry attracted American investment and spawned new communities: Shelter Bay on the forsaken north shore of the eastern St. Lawrence River, Kénogami far up the Saguenay, Kapuskasing, Long Lac, and other whistle stops in northern Ontario which seemed as remote as Siberia. It brought new life to old lumber towns like Buckingham, Hull, Trois-Rivières, Thunder Bay, Liverpool, Nova Scotia; and communities in Newfoundland where the wood, as at Placentia Bay, was better for pulp than for lumber.

The pulpwood industry did not need the tall, straight pine or white spruce prized at the sawmills; it could flourish on the smaller, commoner black spruce, balsam fir, and even, to some extent, on stunted, knotty jack pine. From 1913 to 1929, the beginning of the Depression, the pulp-and-paper industry expanded, particularly in the nine years starting in 1920. Canada became the world's greatest exporter of newsprint. By the middle of the century there were 130 mills consuming nearly nine million cords of wood each year. The number of lumberjacks had increased threefold and more than 100 000 pulp cutters might be in the bush in any given autumn. Camp life had changed. The lumberjacks of the pulp woods acquired tools, techniques, and traditions quite different from the lumber camps. There were pine camp foremen like Ed Hoover of Thessalon who spoke scornfully of "toothpicks," as he called the black spruce used for pulpwood. The days of the shantymen had passed away with the First World War.

For three generations and more, the shantymen had cut their way west, their wake-up cry, "Daylight in the Swamp!" echoing on the Saint John and the Miramichi, on the Ottawa, the Great Lakes, and on Vancouver Island. John MacTaggart, a Rideau Canal engineer who was a friend of Philemon Wright, described "the wood cutter from the wilderness" as "a creature by himself, like the sailor. To know them . . . we must live with them for a time, and partake of all their joys and sorrows; we must run the rapids with them and get wet with spray and sweat."[17] And so we shall.

TALES OF THE TIMBERBEASTS: JOE MONTFERRAND 2

A lot of people think Joe Monferrand was just a story. My God, my grandfather worked with him! He and my grandfather, Michael MacCormick, rafted wood on the Ottawa River together. Sure.

CHARLIE MACCORMICK, PORT-MENIER, ANTICOSTI

When he was 16 years old Joe Montferrand was digging a pit near his home on rue des Allemands in Montreal when a notorious neighbourhood bully, Michel Duranleau, happened along with two cronies and seeing the boy's head protruding from the hole aimed a passing kick. Poor Duranleau. The enraged young Montferrand leaped from the pit and thrashed all three. Although his mother insisted her Joseph was normally a placid boy the neighbours of the Saint-Laurent quarter were impressed and urged Joe to take up boxing, a popular sport in the garrison town.

A year later Joe was in the crowd on the Champ de Mars when a soldier from the English garrison won the title "champion of Canada." Following the custom of the day, Montferrand crowed like a cock to show he was the new challenger and sprang into the ring. He swung just one blow and became the new champion at the age of 17.

Montferrand was born in 1802, the son of a North West Company fur trader, and grew up the same time as the square timber trade. He grew to six feet two and despite his size he had the grace and agility of his grandfather, a fencing master. His favourite trick was standing on the floor and kicking the imprint of his heels on the eight-foot ceiling. All his life his enemies feared Joe Montferrand's boots.

35

He was as strong as a bear. One day, for fun, he seized a rope and pulled a big barge right onto dry land. It took five men to refloat it. He had a whirlwind temper when finally aroused and when the champion boxer of Kingston fouled him repeatedly by butting, Montferrand is said to have broken the man's jaw in four places. When the boxer Bill Collins deliberately smashed Montferrand's glass in a bar, the not-so-gentle giant threw Collins into the fireplace where he lay smouldering until his cronies hauled him out. When one of the best boxers in the garrison, a Major Jones, mocked him in a tavern one afternoon, Montferrand fought the major then and there. *"Insulterez-vous encore les Canadiens!"* Montferrand shouted each time he struck a blow. The major capitulated.

By the time he was 25 Montferrand was working for Bowman and Gilmore in the shanties on the Lièvre River above Buckingham and on the Upper Ottawa. When he became a rafting foreman and went down to Quebec City he once defeated, in 17 rounds on the Queen's Wharf, the champion of the British Navy. He refused to fight for money, however, and most of his battles were to avenge insults — to himself and to his race. He was forever being challenged, like a western gun-fighter.

The scene of his greatest fight was on the bridge spanning the Chaudière Falls between Hull and Bytown. It was here that fact and fable intertwine. In those days the Shiners, the Irish navvies who built the Rideau Canal, were the bane of Bytown. They were a law unto themselves in what was little more than a lawless construction camp, and their fights with *les Canadiens* were famous up and down the Grand River. Their nemesis was Joe Montferrand and once, in 1829, the story goes, 150 Shiners lay in wait for him at the bridge. Montferrand was halfway across the bridge before the Shiners leaped out of ambush and advanced upon him, brandishing cudgels, egging each other on to feats of glory. Finding that the bridge-keeper had closed the gate behind him cutting off his escape back to Bytown, Joe Montferrand crossed himself, invoked the Virgin, and strode forward causing the mob to pull up short. At that instant Montferrand seized the closest Shiner in his mighty arms and, swinging him like a human club, flattened the first row of attackers like so many tin soldiers, knocking some into the white water below. The scene was horrible. Blood ran from the bridge into the river. A crowd gathered on the bank at Hull to watch the Shiners flee down the Aylmer Road.

Hot for revenge, the Shiners waylaid him one day as he was walking by the Rideau River. Thinking to escape, for he was a tireless swimmer, Montferrand leaped into the water only to discover another band of Shiners waiting for him on the opposite bank. They watched him while he disappeared in the rapids but as word spread

JOE MONTFERRAND

Archives Nationales du Québec

Joe Montferrand, hero of the north woods, known from the Gaspé to the Lake States as a lumberjack who could run faster, jump higher, hit harder than any other "timberbeast." A giant of a man, blue eyed and fair skinned like his ancestors in the northeast of France, Montferrand defended the good name of Québécois *bûcherons* against all comers.

through town that afternoon that the great Joe Montferrand had drowned he was, in fact, sitting in the inn of his old friend Agapit Lespérance, drying out.

With his brown hair, blue eyes, and gentlemanly air, he was, it seems, a gallant figure with the ladies, and after his work was done for the day in Hull he would stroll across the bridge and, in that delightful French phrase, "*demander des nouvelles de son coeur.*" He had lost his heart to a girl in Bytown who was also being wooed by a six-foot Highlander named MacDonald. MacDonald was jealous and with his six brothers lay in wait for our Adonis at the infamous bridge. It was one against seven and they were big men armed with clubs but Montferrand wrenched a pole from the guard-rail and, swirling it around his head, drove them off the bridge and escaped into the night.

Inviting his men one day to refresh themselves at a riverside tavern, he found that his old friend the innkeeper had retired and there were new owners. Engaging politely in conversation with the pretty girl behind the bar, he explained he had no money with him and perhaps he should leave. "Stay," she said, "for you look like a man of honour. You will be served." After his men had taken their drinks Montferrand thanked the barmaid and placing himself in the middle of the taproom kicked the imprint of his nailed boots into the high ceiling.

"Voici, Madame," said Joe Montferrand, "a visiting card. You can show it to your clients. My name is Montferrand." People came from miles around to see the famous nail marks and the inn prospered.

He was a stern boss in camp but kindhearted to those in need and like his father gave gifts to widows and children. When he learned that a poor carter's horse had died he bought him a new one. He was religious, drank but sparingly, and from Gaspé to northern Ontario became the hero of the French-Canadian lumber camps. He married at the age of 60 and fathered one son, Joseph-Louis. In those days he was often seen strolling in Montreal's Bonsecours market, a tall, smiling figure, joking with the butchers and the farmers' wives who were selling their produce.

Joseph Montferrand died peacefully in his home at 212 rue Sanguinet on October 4th, 1864. His remains lie in a family plot, the simple tombstone bearing only the words "Famille Joseph Montferrand," in a high and lonely part of Notre Dame des Neiges cemetery in Montreal. There were many *hommes forts* in those days but for *les bûcherons* Joe Montferrand epitomized the epic lives of the 19th century shantymen.

Migrant French-Canadian lumberjacks carried his fame to northern Ontario and the pine camps of Michigan and Wisconsin where he may have been — who knows? — a model for the tall tales of the legendary Paul Bunyan whose stories first appeared, it seems, in the 1850s in the Adirondacks, New York, and Michigan pine camps. In the English-speaking camps he was "Joe Muffraw" and one old Lake States shantyman who had come from Quebec in his distant youth recalled, "Joe Muffraw? We knew about him. There were two Joe Muffraws — one named Pete." Long before Paul Bunyan and his blue ox Babe there were stories of Joe Montferrand and his mythical pet white moose.

Lucien Bergeron of Quebec City remembers such stories from the 1950s during his days in the Lac St. Jean camps up the Saguenay. "I used to hear some of the old fellows talk about Joe Montferrand. To them he was the ideal. He was The Man, hey? He'd walk into a camp and make a big impression, he was The Boss. If anyone was abused, he'd fix it. If anything went wrong, he'd fix it. They didn't talk about Paul Bunyan up there, they talked about Joe Montferrand."

3 THE RAFTSMEN

*Going on deck after breakfast I was amazed to see floating down
the stream a most gigantic raft, with some 30 or 40 wooden houses
upon it and at least as many flag staffs, so it looked like a nautical
street.*

CHARLES DICKENS, DESCRIBING THE ST. LAWRENCE RIVER IN
"AMERICAN NOTES," 1842

For 100 years timber rafts scudded down the St. Lawrence to
Quebec City from Lake Ontario, the Richelieu, the Ottawa, and the
St. Maurice, sails billowing, banners streaming, and smoke swirling
eastward from their cooking fires. Some were floating villages a
quarter of a mile long with crews of 50 men and perhaps another
100 homeward bound from the woods. A typical raft was one containing 1442 sticks of square timber and a crew of 22 which Ruggles
Wright brought down in 1840, a year in which 400 rafts were
sighted on the St. Lawrence.

"When Spring draws on they form the lumber into small rafts
called cribs, and drop down the rapids to market. When they come
to any extensive sheets of still water the cribs are brought into a
grand flotilla; masts, white flags and sails are sported, while with
long, rude oars, they continue to glide slowly along. Thus they will
come from Lake Calumet, on the Ottawa, to Wolfe's Cove, Quebec,
a distance of nearly 800 (*sic*) miles in six weeks. On those rafts they
may have a fire for cooking, burning on a sandy hearth; the places
to sleep in, formed of broad strips of bark, resembling the half of a
cylinder, the arch about four feet high and in length about eight.
To these beds, or lairs, trams or handles are attached so that they can
be moved from crib to crib or from crib to shore."[1]

The rafting of logs is as old as history. Hiram assured King Solomon he would fetch fir and cedar timber from Lebanon to bring to the sea and "convey them by floats unto the place thou shall appoint me." The Europeans had rafted logs for centuries but it's doubtful if they excelled "les rafmanns" on the St. Lawrence and the Ottawa.

To withstand rapids and storms a raft had to be built strong, but it also had to be built so that it could be dismantled quickly at Quebec City and sold as timber. The early rafts on the Saint John River in New Brunswick were simple: logs driven separately down to Fredericton were lashed together, 30 logs perhaps, secured by crosspieces and topped with a second layer to make a "joint." Joints were combined to make a raft 150 feet long. When the river was high and the days long 50 rafts might be seen on the river at one time and a good raftsman could run 100 miles from Tobique in 24 hours.

On the Ottawa the basic unit of a raft was the crib, 20 pieces of square timber locked between two big logs which served as floats. A crib weighed 40 tons and was fitted with oarlocks for 20-foot sweeps. Cribs were coupled together with cap pieces, short planks which fitted over wooden pegs, and when rough water was encountered on the rivers each crib was uncoupled like a railway car and driven separately down the rapids. The worst hazards were falls such as the 60-foot drop at Calumet where raftsmen were known to suffer "Calumet fever," a fear they would be sucked down the falls before they could snub their raft and get it dismantled. Sometimes whole rafts somersaulted over the limestone ledge of Chaudière Falls, logs flying in every direction. Raftsmen might be delayed for weeks collecting battered logs.

The problem was solved by Philemon Wright's son, Ruggles, in 1829, seven years after rafts had started coming over the Chaudière Falls. Wright built a shallow canal three-quarters of a mile long that bypassed the falls and slid entire 25-foot cribs of timber down a series of inclined planes to the pool below. A raft would be dismantled crib by crib at the top of the chute and a pilot and a steersman would ride each crib down the long watery slope. Wright's innovation opened the Upper Ottawa as never before and did more, perhaps, than any single man-made thing to make the Ottawa the greatest logging river in the land. Timber slides were built to bypass the fearsome Calumet and Chats Falls where as many as 2000 raftsmen might come through in one spring. The chutes meant that timber cut in the deep forests of the Kipawa and Lake Timiskaming could reach the Quebec market in one year rather than two. The men no longer had to tear down and rebuild a whole raft eight or nine times on the 600-mile journey. Timber slides were used for 80 years and were frequently battle grounds for raftsmen trying to get their logs through first. Later, to police the river, logging companies formed into a cooperative, the Upper Ottawa Improvement Company. Even with controlled timber slides, or "artificial rapids," there was danger. "There is scarcely a portage, or a cleared point, jutting out into the river, where you do not meet with wooden crosses, on which are rudely carved the initials of some unfortunate victim of the restless waters," the Ottawa engineer Thomas C. Keefer wrote in 1854. "In a prosperous year about 10,000 men are afloat on loose timber or in frail canoes and as many as 80 lives have been lost in a single Spring."[2] Ten men were killed and 100 000 feet of timber smashed in 1835 when a raft got into the wrong channel atop Chaudière and was swept over the falls. Liquor, purchased in the fly-by-night grog shops at 10 pence a gallon, was blamed for many drownings. Long after heavy drinking was banned in the camps it continued on the river drives.

Three-quarters of the 14 million cubic feet of white pine sold at Quebec City in 1845 came from above Chaudière Falls. Although Ottawa rafts were usually smaller, it was not unusual for one to contain 80 to 100 cribs or 2000 pieces of squared timber. Equipment on such a raft included 12 "whites," or sails, one anchor made of oak and weighted with a rock lashed to its crown, one chain cable, five pike poles with hooks, 150 twenty-four-foot red pine oars to steer with, four axes, and 2500 withes. The withes were half-inch willow saplings, twisted as pliable as rope, and tied like tourniquets to "band" pine logs together or to lash oak timber, which does not float, to pine, which does. On the month-long journey to Quebec a crew of 22 might eat four barrels of pork, 644 pounds of biscuits, 30 bushels of potatoes, 156 pounds of dried fish, 125 pounds of flour, drink 12 pounds of tea, and smoke 10 pounds of pipe tobacco. They built crude plank shanties on the rafts to sleep in and each raft flew a banner with the owner's timber mark.

Whether cribs were smashed in the rapids or broken in squalls on Lake St. Peter below Montreal, rafting was a daily hardship. Ruggles Wright recalled that it once took his men eight days to row 26 miles across Lake of Two Mountains. His rafting diary written in the spring of 1835 described a typical journey.

"Sunday 31st May 1835

"Left Hull at 7 o'clock AM with twenty Hands on Board. 1st Red Pine Raft. Morning fine no wind. At 11 oclock wind rose from the south but not so heavy as to stop the raft. Rowed considerably to clear the point. Men employed making their cabins. At 12 oclock P.M. wind drove us in to the small sny (backwater) opposite Doles. Raft run on shore. It rained & was so Dark could not see do any thing. One of the men got his foot badly hurt.

"Monday 5 oclock AM 1st June 1835

"Got out of the sny with very little trouble. On examining the raft found one Crib badly Damaged and float of another Broke. The wind was heavy from the north and Drove us ashore 2 miles below Doles. The men employed banding & repairing the Cribs. At 5 oclock PM wind fell. Pushed off next morning and found ourselves at Hamilton Wharf (at the head of Long Sault Rapids) 2 men sick . . .

"Thursday 2nd June 1835

"Wether fine. No wind. Had a great Deal of Trouble to find Cook. At last found him but it was so late we could not run only one band (through the rapids). Paid for liquir 7/6. Had a great Deal of Rain to in the afternoon . . .

"Saturday 6th June 1835

"Wether fine. No wind. Run the last band over the Long Sault and the whole of the Raft over Carrillion. Stopt all night at the foot of Carrillion. Had the misfortune to get one mans Arm Broke running Carrillion . . ."

By June 15 the raft was in Rivière-des-Prairies behind the island of Montreal. A week later, after a series of mishaps which included losing their anchor and having to hire a boat to grapple for it, they were out into the St. Lawrence where a sudden change of wind into the north ran the whole raft ashore opposite St. Sulpice.

On Lake St. Peter, 23 miles long and so shallow the waves kick up even in a small wind, they hoisted sail and promptly ran into a storm. On Monday, June 29, one of the new steam boats from Quebec came up and took them in tow and at 4 P.M. they moored off Spencer's Cove, Quebec City, 30 days after they had set out. Safe arrival, however, did not end their troubles. On Saturday, July 25, with the raft still moored outside Spencer's Cove while Wright haggled with the firm of Usborne and Atkinson over the price of his timber, a storm blew up.

"Every man useing his exertions to save his Raft. Wind increased with rising Tide. In the afternoon we thought our raft would go to pieces. During the Night lashed the top Timber and got extra cables and secured it as well as we possibly could

Like the rest of the raft, the cook's section ▷
ran down steep timber slides and rapids
and down through summer gales on the
St. Lawrence and was strongly built to
withstand wind and waves. The roof was
made of loose planks, part of the cargo
which was sold at Quebec City.

Notman Photographic Archives

The Chaudière Falls in the early 1870s before
they were tamed. These 40-foot falls were a
barrier to logging the upper Ottawa until 1829
when Ruggles Wright built a canal, a timber
slide, to bypass them. The entrance to the slide
was 300 yards above the falls and the slide termi-
nated well below the falls after a run of three-
▽ quarters of a mile.

The Public Archives of Canada   C 23028

Several times a day the crew would man
the 30-foot oars to keep the raft in the
current or sweep it through calm water
when the wind failed. A raft might contain 2000 separate timbers and weighed
thousands of tons.

The Public Archives of Canada   C 4620

Raftsmen guide two cribs, or sections, of a timber raft down the slide built in 1843 to float timber safely around the 60-foot Calumet Falls on the upper Ottawa. The lead crib has reached one of the level stretches of the slide which acted as brakes between the steep inclines. A lumberman left the following description of his descent: "The slide gates are thrown open. The water surges over the smooth, inclined channel. Our crib, carefully steered through the gateway, slowly moves over the entrance, advances, sways for a moment, then with a sudden plunge and splash of water rushes faster and faster between the narrow walls, then dipping heavily it leaves the slide and is in the calm waters beneath."

◁ *The Public Archives of Canada C 8734*

but fortunately on the Ebb the wind moderated a Little and our Raft rid out the Storm without Material injury but we Learnt that their was many others wrecked."

So many rafts were lost on the St. Lawrence that in 1856 one million feet of square timber and sawlogs were found on the shores of Anticosti, the lonely island at the mouth of the St. Lawrence.

For three generations Quebec City was a roaring timber port, some said the biggest in the world, shipping wood from half a continent to Liverpool, Cardiff, and London. Rafts came there from the St. Maurice, the Ottawa, Vermont, New York State, the shores of Lake Ontario, and from Michigan. Timber even came from Kentucky, white oak trundled up to the St. Lawrence by canal or rail and rafted to Quebec for shipment to avoid the British tariff on American timber. Ruggles Wright, still haggling over his timber and amusing himself with visits "to see the exhibition of fleas" in the city, reported on August 26th that "25 square rigged vessels arrived this day." In one summer more than 1300 timber ships might clear the port, hundreds of them all loading at the same time. The navigation season for sailing ships was brief and the port was hectic. Testifying before a government timber commission in 1849, Wright recalled the desperate measures the merchants used to get their timber away. "I have actually known, been present, and seen men hired and armed for the protection of a commission merchant's boom and directed, whatever might be the consequences, to shoot the first man who should attempt to attach a raft to the boom, the merchant observing at the same time that he had 30 ships to supply with timber next day, which he would be wholly unable to do unless he kept the way clear by some stringent means."

On shore the shantymen and sailors, English, Scots, Irish, French Canadians, Yankees, roistered in the taverns and fought in the alleys off Champlain Street in the basse-ville, haunt of the crimps who shanghaied drunken lumberjacks to complete the crews of leaky, hard-driven timber hulks. The raftsmen were targets for moralizing writers of the time and were taken to task for "idle indulgence, drinking, smoking, and dashing off in a long coat, flashy waistcoat and trowsers, Wellington or Hessian boots, a handkerchief of many colors around the neck, a watch with a long tinsel chain, and numberless brass seals and an umbrella . . ."[3]

The mark of the timber drogher, old ships which had seen better days in finer trades, was the four ports cut in her bow. They called at Quebec City twice a season, in June and late August, and on their westward passage in ballast were fitted with temporary bunks as cheap immigrant ships. In 1834 hundreds of immigrants were drowned when 30 timber ships were lost at sea.

At the timber coves in Quebec City, rafts were broken up into acres upon acres of squared pine and oak logs to await shipment to England. At the height of the timber trade in the late 1850s as many as 600 ships at a time might be seen loading timber and 1500 cargoes were shipped every summer.

The Public Archives of Canada C 6073

It took three weeks to load a ship through square timber ports in bow and stern, heavy red pine at the bottom and the whole load balanced so it would not shift. Even so, many foundered each year on the voyage to England and sailors called old timber droghers "leather coffins." In this 1872 photo, the loaders are topping up the cargo with "deals" — three-inch planks. "...the rafts are finally broken up, and from the acres of timber thus accumulated, the large, ocean-going ships are loaded. Near the vessel men run actively over the floating timbers, and with the help of pike-poles select the cargo. Each stick or spar is lifted by means of a chain slung from a spar on deck, and brought to a level with the large receiving-port near the vessel's bow. It then rests on a roller, and is easily shoved in, and stowed away. 'Deal' planks are brought alongside the timber-ship in large barges moored fore and aft of the ship, and the deals thrown in through the ports. When the steadily-increasing load within the hold sinks the vessel to its lower ports these are closed, and the loading is resumed at those immediately above."

G. M. GRANT AND A. FLEMING, "LUMBERING" IN *Picturesque Canada, c. 1882.*

47

The droghers were loaded at 35 "timber coves" which stretched 10 miles along the waterfront and spilled across to the south shore. A cove was a storage pond, 1800 feet wide, protected by two stone piers jutting 150 feet into the tidal river. At Wolfe's Cove, Sillery, Spencer's, a cove owned by the Ursuline nuns, and many others, the rafts were dismantled when the tide was low, the timber "brightened up" by broad-axe men who removed the travel scars. There they were measured and graded by government cullers who stamped merchantable export logs with an *M*. Gangs of stowers, swingers, and hookers — 5000 in a good season — winched up the dripping timbers with tackle and windlass and packed it into the holds in the humid heat of a Quebec summer. The gangs were mostly French and Irish, many of them shantymen earning extra cash. Lumber and spars were piled on deck, a top-heavy hazard to navigation. Between May and December in 1872, 57 timber ships were wrecked and abandoned in the Gulf of St. Lawrence and sailors came to call the droghers "coffin ships."

Behind the coves and sail lofts and ship chandlers in Lower Town lay rue St. Pierre, the short and narrow Peter Street, centre of the trade since the 1790s when rafts came down from the Richelieu River and Lake Champlain and from the Bay of Quinte.

Timber had been rafted from the eastern shores of Lake Ontario since 1790, when Samuel Sherwood floated masts down from the Trent River, and the trade from the Upper St. Lawrence area continued to the end of the 19th century. The rafts were bigger than those from the Ottawa, their basic unit not a crib but a dram — possibly 250 or even 500 sticks — which measured 300 feet by 60 feet and took 15 men 30 days to build. The foremen were usually French Canadians: François Landrigg, Julien Giroux, and Aimé Guérin; and the crew men like Tom Mudturtle and Charlie Doubleskin, Iroquois from the reserve at St. Regis near Cornwall or Caughnawaga across from Montreal.

A raft generally took 20 days to travel 500 miles from the banding grounds on Garden Island near Kingston to Quebec City. Licensed pilots with 30-man crews came aboard to take each dram down the three major sets of rapids: the Long Sault which spilled for 20 miles into Lake St. Francis; the Coteau, Cedars, Split Rock, and Cascade rapids from Valleyfield into Lake St. Louis; and finally the Lachine rapids at Montreal. At each rapids the drams were uncoupled from each other and piloted with 30-foot sweeps down the cataract at 20 miles an hour. There were English-speaking pilots at Long Sault, French at Coteau, and at Lachine there were the Iroquois. "To hear the withes cracking and the timber grinding and feel the motion under one's feet as the huge sticks are twisted and bobbed up and down is so thrilling and bewildering that I had no time to think," wrote George Thompson.[4]

The worst rapids on the St. Lawrence, at
Lachine near Montreal, 1901. Crews of
expert Iroquois from the Caughnawaga
Reserve came aboard from Nun's Island
to pilot the timber safely through the
white water. After the rafts disappeared
from the river the sons of Iroquois raftsmen became the cat-footed high steel
workers who built bridges and sky-
scrapers.

Notman Photographic Archives

The Public Archives of Canada   C 2344

Year after year, rafts were smashed in storms on the St. Lawrence, particularly
in the wide stretches of Lake St. Peter and Lake St. Francis. A typical wreck
was reported May 10, 1831, in the *Montreal Gazette*: "We learn that a raft
coming from Salmon River (west of Kingston, Ont.), the property of Mr.
Wells, went to pieces near M'Gee point in Lake St. Francis during the storm
that prevailed on Thursday and we regret to add that 11 out of the 15 who
were on the raft perished."

"Just as we were about to enter the first (Coteau) rapid and the dram bowling along at a lively gait, every Man Jack of them pulled his sweep oar in and dropped to their knees. Of course I thought something dreadful was about to happen; I was standing close to the pilot in the center of the dram and turned to ask him what the trouble was, and he, too, was on his knees crossing himself. My knees shook and my teeth rattled, when suddenly the pilot jumped up and started to swear, and I caught sight of the crew pulling at their oars like heroes. This reassured me and I took a chew of tobacco to steady my nerves. I afterwards learned that the French Canadians always repeat a prayer before entering the rapids, as also do the Indians . . .

"By the time I reached Lachine Rapids on my first trip down I had got quite brave. The last mile or so of the river before entering the rapids, which is run in single drams at intervals of a few minutes, the stream looks quite peaceful. I was, therefore, not much alarmed, and even after we entered the rapids I did not see any particular reason for getting into a funk, so when suddenly the big jump came in view and the pilot yelled in my ear that there was only one place in it about 100 yards wide over which we could safely pass, and he was afraid the dram was not in that channel, my hair fairly began to stand on end and I could see by the way those splendid fellows were pulling their oars there was no 'monkey' business about it, and it was a sight to watch the Indians; every stroke was in unison and made with military precision. In an instant they would reverse the stroke at a signal from the pilot, for the roar of the rapids would drown the report of a cannon. The crew is equally divided, bow and stern, while the pilots stand in the center. Our dram was got back into the channel and in a few moments we were over the big jump, but the enormous waves drew the bow of the dram under water and the men in the bow had to hang onto pieces of rope which were fastened to the timber to keep them from being swept off, and even the pilot and I, standing in the center of the dram, did not escape a ducking. The day previous a dram had missed the channel and 10 men were drowned."

By the late 1800s tugs were used to tow the rafts and Thompson recalled how a storm caught Big Paddy Maher's raft "suddenly in the night" 10 miles out on Lake Ontario. "The assistant foreman was also an Irishman by the name of John Montgomery, who was as stiff an Orangeman as Paddy was a devout Catholic, and they say Paddy started to pray while Jack began to swear. The night was so dark the captain of the tug could not see back to the raft, neither dare he run his tug back among the wildly tossed timber. All the captain knew was that the raft was breaking up, and instead of throwing off his tow line held right on. To uncouple the stern dram was what Montgomery wanted to do, and let her drift ashore, and take chances when she struck of getting off; to remain much longer meant sure death one way or the other, either by being crushed to death or drowned. Some of the crew were frantic, and nearly all badly scared, so that Jack could get none of them to help him . . . the thing (to do) was to cut the chain, which he succeeded in doing with an axe, after hours of toil, the tossing sticks of timber making it dangerous work. The wind drove the dram with the crew ashore just before daylight but it was on a sand beach, and the men got safely ashore losing nothing but their clothes. Without a doubt the whole crew would have met their death but for the cool courage and brave determination of Montgomery . . .''

Occasionally a raft was lost for other reasons. A crew tied a raft at the foot of Rice Lake and, "being votaries of Bacchus and tormented with an incessant and inextinguishable thirst, they adjourned to a tavern to spend the night in the workshop of that jolly god."[5] The raft broke away and floated down the Trent River with not a soul aboard.

Sober, they were the best rivermen in the world. When General Sir Garnett Wolseley needed boatmen to ferry his redcoats up the cataracts of the Nile in the Sudan war in 1884 he remembered the Canadian boatmen who had taken him west to quell the first Riel rebellion. He brought 400 of them to Egypt — Scots from Peterborough, French and Irish from the Ottawa and Trois-Rivières, and Iroquois from Caughnawaga.

Over the years strange and wonderful craft were invented to transport logs. On July 28, 1824, with a brass band serenading 5000 spectators, Charles Wood from Scotland launched a hybrid – half ship and half raft — near Quebec City and named her *Columbus*. Her tapered hull was a solid mass of square timber from her flat bottom to her deck. She was 301 feet long, 51 feet wide, and weighed 3690 tons, one of the biggest vessels ever seen at the time, and carried nearly 100 men in quarters hollowed out of timber. She took seven weeks to cross the Atlantic and, although Wood had intended to break her apart and sell the whole lot in England, at the last moment he decided to sell only her deck cargo of lumber and send her back to Quebec for another load. She was lost on her return voyage although apparently her crew survived. The next year Wood built a larger monster, the 5000-ton *Baron of Renfrew*. She was wrecked on her maiden voyage in the English Channel, her timbers washed up for miles along the shores of Normandy.

Hugh Robertson of Saint John, New Brunswick, was more successful. At Fingerboard Beach in the Bay of Fundy near Joggins, Nova Scotia, he built 22 000 logs into the shape of a cigar 150 feet around at the middle and 600 feet long. The local housewives donated butter to grease its launching skids and two schooners towed it to New York City where it was the talk of the town in 1888. Like

Lockwood Survey Corporation Limited, Toronto, Canada

One of the last of the Abitibi Paper Company tugs towing a raft of 10 000 cords of pulpwood from White River on the northeast shore of Lake Superior to the mill at Sault Ste. Marie. Thousands of logs, corralled within a mile-round "bag boom" of buoyant Sitka spruce logs chained end to end, were towed at the end of a 1600-foot cable. Since the tug could travel at only one mile an hour, the trip took a week of steady hauling. The greatest hazard, apart from storms, was a headwind which might blow the tow backwards.

In August 1888, Hugh Robertson of Saint John, New Brunswick, launched a new type of raft, shaped like a giant cigar, at Fingerboard Beach, Joggins, Nova Scotia. It was 600 feet long, 150 feet around, weighed 15 000 tons, and contained 22 000 logs. It was towed to New York by two schooners. If the logs had been shipped in the usual fashion, 40 schooners would have been required.

N.S. Museum Collection

Photograph by MALAK, *Ottawa*

Pulpwood on the Ottawa. If this scene looks familiar take a look at the back of a Canadian one-dollar bill. Long after the old pine rafts were gone from the river, booms of pulpwood such as this were brought down by the sturdy grey tugs of the Upper Ottawa Improvement Company.

many other New Brunswick lumbermen Robertson took his ideas to the Pacific northwest, towed great redwood logs to San Francisco, and built what was, then, the greatest man-made object ever seen on the coast – a raft containing 11 million board feet. Before World War One a British Columbia logger, G. G. Davis, faced with towing logs 400 miles to Vancouver from the stormy waters of the Queen Charlotte Islands, improved on Robertson's cigars by lacing logs with wire cables pulled tight by donkey engines. A typical Davis raft, bound with 90 tons of chain and cable, was 200 feet long, 30 feet high. Davis could tow his rigid, streamlined rafts through seas that would have smashed a conventional towing boom.

On the lakes and rivers of the east, pulpwood was towed by tugs. Up to 200 buoyant 25-foot Sitka spruce logs would be chained into a circle perhaps a mile around and containing 600 000 12-foot pulpwood logs. "We'd go about a mile an hour towing a boom on Lake Superior and a trip would take eight or nine days. Once we got a gale of 70 miles an hour and the booms parted and the tow broke and we were blown backwards for 80 miles. The main problem is to make sure you are far enough off shore. It's the onshore winds you worry about. We carried oil lanterns on the booms of the raft, on the nose piece, the back, both sides, but they were visible only for one mile. One time the tug *Gargantua* was coming down Lake Superior with a raft and an American boat got tangled right up into the raft. The tug skipper couldn't stop and he towed the American boat 17 miles in the opposite direction to what the American boat had been going."[6]

By the late 1800s Montreal had replaced Quebec City as the big timber port on the St. Lawrence. The lumber trade had grown bigger than the square timber business and Montreal was the centre of the lumber trade to the United States. The Lake Ontario ports, Oakville and Toronto, were shipping lumber. Steamships had replaced the timber droghers and unlike the sailing ships could easily ply right up to Montreal to load the square timber still being shipped to Britain.

In 1908 the last square timber raft to come down the Ottawa and on to Quebec City was delivered by an 80-man crew. It came from J. R. Booth's Coulonge River limits, contained 150 000 feet of pine, and was worth $100 000. After that, timber, like lumber, was shipped by rail or in barges. At Quebec City, once the biggest timber port in the world, the coves had been abandoned, the booms left rotting on the shore.

GREEN GOLD: THE TIMBER CRUISERS

4

Until the 1900s good timber, like good labour, was cheap and plentiful and a lumberman could choose his "logging chance," or timber berth, as casually as he might go fishing. Equipped with a couple of blankets, flour, salt pork, tea, a light axe, and a compass he walked or canoed into the bush when the black flies had thinned out in August, and when he found a stand of pine within hauling distance of a stream he built a camp. As operations grew he might hire a bush-ranger, a woodsman who knew where good timber stood. In the thick primeval forest the bush-ranger would climb a tall tree, spot a "vein" of dark pine amid the brighter foliage of lesser trees, drop a branch to the ground to point the direction, climb down, and hike off on a compass bearing to have a look. He could estimate at a glance, within a thousand feet or so, what a big stand of trees would yield in sawn lumber down at the mill. When the lumber business grew more demanding in the 1890s the bush-rangers refined their estimates by running a couple of compass lines as far apart as they could see. They counted the trees on the sample "strip," estimated the number and size of logs that could be cut from each tree, and multiplied the results with a pencil stub each evening by the light of a camp-fire. "Different ways are adopted to arrive at quantities by different men; the figures obtained by the rangers all bear a close affinity to each other and sometimes are amazingly alike. Upon the reports of these men deals of great value are made. Rangers of experience enjoy the confidence of lumbermen of the country and to such an extent as to induce them to invest millions on their judgment."[1]

Bush-rangers came to be called timber cruisers as they improved their skills. In British Columbia in the early 1900s they were almost as common as prospectors, and a man looking for "green gold" could drive a post in unoccupied Crown land, measure a square mile, and rent a timber berth for $140 a year. "My old man," said Edwin Debeck of Victoria, "was cruising in the 1890s . . . you landed on the shore, ran into there half a mile, a mile maybe, took a look, come out and that was a cruise . . . It was quite an adventure, you know, for a young fella."[2]

During the 19th century eastern loggers cut in the Acadian Forest Region of the Maritimes and in the Great Lakes–St. Lawrence Forest Region which runs in a broad green band west by north from the Gaspé to Thunder Bay and on to the Manitoba border. Those forests contained oak, maple, and other hardwoods as well as hemlock, spruce, balsam fir, and the stately pine which had brought such sudden wealth. The pine was one of the few trees Jacques Cartier recognized when he stepped ashore in what is now New Brunswick in 1534; but it was a pine which grew so large that French and English explorers carried seedlings home like trophies and planted them at Fontainebleau in France and Longleat in England. As late as the mid-1800s there were still a goodly number of those original, majestic, primeval pines, "frequently 15 feet in circumference near the ground, free of branches for 70 or 80 feet, and often more than 120 feet in height. Some trees, after being hewn square, and the limbs, within 20 to 30 feet of the top cut off, have measured eight to nine tons of 40 solid feet each."[3] A good hewer would take two 40-foot square timbers from each tree, sometimes three. The white pine was valued for anything from ship masts to matchwood and the red pine was used for construction timber.

The first official estimate of standing white pine by the Department of Agriculture in Ottawa in 1895 gave Ontario 19 billion 404 million feet, Quebec 15 billion 734 million feet, and the Maritimes, which meant mostly New Brunswick, 2 billion 200 million feet. Within little more than a generation much of this pine was to fall to the axe and to fire and loggers then turned to spruce and balsam fir. But the true home of the spruce and balsam was farther north in the Boreal Forest, a million square miles of "Christmas trees" stretching 600 miles north and ending in the tundra as a scrawny "forest of sticks."

In the Boreal Forest the toughest, most ubiquitous tree is the black spruce. In swampy ground it averages 30 to 50 feet in height and perhaps 10 inches around, but is known to grow almost as big as a small pine and is usually shunned by its fairer sister, the white spruce, which averages 80 feet and two feet around on higher ground. While prized for lumber, the white spruce is less prolific. These and the 70-foot red spruce of the Maritimes and the balsam fir, like 50- or 60-foot church steeples, mantle one-third of Canada's forest land as thick as wool on a sheep's back. They were the softwood trees which fed the pulpwood industry although in later years jack pine, which grows 40 to 60 feet and one foot around, has also been used for pulp. Originally, these softwood trees were often used as railroad ties.

In the Rocky Mountains the eastern forest shades off into other spruce, the western white spruce and the Englemann, and the lodgepole pine, and at the end of that long green sweep of trees from Atlantic to Pacific lie the coastal forests of British Columbia where trees have been found as tall as 20-storey buildings.

On the coast, mixed with giant cedars, Sitka spruce, and western hemlock, rules the Douglas fir, named for the Scottish botanist David Douglas who identified it in 1823. One of the most prized trees in the world for lumber and construction timber, it grows to 150 or 200 feet, 9 feet around and sometimes as much as 300 feet with girths of 15 feet. The coastal forests stretch inland 50 miles before they merge with the trees of the B.C. interior, which are more like those back east.

In the east the new pulpwood industry, with its great appetite for long-fibered spruce, turned after the First World War to the Boreal Forest, the vast region known to few except the Hudson's Bay Company traders and a handful of government surveyors such as Alex Niven who had blazed base lines and meridian lines between Georgian Bay and James Bay around the turn of the century and had been told to keep a look-out for suitable forests of pulpwood. "Even in the 1920s and 30s there was surprisingly little known about the geography up there. Cruising in the Timogami area of Ontario in 1929, we were not only naming the lakes, we were *finding* the lakes."[4]

To log that rugged country, far from the settled river valleys of the old established lumber industry in the south, better cruising methods were needed and American foresters trained in German methods at Yale or Pennsylvania State University were imported. Canada had no forestry schools of its own until the University of Toronto established one in 1907, the University of New Brunswick at Fredericton in 1908, Laval at Quebec City in 1910, and the University of British Columbia in 1921. Old woods bosses like Harry Dennison at Sault Ste. Marie, Ontario, who put no faith in book learning, were sceptical. Dennison insisted that a bush-ranger such as Peter Lesage of the Garden River Indian Reserve, born and bred in the woods, could out-cruise any college boy. But the new pulp companies were in-

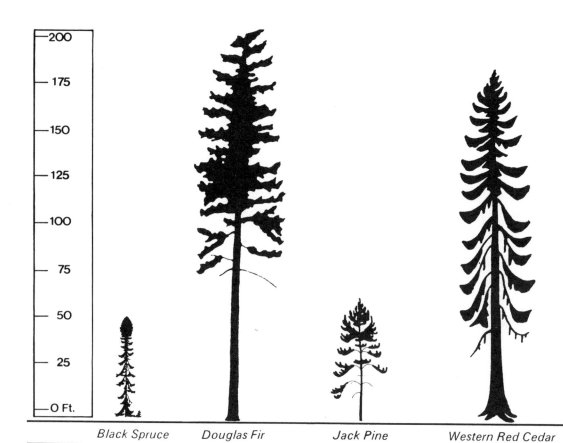

Black Spruce   Douglas Fir   Jack Pine   Western Red Cedar

Black spruce. This smaller, tougher cousin of the white spruce thrives in the swampy Boreal forest and reaches a height of 30 to 50 feet, with a diameter of 6 to 10 inches. With branches jutting out like a candelabra, these trees sometimes grow to a height of more than 100 feet and a diameter of three feet.

Douglas fir. One of the most valued timber trees in the world, this native of the British Columbia coastal forests averages 150 to 200 feet at maturity, sometimes reaching 300 feet. Diameters of nine feet are common and 15 foot diameters were not uncommon among virgin stands. It is used for building and was the mainstay of the B.C. lumber trade, as the white pine was in the east.

Jack pine. Used in building, for railway ties, and in production of pulp and paper, it usually grows from 40 to 60 feet high and 12 inches around, but sometimes reaches 80 feet in height and two feet in diameter.

Western red cedar. Normally grows to 150 feet in height and six feet in diameter. It provided wood for shingles because it did not warp easily.

White spruce. One of the mainstays of the pulp-and-paper industry, along with black spruce and balsam fir. It grows to 80 feet with a diameter of two feet and sometimes reaches 120 feet with a diameter of four feet. Valued as lumber for its strong, resilient wood, its resonance made it good material for making musical instruments.

Western hemlock. Used not only for lumber and pulpwood, but also for its red inner bark which contains tannin — a substance used in the tanning of leather.

Eastern white pine. The monarch of the eastern Canadian square timber trade in the 19th century, used as masts for ships and as lumber to build homes. The most valuable softwood tree in eastern Canada, it was also the tallest, reaching 100 feet in height and three feet in diameter, and sometimes growing 175 feet or more and five feet in diameter. Formerly called "yellow" or "Quebec" pine.

Balsam fir. A staple of the pulp-and-paper trade, but also marketed as lumber and as the most popular of Christmas trees. It grows in the shape of a church steeple, 50 to 70 feet high and up to one or two feet around.

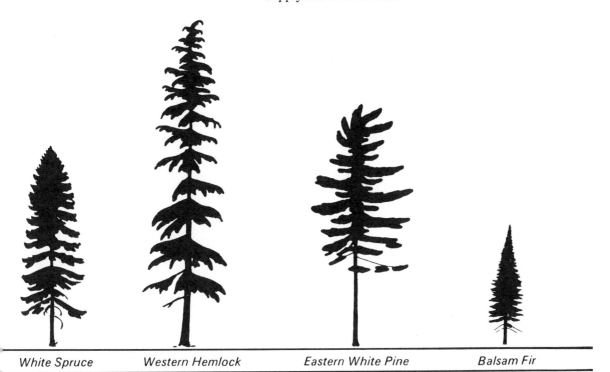

Environment Canada — Forestry Service Booklet: Canada — A Forest Nation. Reproduced by permission of the Minister of Supply and Services Canada.

| White Spruce | Western Hemlock | Eastern White Pine | Balsam Fir |

Before the appearance of university-trained timber cruisers the forests were explored for likely timber "limits," or "berths," by bush-rangers with experience both in the lumber camps and down in the mills where they had gained a shrewd idea of what a tree would "saw out to." With rations of salt pork, tea, flour, and molasses, they would plunge into the woods for a week or two, hunting like prospectors for a good, big "vein," or clump of pine, or for stands of spruce or balsam fir where they could cut 10 cords to the acre for pulpwood. The woods they cruised were usually like great patchwork quilts, with hardwood on the ridges, evergreen on the flats and slopes, and lakes and rivers galore.

Ont. Ministry of Natural Resources

59

clined to agree with Ellwood Wilson, the Yale Forestry School graduate who pioneered modern timber cruising on Quebec's St. Maurice River in 1905; like army generals the companies needed accurate maps and information to operate. It was not enough, argued Wilson, merely to know where the wood and the streams were, with a guess at the amount. He wanted to know how much of a timber limit was swamp or burnt-over, whether the trees were growing or dying and how long the supply would last, how much it would cost to log the area, and what the risk of fire might be. He found it strange that hard-headed lumbermen, who would not dream of buying a few hundred dollars worth of equipment without close scrutiny, thought nothing of spending many thousands on logging operations merely on the say-so of an illiterate bush-ranger. "Now that fire and the axe have destroyed so much of our available supplies and the multiplication of wood-using industries for larger and larger quantities of wood year by year," he said, "it is absolutely necessary to take account of what we have left." He set out to do just that, sometimes with great hardship, as at Lac Marcotte up the St. Maurice in late November 1910.

Ellwood Wilson's Story

"I had gone about 600 feet from the place where we went onto the ice and was about 300 feet from the nearest shore when without any warning the ice seemed to give way in all directions dropping me into the freezing water. I swam to the edge of the ice nearest the shore and tried very carefully to get up on it, but it was too thin. I tried this in several places, breaking the ice in front of me toward shore in the hope of finding a place where it would bear my weight.

"While this was happening my companion had gone back to shore and cut a long pole which he slid out to me. This I placed across the narrowest part of the break and got almost onto the ice when it broke again and down I went head first into the water. I was getting so chilled now that I could hardly swim. I made for my sleeping bag floating nearby and with that to hold me up swam to the ice nearest shore. Sliding the bag under my chest I tried to work myself out onto the ice. I got my whole body out with only my feet on the bag and was just congratulating myself when the ice gave way again. On coming up I was so numb that I took a turn of my tump-line around my body in case I should lose consciousness. I did not know how I was ever going to get out and was childishly angry at not being able to and the thought of having to drown.

"Twice my man had started out on the ice after me, but I made him go back, realizing that if he went in we should both drown. I called to him to cut a long, dry pole and to tie three tump-lines to it and slide it out to me. I got hold of the pole and lying on my bag and breaking the ice in front of me he drew me to a point where the ice was thick enough to crawl on. By now, 25 minutes after my first plunge, I was very numb. To cap the climax we both went in again about 15 feet from shore, but fortunately only up to our chests. After getting out I completely lost consciousness.

"When I came to I was sitting naked on a log in the snow being rubbed with a dish towel. He had some dry underwear in his duffle bag which we put on. As I had all the matches, and they were of course wet, we gnawed a piece of hard tack and both crawled into his sleeping bag. At least half a dozen times in the night he woke me up saying 'For God's sake let me turn over.' When we woke in the morning our clothes were frozen solid; my breeches were standing up as though a man was standing inside of them. Having slept with the matches under my armpit, they were quite dry, and we soon had a good fire and some breakfast."[5]

Cruisers commonly worked in the winter when travel was faster, the swamps and lakes were frozen, and food kept better, but blizzards and subarctic cold were threats to survival. Walter Kishbaugh's diary of a cruise north of Lake Abitibi was typical.

> "Saturday, January 14th, 1922
> Niven's Base Line — Mileage 192 — Camp #7
> Cloudy and Snow
> "After a very restless night of fitful dozes I rose at 3.30 and lit a fire. After a glance at the thermometer I realized why I had been unable to get warm. It registered 56 degrees below . . . a blinding blizzard sprung up during the P.M. and our trail was well covered when we travelled back to camp . . .

> "Friday, Feb. 3rd, 1922
> Camp #10 — 1 mile S of Speights Line — Mileage 36
> "Cold with heavy wind and fall of snow in AM. We broke camp at 8.30 and were on the trail in the midst of a severe wind and snow storm. Dick, one of our huskies, had been sick for some time and had to turn him loose today. Ted has a bad attack of distemper and we let him trail behind the loads. He followed about a mile in the rear. Pete played out on the trail and had to be turned loose also, so we had three useless dogs today. The wind was severe on the lake today and everybody nearly froze."

Kishbaugh and four other young American foresters had been sent to look for timber limits between Cochrane and the mouth of Abitibi River near James Bay.

"Cold? Oh, boy!" he recalled. "Sixty-five degrees below zero one night. We put up a tent every night, tramped down the snow and put brush down and big, heavy felt blankets that came off the Iroquois Falls paper-making machines. Each of us had a dog team. It was the first time we ever drove dogs but there was nothing to it, four dogs in a team, you just follow the leader. We ate well, porridge for breakfast, soup at noon, dried food, potatoes, peas. We'd play poker every night. We met Indians going south, trapping, travelling alone, just one man and a dog team and we stopped and talked to them and told them how the trail was on the way south. The country is quite flat and you don't go far from the river, perhaps a mile, before you run into muskeg and we found there wasn't enough wood to cut commercially. It didn't take us long to be able to judge the amount of timber to the acre. We covered the country right down to the mouth of the Abitibi River where there was an Indian settlement and just turned around and came back. We spent Christmas in the bush and every day was the same. We were there all winter, as long as we dared, until the spring breakup — five or six months. I think it was the first big cruise in Eastern Canada. That was more than 60 years ago."

In such harsh conditions cruisers learned to make camp with speed and precision. In a seven-man party four would bed down the dogs, cut firewood, and cook a pound of corn meal and one-third of a pound of tallow for each dog while the other three men unloaded toboggans, erected tent and stove, and stuck spruce twigs into the packed snow inside the tent to make a springy bed. A tarpaulin and blankets or sleeping bags were laid on the twigs. A log served as a seat and behind it was stacked tamarack, dry spruce, and green birch for the stove. Everything had to be carefully repacked or hung on the ridge pole so it would not get lost in the snow. One of Kishbaugh's men lost a leather dog harness and found it only two days later in the soup pot where it had become part of the stock.

"You'd bank snow around the edges of the tent so there would be no draughts," said forester Earle Wilson of Toronto. "We had a little oval stove, like a Quebec heater, light sheet iron — 15 pounds. The pipe went out the back of the tent and the stove was on stilts you drove down through the snow, which might be three feet deep. After five days the snow would start breaking down and you couldn't stay there any longer. We moved on every five days. We'd put jack pine in the stove and then green birch and lock the damper tight as a drum and it would last nearly all night. The dogs we chained to a tree and they would stay out there in the cold, just curl up, and if there was a snowstorm they wouldn't be up and move around in the morning until the people moved. We'd start cruising at daybreak and cut tin cans open on one side to put a candle in to see to read our compass. By 2 P.M. we would have cruised six miles out, offset one-half mile, and cruised six miles back. In one winter and part of the next summer, this was in the 1920s, we covered 980 square miles in northern Ontario, with cruise strips running one-half mile apart.

"Each man took one six-mile-long cruise line and these were one side of a township to another. The township lines had been blazed around 1909 by Ontario land surveyors. Farther north the lines were nine miles apart. The only information on those maps was what the surveyor saw when he crossed rivers or high rock hills or areas burned by fire. The compassman would steer a course ahead of you and make a trail that you would follow and if he was good and there was no magnetic distortion he'd come out within 100 yards of a survey post at the other end. The cruiser had to identify the changes in the types of trees, the forest mixture, and we'd estimate by eye the cords per acre of pulpwood within a quarter acre sample plot — 59 feet around us in a circle. How many trees were in the plot, what they were averaging, maybe eight inches in diameter at breast height. We'd estimate the age, 40 or 60 years.

"In 1924 I cruised up the Péribonka, 200 miles north of Lac St. Jean above Chicoutimi in Quebec. I think it was the first time anyone explored into that region because there were no Indian trails, even. No sign of anything up there. It was good timber. There were 20 of us but we didn't have good food on that job: sow belly, prunes, beans, very little that would prevent scurvy, and everybody got boils so damn bad they could hardly work. We were pretty strong guys in those days. We'd carry 80 pounds, an 18-foot canoe weighed 90, some could carry 100 pounds over a portage. The Péribonka ran due north, a big river, about as wide as the Ottawa and full of black flies."

By the 1920s cruising was becoming a science. The cruising team would measure and describe all the trees on a strip right through a township, 11 feet on each side of a compass line, perhaps six strips or more through a township. The six-mile meridian lines ran north and south and the base lines east and west, marked with spruce or cedar posts. First came a compassman with a "two-chain," which once was a steel-link Gunter chain used by 19th century land surveyors but which by the 1920s had been refined to a 132-foot steel tape anchored to the back of a man's belt. Checking his course with frequent compass readings, he would halt at the end of each 132-foot span, "hang" a blaze mark on a tree with his light cruising axe, and walk on. The caliperman with him would sample the diameters of trees with his 30-inch wooden calipers, and the tallyman, usually the leader of the crew, would note down the forest types which followed the contours of the land, the hills and streams and valleys.

Since a stand of white pine, for example, would tend to run along a hillside, the strips were cut across the contours of the land so as to include a sample of all types of trees. A crew would cruise about 10 per cent of an area to be cut, jotting down information to be worked up later into detailed maps. They would sample the ages of the trees with a steel borer which pulled a plug out of a tree so the rings could be counted, the light lines of summer growth and the dark lines of winter.

A cruiser rarely, if ever, got lost although a few admitted to "getting turned around a bit." "I was out two nights one time, but you know the way out. You've got a compass and you've got creeks to follow. The trouble with people is they panic. You could go a long time, a week, without food. You just sat down and made a fire to think things out."[6] Fleetwood Pride from the Saint John River in New Brunswick once found a lumberjack lost in the snowy woods and asked him, "When you found you were lost, why didn't you take your back tracks?" The man replied, "Goddamnit, I've been hunting for them all day!" So Fleetwood Pride took him by the shoulder, turned him around, and said, "There they are, damn it. They must have been *following* you all day."[7]

Jack Matthews recalled that for six days in 1928 his northern Ontario cruising party had only beans and tea. "We didn't have any sugar left, we didn't have any salt. We just had beans. There was no fish to catch in that part of the country. So we had boiled beans for breakfast, you'd take a baking powder can of boiled beans for your lunch, and when you came home in the evening you'd have more boiled beans. One time, for 10 of us, we had about a pound of bacon and a handful of rice and we ran into some blueberries and picked like mad, thinking, well, blueberries are good to eat. But the cook was a little dumb. He took the bacon and fried it and chopped it into little pieces and got a big pail of water boiling, put the rice in, put the bacon in, and dumped in the blueberries. Jeez! You never saw such a gruesome purple-looking gruel in all your life. It tasted like nothing on earth. It had no flavour, just thin, purplish gruel, but if you got a little chunk of bacon it didn't taste too bad."

The Moon of the Broken Snowshoes: Hulme Stone's Story
"In winter we'd get six weeks of good cruising weather and we'd do twice as much as we'd do all summer. From February until the frost disappeared you'd break a lot of snowshoes breaking through the crust. 'The Moon of the Broken Snowshoes,' the Ojibway called it.

"At night there'd be a good inch of crust and you could go to beat the band. Often you didn't need snowshoes. By mid-afternoon, however, you'd have to get off it since it was too soft. I was trapped a couple of times by this and just sat down and made a fire and waited until it firmed up again. You'd carry tea and your little cotton lunch sack. We're talking about early 1924 now, down the Sand River in that rough country between Lake Superior and Mile 130 on the Algoma Central Railway above Sault Ste. Marie. We didn't have dogs; we pulled the toboggans ourselves with a harness — one pushed with a pole and one pulled. We carried 200 to 250 pounds on a toboggan.

"We'd be out a month or six weeks. The townships there were mostly six miles wide. You found the three-mile post on the base line and ran a centre line by compass up through and you worked off that centre line. Ran out three miles from it to the township line, offset half a mile along that, and then came back to your centre line. Those were interesting times because Ben Avery, a forester at the Soo, was developing new systems. I'd cruise the thing first, then lay out the cutting area by watersheds on a sustained yield basis. That is, instead of harvesting annually as an ordinary farmer does, you were supposed to be able to go back and cut spruce in 60 or 65 years due to natural regeneration.

"In 1924 I had Henry Dow and old Mose Lesage, two boys from the Garden River Reserve, as compassmen. They loved the bush and they'd only take about three compass readings in three miles. That was the life of those fellows, cruising. We lived in tents all the time. Funny thing, those fellows were brought up on rivers, in canoes, and not one of them could swim a stroke. Lumbermen in general — some could swim, some couldn't. A lot of them couldn't.

"Joe Belanger was an old Indian, about 60, and a hell of a great cook. We'd take desiccated potatoes, dried onions, dried carrots, canned butter, bacon, hams, flour, sugar, tea. In the summer-time we'd gather up the arrow weed for him and he'd hang it in a bag. White, solid little flowers and a fern-like leaf. He made medicine tea out of that. If we got snow-blind, which we did often in spring from the glare, we'd have to go and pick Old Joe the tips of cedar trees, little buds, and he'd make a hot poultice and put it on your eyes and they'd be fixed in about 24 hours. We'd put charcoal under our eyes to try to cut the glare. I used to take him fishing in the evening in our canoe. We crossed a lake with nice green, clear water but it was an eerie-looking bottom on this lake. He said suddenly, 'Stone! Turn around. Wanibiju water!' That's the Ojibway devil. So I turned around and we went to fish in another lake. We used a four-holed tin stove and the pipe was small and Old Joe's eyes got bad from this smoke. The next morning he brought me an empty lemon extract bottle. 'Stone, you go by that lake today? Fill that bottle with Wanibiju water.' I forgot all about it — just remembered on the way home — so I filled the bottle not from the Wanibiju Lake but from the same lake we were camped on. I asked him next morning, 'How are your eyes?' 'Oh, Stone,' he said. 'I can see moose three miles.' All he needed was a little water in his eyes.

"Once Henry Dow and I had been out to Chapleau and were coming down Montreal River. That was the greatest Indian country — Cree. There were signs on the trees and the little cradle boards they carried the babies in, hanging in the trees on the portages where they took the baby out. Moss was hanging up to dry — the baby's diapers. There was an old couple ahead of us and they'd camp on the bottom of the portage overnight and we'd camp on the top side. I found a little red corner of bandanna and picked it up and there was a little piece of plug smoking tobacco tied into it and I said, 'The squaw has forgotten her tobacco.' 'Oh, no,' Henry said. 'She didn't forget. She leave that. Wanibiju he come along and see that and sit down and smoke and they get away.' "

Except for moose in the autumn rutting season and for bears rummaging in the cook-camp garbage, woodsmen had little trouble with animals.

Bears were more a nuisance than a threat. "They had a funny way — 'woof,' and a kind of sigh — and they ran faster up hill than down, 35 miles an hour. We met a mother bear when she had cubs but she just turned the cubs around and gave them a slap."[8]

— "Back of Agawa on Lake Superior 50 years ago we had packed our supplies 16 miles and built a high platform of round poles and put the meat and sugar on top wrapped in tarps and the canned goods underneath. We had a can of fly tox and put it on top and moved on. We sent one of the fellows back for supplies a few days later and he returned with that can of fly tox with big teeth marks in it. A bear had got hold of it and drank it. Well sir, that big balsam tree beside the cache, the bear had gone up that a couple of times, you could see his marks. You could smell the fly tox. He had taken a big drink of it. You could see where he'd vomited a big hunk of stuff full of fly tox. I guess the bear is still going. He never bothered us again."[9]

— "Now here's a true story you can put in your book. This really happened." Len Shewfelt of Thessalon, Ontario, is the sort of man who does not retail fables. "We were on the Serpent River camped at this end of Quirke Lake right where the river comes in. The boys were having lunch when they saw an animal swimming from an island less than half a mile out from the mouth of the river. A whole bunch of these Frenchmen ran and got into a boat, a big 30-foot pointer. They didn't know if it was a deer or a bear or what, but it looked like a bear. They caught up with the bear but were rowing too fast and went right up on it. He put his paw up and swung himself right into the boat. The fellows beat it to the back of the boat but it kept right on going from momentum and hit the shore and the bear ran off."

Most of them considered wolves harmless and around Sault Ste. Marie they had a saying — "I never knew a man that was et by a wolf" — but there were always a few lumberjacks who argued otherwise. J. B. Benson, who cruised the Gatineau in Quebec and the Restigouche in New Brunswick, wrote that "wolves were plentiful in the 1850s in every part of the Canadian woods . . . as a rule arrant cowards, a shot will generally cause them to drop their tails between their legs and run. In packs at night they gain courage and are then unwelcome visitors."[10] Benson claimed he was walking through the bush alone one night when five wolves began to follow him and when he ran they closed in on him. He dropped his leather mitts. "Soon I heard a succession of growls and snarls and on looking back saw they had all stopped pell mell and were having a scrap over my mitts." Before Benson reached camp the wolves caught him, "their hair on end, frothing like demons at the mouth. I shall never forget that fight." He said he was tiring fast when a gang of teamsters came to his rescue and drove the pack off. Most woodsmen find Benson's other encounter — with a rutting bull moose — more credible. "Mr. Moose came upon me so suddenly that I barely had time to shin up a birch tree. He fairly reared up against the tree in his endeavor to reach me, struck at the tree with his fore feet and pawed up the ground around the tree until I almost began to think he was bent on uprooting it. His hair stood on end and his eyes blazed fiercely. The rascal kept me there for about two hours."

Most cruisers, however, swore that the woods were safer than a city street and when they carried guns it was not for protection but to hunt fresh meat. Paul Provencher from Trois-Rivières, Quebec, preferred to hunt with bow and arrow. In his 40 years as a forester, the descendant of a 17th century *coureur de bois* named Sébastien, Provencher cruised the North Shore of the St. Lawrence.

Paul Provencher's Story

"From Baie Comeau it was all wilderness for 600 miles right up to Eskimo Land, Fort Chimo, and Ungava Bay. That was the territory I covered for years making the first forest inventory. We went straight up to Ungava Bay on foot with Montagnais Indians from Lac St. Jean, 40 men. It was winter work because the grub wouldn't spoil and we could cover so much more territory with dog teams than by canoe, but there were days in January and February when the storms would immobilize you for three days at a time. I supplied my men with felt to put under them so they wouldn't catch cold in their kidneys, even though we slept on balsam boughs. I've seen it go 62 below. You could hardly light a fire outdoors; it seemed to lack oxygen.

"I ran short of grub once when I did a reconnaissance with an Indian guide and we had to live off the land. We ate beaver, lynx, anything we could find: owls, gulls, partridges, ptarmigan, squirrels. When it was windy, 25 or 30 miles an hour, you'd go into the woods and not dare show on a lake. The first thing hit by the wind was the genitals. I asked the Indians, 'Gee, how do you protect yourself? Sometimes I have so much trouble with mine I don't know if I'm going to lose the whole damn thing.' They said, 'Take an old sock there and press the whole thing against your belly and you'll never feel no damn 40 degrees going through.' Some tried weasel skins but they were too slippery.

"Our timber limits ran north about 200 miles to Lac Mouchalagan and Summit Lake where the water drains both ways, up to Ungava Bay and down to the St. Lawrence. We had an early Russian motorized toboggan but didn't like to use it in case spare parts were needed in 60 below zero weather. A dog, on the other hand, could live and work in 60 below zero weather. I studied those dogs and found I could add one hour a day to their speed by having a dog in heat as the leader. I exploited the sex life of those dogs. I wouldn't have depended on that Russian toboggan, that was no damn good.

"I surveyed from Bersimis River east along the St. Lawrence to Moisie and all that country and I travelled north to the height of land and Fort McKenzie. My longest exploration was 10 months. I started in November and came back when the snow was falling the next year, 1929–30. Before that only the main rivers had been surveyed. When aerial photography came in, it was different."

After the First World War the cutting of pulpwood expanded rapidly up into the Boreal Forest, and quick timber surveys were needed. In 1919 at Grand'Mère, Quebec, Ellwood Wilson borrowed two superannuated Curtiss HS2L flying boats from the federal government and bought two cameras. "As far as I know it was the first cruising of pulpwood by aerial surveys. The ideas of using the air had been thought of before and some sketching had been done by different people, but our base maps in that country were so terribly inaccurate — lakes, instead of being irregular with bays in them, were just a circle on the map."[11]

Aerial cruising spread to Ontario and a few jobless veterans of the First World War Royal Flying Corps gave up their death-defying weekend flying circuses and founded the almost equally hazardous

Charles Cameron, cook with Earle Wilson's cruise party in 1922, portages his portable kitchen around the rapids on Missinaibi River north of Chapleau in northern Ontario. This was a gag shot, posed for fun, but a portage load of 100 pounds was not uncommon.

Courtesy of Earle Wilson, Toronto

The Public Archives of Canada   C 22736

Among the first aircraft used in timber cruising in the early 1920s was the Curtiss HS2L, an amphibian, 40 feet long, 14 feet high, with a wing span of 74 feet. Both pilot and observer sat in open cockpits in the nose.

trade of the bush pilot. The first big aerial cruise was organized by the Ontario Department of Lands and Forests in 1921 to map 15 000 square miles of forest in northwestern Ontario. The Curtiss flying boats had 330 horsepower Liberty motors, a top speed of 70 miles an hour, and enough piano wire lacing the 70-foot wings to imprison a canary. The open cockpit in the nose, although a cold perch and precarious, gave excellent visibility for both the men with cameras and the foresters who liked to sketch their own maps of the forests 5000 feet below. It was, said Ellwood Wilson, exactly like having a coloured relief map spread out below for study. He said a forester could get a better idea of 50 square miles of unknown territory in two hours' flying than he could after spending two weeks on the ground. In the six years ending in 1927 aerial artists sketch-mapped some 30 000 square miles of Canadian forest long before aerial camera techniques reached maturity. One of the best was Holly Parsons, a young forester from Toronto.

Holly Parsons' Story

"I did my first flying in 1922. Those planes had a gliding angle like a falling brick. The pilots were having trouble with forced landings and would not fly under 5000 feet but later we flew about 3500.

"The colour and density of the crowns of the trees not only tells you the species but the age class and in many cases the quality of the timber underneath. You could not see much of what was under the crowns but the various intensities of green would tell you whether it was spruce, white pine or red pine, hard maple, or tamarack. As to heights of stands, if the crown cover was fairly consistent you knew it was a mature stand. If you could see holes in the stand you knew it was overmature. If the crown cover was flat but coming up almost to the height of the mature stands you knew it was an advanced second growth stand of timber, usually the result of a forest fire. It got so I could tell the age classes of stands up to 50 years. My early ground cruising was the foundation for my work.

"I put in at least 10 000 flying hours over 50 years and mapped 100 000 square miles at various scales for 79 different outfits and flew with 80 pilots. Up around Hearst in northern Ontario, where I was going for 25 years, I knew the trees by their first names.

"We had this pilot who was quite a character. At the Soo they built a dove-cote on top of the hangar and got two homing pigeons from Holland at $125 each. This lad flew out to Steep Rock, a long jaunt in those days, and they gave him a homing pigeon. He had a forced landing out around Atikokan and looked for the emergency rations but somebody had forgot to pack them. So he built a fire and wrung the pigeon's neck and ate it, a $125 blue plate special.

"We were doing work for Gillies in Quebec one winter and Charlie Lawson was the pilot. It was 40 below zero and the snow on the crown cover made identification almost impossible. Around Mattawa the motor started to splutter. We found out later the carburetor was icing. Charlie had just come back from British Columbia and wasn't used to the cold, I guess, because if he had shoved the manifold heat to it the carburetor would have thawed out. We started to come down and there was a little clearing and I could see a man there and a flock of sheep and he turned and headed for the house as fast as he could. We came up out of the clearing and just cleared the tree-tops — we took about eight feet off one tree — and we skittered across the crowns of the trees to the next clearing and came down and were heading right for a log building and we tried a ground loop and tore off the undercarriage and one wing . . . and the conversation languished. Over the years I had to walk out of the bush four times. One time I had no compass so I had to use my watch — the sun has to be out and you point your hour hand at the sun and halfway between that and 12 o'clock is due south.

"When those H-boats had to come down the boys got so smart they picked out a second growth stand with lots of cover and they'd land right on top of that and the 70-foot wing span held them up, you see. Then they'd shinny down the trees. The planes had three gas tanks of 40 gallons each and the 120 gallons was good for only three hours of flying.

"Aerial sketching is a lost art now, there's nobody doing it and somebody should. With aerial photography your maps may be four or five years old but with aerial sketching a guy could take off and get fresh information right away."

The early aerial cameras — the first were used in captive balloons during the American Civil War — could take only oblique pictures, the camera held at an angle. The photos did not show the different types of trees as the sketches did. Using the techniques developed during World War Two, however, aerial forest cruising came of age and along with stereoscopic examination provided the fastest forest surveys. Refinements included a system developed by a Canadian forester, H. E. Seely, for measuring the height of trees from the length of their shadows shown on the aerial photos. Cruisers, however, were still needed on the ground. Equipped with stereoscopes to read the air photos they continued to slog through swamps in summer and snow in winter to measure trees and tally species.

As early as 1908 the *Canadian Forestry Journal* claimed that "the essential difference between a forester and an old-time lumberman is that one makes provisions for the production of future crops, the other does not."[12] Certainly by the 1930s foresters from the Canadian schools were entering all phases of logging. In the beginning, after the First World War, young forestry school graduates were hired for inventory cruising to find where the timber was, estimate quantity and quality, and map the country for logging. They were, in effect, better-equipped versions of the old bush-rangers who called them "bug hunters" in wry recognition of their scientific training. Then the foresters got into fire protection and into "control work" wherein they planned each winter's logging "show," or operation, and followed up to ensure there was no waste. Finally they got into reforestation and forest management.

Over the years Canadian schools have trained 4000 foresters, some of them working for international agencies as far afield as the Malaysian jungle or the highlands of Africa. They would, doubtless, be a source of wonderment to men like Titus Smith who was one of the first timber cruisers in this country back in 1801 before the timber trade had come of age. Smith, a land surveyor, or "land looker," as they were sometimes called, was commissioned by the government to hike into the unexplored back country of Nova Scotia to report on "the quality of the land and the character of the timber, especially for masts." In those days, it seemed, the pine and spruce would last forever.

THE SEASONS: FALL CHOPPERS AND SAWYERS 5

The choppers and the sawyers,
They lay the timber low,
The swampers and the skidders,
They haul it to and fro.

THE SHANTYBOY'S SONG, CIRCA 1840s

Choppers and Sawyers

The tree fellers, or fallers, as they are called in British Columbia, were the shock troops of the forest. They were the first to trek into eastern camps in September and before the frost came the thwack of their axes echoed across the watersheds and down a hundred river valleys.

The lumberman's year began as the farmer's year was drawing to a close and, like the farmer, the lumberman had his slowly turning seasons. Deep winter, after Christmas, was the season of the horsemen, the teamsters who hauled logs to the river on roads built of ice and snow. Spring was the time of the river drivers, the "river hogs," or "white water men," who sluiced the wood down to the mills. Autumn, except in coastal British Columbia where the milder weather permitted work all year around and where style and pace were different, was the season of the axemen and the sawyers..

The lumberjack used an axe with a narrow head, or poll, which weighed as much as the blade and thus gave more weight to his stroke. Poll axes had replaced European axes in the 18th century and weighed three to five pounds on a hardwood handle of hickory or maple. An axeman usually "hung," or fitted, the handle himself and ground the blade to a fan-shaped edge on a grindstone he turned slowly and kept wet so that frictional heat would not destroy the temper of the steel. The lumberjacks favoured the "Black Prince" or the "Sampson," made in Montreal, or an axe made in Ottawa by

73

"Hurling down the pine." A sawlog gang cutting down a tree with axes and bucking it up into 20-foot lengths with a two-man saw. Until the 1870s, and the introduction of better saws, only axes were used to fell the trees. The axeman on the right is making an undercut on the side toward which the tree will fall. In the centre sketch the lumberjacks are brewing up undiluted, "barelegged" tea, strong enough to "float an axe" at their "dinnering out place."

Archives Nationales du Québec

Broad-axe. The greatest of the axes was the broad-axe, first cousin of the executioner's medieval chopper. It weighed 12 pounds, its 12-inch blade bevelled like a chisel, and was used not to cut down trees but to hew fallen pine and oak to a plane-like smoothness for the 19th century square timber market in England.

West coast falling axe. It was developed especially for the thick trees of the Pacific Northwest. It had a longer, narrower blade than eastern axes and a longer handle.

Henry Walters who had learned his trade in Sheffield, England.

An axeman's skill was such that he could drive a stake into the ground 30 feet from the tree he was about to fell and hit the stake with the falling trunk. He was instinctive master of the ways of the fulcrum and could steer a 100-foot pine, or even a 200-foot B.C. Douglas fir, to the direction he wanted by the size and cunning of the notch, or "cowsmouth," he undercut on the side the tree was to fall. His notch, perhaps a quarter of the way through a tree, was horizontal at bottom and sloped up at an angle of 40 degrees. A lumberjack prided himself on the smoothness of his axe cuts. The final cut — the back cut — in the side away from the fall, did not quite meet the first notch but formed a narrow hinge of wood which controlled the tree as it came slashing down like a flail amid a long-drawn wail of "Timber-r-r!" A dozen different things — a difference in the grain, in the growth of branches, in the health of a tree and whether it had rotten parts — could influence how it fell. A cutter could gauge the wind as well as any seaman because cutting trees in a gale was as dangerous as jousting with windmills. There were other problems: "On the Metabechuan one winter," said Pierre Desbiens, "I was cutting a big spruce when all of a sudden I fell through the snow up to my shoulders. It was a bear's winter den. I scrambled out and grabbed my axe and slashed the bear on the head and killed it."[1]

Cutting trees with axe or saw, hour after hour, day after day, was brutal work. Camp paybooks are mute witness to the number of greenhorns, aching in every joint, sweating, half asleep with fatigue, who gave up and went back to town. "I remember they got a gang from Buffalo, New York, one time. It was 1918 and there was so much work around here they couldn't get enough local men. These fellows come up with just little street shoes and light clothes in the winter-time. They'd never worked in the bush before. I never forgot that. Why did they hire men like that? I felt sorry for those fellows, because a bush job is like anything else, you have to get a man who knows how to use an axe and saw. They didn't stay long."[2]

On the west coast the trees were so big the loggers, used to eastern forests, had to learn new skills. With Douglas fir some 200 feet high and 12 feet around at the base, the eastern poll axe was too puny, so in 1880 they developed their own west coast axe, double-bitted with a narrow foot-long blade that got into the heart of the tree. The flaring butt of one of those ancient west coast monsters was tiresome to cut through, sticky with sap, hard to haul, and too big for the mill, so they learned to cut high above the ground. Instead of building cumbersome platforms they fashioned cunning springboards four feet long and tipped with iron, which they wedged into notches. The spring in the boards made the chopping easier, and to change position a faller cut a new notch, embedded his axe in the tree above his head,

Two British Columbia "fallers," perched on "springboards" slotted into the tree trunk five feet above the ground, hack out a notch with the double-bladed axes developed for such thick timber before finishing off the job with their long cross-cut saw.

*The Public Archives of Canada
PA 31617*

Logging camp near Foleyet, Ontario, in 1917. There was a superstition that a man who sharpened his axe on Sunday would cut himself on Monday. Some shantymen honed their axes so sharp they could shave with them.

*The Public Archives of Canada
PA 61805*

and clung to the axe with one hand and adjusted his board with the other. He left his stubby board only when, with creak and crack and thunder, the tree came down, and with axe flying one way and springboard another he leaped into the underbrush with a wail of "Timber-r-r-r! Timber down the hill!"

Woodsmen, like castaways, had to amuse themselves with whatever came to hand. "I'd take this axe," said Wilmot MacDonald of Chatham, New Brunswick, "and throw it maybe 40 feet and it would turn over once and stick into a dry tree. It just comes naturally when you are working like that in the woods."

In the old days when axe cuts were the cause of more than half the accidents, a common cure was chewing tobacco. "The cook would warm it up and make a poultice," recalled Geoff Randolph, "and jam it into the wound and that was supposed to draw the poison." "I got a real nice axe and sharpened it every night," said Murray Bean of Bruce Mines, Ontario, "and I think it was on the 9th of December, I cut my big toe off. They brought me down 32 miles in a sleigh. That would be in 1922. Doc Grigg he took and rounded the bone of my toe off and by golly it hurt. He never froze it or anything but it healed and I never had any trouble with it and went back to work in February. I was 16 years old."

The axemen from the early shanties on the Saint John River, the Miramichi, the Ottawa, and the Trent would seek out a white pine and smooth the ground around it, particularly if the tree was to be sold as a valuable mast.

"Its trunk," said one 19th century lumberjack, recalling those virgin pines which are no more, "was as straight and handsomely grown as a moulded candle and measured six feet in diameter six feet from the ground . . . in length 140 feet, about 65 feet of which was free from limbs, and retained its diameter remarkably well. I was employed about an hour and a quarter felling it. It is thrilling business to bring those great pines down. The ground trembles under the strokes, while the reverberating echo of its fall, as it rings through the mountains and valleys, may, on a still morning, be heard six or eight miles."[3]

To haul such monster spars out of the forest and down to the water without breaking them was high adventure. Robert Harrison of Norwood, east of Peterborough, Ontario, remembered how it was "to command 22-span of spirited, active, powerful horses hitched to a 'bridled' mast sleigh (chains wrapped or bridled around the runners to act as brakes) to prevent the liability, while crossing steep ridges, of being 'jacked' as the mast broke over the hill crests and rushed headlong towards the valley underneath, with teamsters mounted and every horse of the 44 galloping for life at full speed . . ."[4]

The square timber crews, more numerous, were almost as highly skilled as the mast makers. The largest stick of square timber cut on the Trent was seven feet six inches around and was such a giant that "every man in the shanty, cook included, got on the piece and danced jigs and reels and hornpipes on its surface to the music of the fiddle."[5]

After a tree was felled the crew worked as smoothly as a team of gunners. The "liner" lopped off the crown, the "rosser," his rossing iron a short, sharp hoe, scraped off two long strips of bark down to the red inner skin, from one end of the trunk to the other, and the liner then took a 50-foot length of twine, coated it with chalk, anchored each end to the log like a bow and "twanged" it against the log to make two straight chalk lines along the rough strips cut by the rosser. Then the "scorer" leaped atop the trunk and every four feet, on both sides of the log, notched a V almost to the chalk line and cut out four-foot slabs between each notch. "His axe swished through and bit into the timber with such rhythm and speed that it resembled the vane of a windmill whirling in a brisk breeze."[6]

Finally the skilled hewer stepped in with his broad-axe to "hew to the line" and finish the sides off smooth. He placed his leg against the log and cut down diagonally across the grain, walking backward with each stroke. The masters, like Bill Hogan on the Black River, up the Ottawa, could hew 14 inches with each stroke and finish the surface off as smooth as if it had been planed.

Poll Axe

The broad-axe man signed his initials with a scribing iron on each log. "How long did it take to become a hewer? Maybe you'd never get it," said Steve Lewis of Devil's Lake, Ontario, who had worked as an axeman in the shanty days. "It was an art, but some were amazing. Old Steve Enright's gang could cut eight to eleven sticks a day but the average was six." To shape a 100-foot pine tree into an octagonal mast ready for final sanding took a good broad-axe man a full day. Main masts for the British navy had to measure 75 to 100 feet, two feet around at base, and a foot and half at the top.

Double-bitted Axe

A balk, or stick, of square timber, on the other hand, might run 40 to 60 feet and was squared to a "proud edge," say 12 inches by 12 inches. It took less shipping space than round logs and was ready to saw into lumber in the saw pits of England, where merchants sold it as "yellow pine."

The greatest problem with the square timber trade was its waste. One-quarter of each tree was slashed and left lying in the forest, dried tinder for summer lightning and forest fires. Only in 1860 did the British merchants begin to worry about the waste and to protect their supply by importing octagonal "waney" pine on which the hewer with his 12-pound broad-axe, its 12-inch blade bevelled like a chisel, left three inches of the natural wane, or curve, of the trunk on each of its four corners. This wasted slightly less wood on each of the squared sides.

Broad-axe

Ont. Ministry of Natural Resources

A square timber gang in 1890 "scoring," or roughing out, the dimensions of a piece of square timber to prepare the 60-foot length for the final artistry of the hewer with his broad-axe.

Ont. Ministry of Natural Resources

Two hewers on the Ganaraska watershed of Ontario smooth the sides of a "stick" of white pine square timber with broad-axes. On the Black River, off the Ottawa, shantymen sang proudly of a hewer named Bill Hogan who could smooth off a good 14 inches of the log with every blow of his axe.

> He swung his axe so freely,
> He did his work so clean,
> If you saw the timber hewed
>   by him,
> You'd swear he used a plane.
> *Hogan's Lake*

The Public Archives of Canada C 75265

Ottawa Valley broad-axe men finish off a stick of square timber "smooth as butter," leaving it sharpened at each end like a pencil. These ends absorbed the shocks and dents as the timbers were driven downriver. They were cut off clean when the timbers were readied for market at Quebec City. On the log behind the hewers, scorers are roughing out the log.

Before the mid-19th century, sawlog gangs were following the square timber makers into the pineries to cut logs for the lumber mills and the growing market in the United States. Although the timber hewers scorned them as mere "log rollers," the sawlog gangs could cut more trees and cut them faster — perhaps 15 in a day — and these were bucked up into 75 sawlogs of 20 feet each.

Steam mills, which burned slab wood and debris from the logging, were springing up, the first in Saint John, New Brunswick, in 1822. "The ravenous sawmills in this pine wilderness," wrote H. W. Withrow, "are not unlike the huge dragons that used in popular legend to lay waste the country, and like dragons, they die when their prey, the lordly pines, are all devoured."[7]

The slow, deliberate ways of the masting gangs and the square timber shantymen were giving way to the rush and tumble of the lumber trade. Screaming gang saws, many blades fitted into one frame, appeared in the mills in the 1830s and whirring circular saws replaced the slow up-and-down Muley saws. Although there were saws in the mills, the men out in the bush were still using the primitive axe to cut down trees. Surprisingly, the saw was not used to fell trees until the 1870s or 1880s although a crude version of the crosscut saw had been used since early in the century to buck up the fallen logs. The problem had been the tendency of the saws to jam in the tree and this was finally solved by inserting cleaning teeth, or rakers, between the cutting teeth to remove sawdust and shavings. Men carried bottles of coal oil to clean resin off the saws and a brace of wedges to hammer into the saw cut to control the line of fall. It was all a lumberman's life was worth if he could not figure in advance which way a tree was going to fall. They tell the story of the foreman who came across a greenhorn sawing away, raggedly, like a beaver. When the foreman asked him which way he thought the tree might topple the sweating city man replied, "How the hell should I know? I came here to be a lumberjack, not a crystal gazer."

When Shurley and Dietrich of Galt, Ontario, introduced the raker-tooth crosscut saws, the "Maple Leaf" and the "Lancetooth," in 1874, two sawyers, one on each end of the saw, could fell twice the wood cut by two axemen. It was faster, if not easier. "If a person worked for three or four months," said one British Columbia sawyer, "it was not uncommon, if he weighed 180 pounds, to lose 30 or 50 pounds. They were right down to bone and muscle because when you pulled a saw back and forth all day that's hard work."[8] Although the history of the crosscut saw is obscure, a similar tool, the pit saw used for cutting logs into boards, was described in the Old Testament; one sawyer standing above a log and the other in a pit below getting sawdust in his hair.

With the introduction of the crosscut saw for felling trees a new man came to the camps, the saw filer, to rank with the foreman and the cook. The saw filer needed a good eye and good light, and some jealously guarded their jobs by making a big mystery of their trade.

Under a skylight in the blacksmith's hovel, the filer set up his wooden clamp to hold the saw blade, a tooth gauge, or "spider," to set the rakers and joint the teeth to proper height, a swage, and a set hammer, flat files, and a hand anvil. Cutting teeth had to be all the same length and bevelled, and the rakers had to be shorter than the cutters by the thickness of a nickel. The filer sharpened 12 to 15 saws each day, sharpening them for the type of wood to be cut and to suit each sawyer: men with short, quick strokes needed shorter rakers than those who rode the saw with hard, slow strokes. In cold weather the filer had to change the set of the teeth for frozen timber. You could "haul the guts out of a man" with a dull saw.

In the eastern pine forests two men with a crosscut saw averaged 100 logs a day in good timber. "It doesn't hurt a man to work, you know," said Murray Bean at Bruce Mines, Ontario. "His muscles build up to it. The first time I went to a logging camp when I was 16 I started sawing wood and the first week I couldn't even raise my arms this high. But after a while it didn't bother me." Each weekend the amount of wood a man had cut was chalked on a "bucking board" on the bunkhouse wall and there was constant competition to head that list. It was a matter of pride and prestige but brought no bonus.

The two-man crosscut saw cut the big pine and a smaller one-man three-foot version cut the spruce and balsam down for pulpwood until the 1920s when the Finns in northern Ontario popularized what they called the Swede saw, bucksaw, or pulp saw. This was a stream-lined farmyard bucksaw of the type which had been used for buck-ing up firewood on a sawhorse or sawbuck, from which it took its name. The farmyard bucksaw had been a poor felling saw, but the improved bucksaw had a thinner blade which could cut spruce down twice as fast as the crosscut saw. The bucksaw was too small, how-ever, to replace the crosscut saw in the pine woods.

"The first bucksaws we had were straight teeth, no rakers, and the boys in camp discovered that by leaving two teeth and taking out every other two you could cut a lot faster. Then the next thing, somebody had introduced the pulp saw blade with raker teeth and that was faster still. You had to be pretty expert to cut two cords a day but some cut four."[9] It took a healthy young man two months to learn to cut two cords, say about 40 average spruce trees eight inches at the stump, in a day.

The Finns helped make the bucksaw the standard pulp camp saw. "The first thing they did when they got to camp they'd go out and find a nice, small, dry spruce for the cross-piece. They never carried

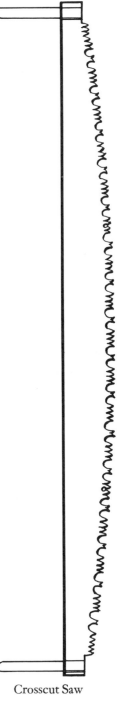

Crosscut Saw

Amid the tangled underbrush of the Vancouver Island Douglas fir forests, two "fallers" topple a tree with a crosscut saw near Port Renfrew in April 1940. A "bush ape," fresh from the fleshpots of Vancouver, could lose up to 50 pounds in a couple of months at such work until he was mostly bone and muscle.

British Columbia Forest Service

The saw filer, like the blacksmith, was a specialist. He needed good light to file the cutting teeth and raking teeth on crosscut saws which ranged in length from 5 ½ feet to 12 feet or more.

"It was a hard job filing a crosscut saw," said Fred Kinnehan. "Every sawing crew had two saws. Every night a sawyer would bring a saw in to the filer and exchange it for a sharp one to use next day."

This filer was working on Cracroft Islands, between Vancouver Island and the mainland of British Columbia, in 1919.

The Public Archives of Canada C 56694

a cross-piece from camp to camp, just the two end pieces of the frame and a blade rolled up in a rag. For the tension they'd buy a rope for 25 cents, just ordinary rope, and they'd put a stick, or 'swifter,' in the rope and tighten the tension and lay it up against the cross-piece. They'd loosen the rope at night so rain would not shrink it and pull out the cross-piece."[10] They liked to make the frame from alder, they said, because there was a spirit in alder which kept a man from cutting himself. They also had a trick of making blades from phonograph springs. "You attached the spring to a tree and unwound it and then you had to file teeth into it. They would make the blades a bit at a time in the evenings. They would make small teeth, easy to saw, for with big teeth, that's heavy work. The small teeth were good for winter sawing when the wood was frozen."[11] In the 1930s factory-made, steel-frame pulp saws became common. Some of the best came from Sandviken, near Stockholm, Sweden, where the Sandvik Company records show they were exporting as early as the 1880s — "a quantity of pulpwood saws imported by Alfred Andersen & Co. of Minneapolis for use in the forests of Quebec."

The bucksaw blade was easier to file so the crosscut saw filers disappeared. "How do you file a bucksaw? Eyes . . . eyes, and the right angle on the blade. You have to set the teeth so when you look down a blade you can see a groove where you can slide a needle down. Depending on whether it is green wood or dry the groove will be narrower or wider."[12]

Unlike the eastern pine, which might be cut two feet above the ground, the pulpwood spruce and balsam fir were cut about four inches above the ground so that the pulp cutters had to bend almost doubled over. Their usual practice was to place the saw on the far side of the tree and saw towards themselves. "The pulpwood was harder work than the pine. You practically had to get down on your hands and knees to cut the trees off close. It was heavy work, too, because you had to pile that four-foot-long stick, sometimes 12 inches around at the stump, by hand."[13] Bolts of pulpwood four or eight feet long were piled, with the aid of a short pulp hook shaped like a sharpened question mark, in "cord cradles" four feet high. A cord weighed about two tons. Two men lifted eight-foot logs but the four-footers were piled by the cutter alone.

In sawlog camps where wages were low and bed and board thrown in by the camp operator, everyone from choreboy to foreman was paid a monthly wage. By the 1920s, however, piece-work was introduced, at first for the broad-axe men cutting railway ties, a lucrative trade since every mile of track required 2600 and 3200 eight-foot ties, depending on whether the track was spur line or main line. Piece-work was especially popular in pulp camps, where cutters were paid by the cord, among "bull workers" who could cut two

Abitibi Paper Co. Ltd.

Axemen in the spruce and fir forests of northern Quebec. The double-bladed axes were used in the pulp woods for cutting, or "swamping," out trails since one blade could be sharpened to a keen edge for cutting and the other left blunt for grubbing up roots.

To fell a slim pulpwood tree with a Swede saw or bucksaw, the cutter had to stoop and saw towards his body in order to cut the tree a few inches above the roots and not waste good wood. It looked like an awkward position but the cutters maintained it was the best way to get the job done.   *Abitibi Paper Co. Ltd.*

84

cords or more a day. Greenhorns found piece-work a misery. "Old Chris Towell kept telling me to do this and do that but I'd go to work like crazy and cut only four trees, maximum, before noon. I was paid $1.75 a cord but I pretty near went broke and was in the hole $8 for my board and meals."[14] Each pulp cutter worked on his own 60-foot strip of trees and stacked his wood to await the sleigh haul.

"Everyone had to cut two cords a day. If he didn't we'd have to get him out and let somebody else have a chance. We'd have 100 men in camp and the object was to cut 100 000 cords by the time the snow was deep and the sleigh haul could begin. If you didn't get the 100 000 cords by then you would keep men on cutting until you did but it was miserable cutting pulpwood in the snow."[15] Sometimes pulp cutters worked on snowshoes and shovelled down to the base of a tree to chop. "In Quebec camps the snow was so deep, sometimes I saw guys throwing bolts of pulpwood five feet up into the air to get it onto the road where another guy would load it on a sleigh. That's how deep the snow was."[16]

"It is only with practice that a man becomes a good lumberjack," said William Savard at Chicoutimi, Quebec. "A lumberjack 'never cuts the same tree twice,' that is to say, uses the same technique on each tree, for every tree is different. Engineers have written books on ways of cutting a tree but you can only learn the techniques with practice. Once I was teaching twelve young men how to cut. Even after I had been teaching them for a month a 40-year-old *bûcheron* with experience could cut twice as many trees as they could. It is not something a man can improvise, no matter how strong he is. Physically it is not harder for an older man to cut a tree down than it is for a younger man. It is the way you do it that matters. It was my father who first taught me. He would show me how to notch, how to throw the axe right into the middle of the tree, how to cut in the same direction as the wind."

Joe Proulx, although taller than most at six feet, was probably as typical a *bûcheron* as one might find. At the age of 75, still straight and strong, he lived in a small, neat room in a Cochrane, Ontario, railway hotel.

"I don't like bush work no more," he said. "But when I was young the job I liked best was cuttin' log. To be a good cutter you had to have good timber, that was the first thing.

"I went to work when I was 13, a swamper, cuttin' out trail. That was 25 miles back in the bush behind Pembroke, just poles for a bed and the grub was beans, pea soup, bread, pork, and porridge sometimes. *Tabernac'*. Then I went to work at Tupper Lake down in New York State. Most of the guys came from Quebec. I was only a kid, but big, me. Wages were better in the States. That's the place we all had to sleep under one big long blanket. Someone showed you a bed, 'you sleep there between them two guys.' Oh, *maudit*!

"I worked for J. R. Booth at Timiskaming, some nice red pine trees there, four or five logs long. That was during the First World War, the time of the Spanish flu, 1918. Some died of it, 15 died of it in the camp I was in, but I never got it.

"We used to go out at 7 A.M. in the winter there and wait for daylight. If there was a blizzard we might not take the horses out. But it's not as cold as it used to be. At Iroquois Falls in northern Ontario it was 75 below zero there one winter, 1940. I was working that day but there was no wind. Oh, it was cold. Holy *Calice*. We got fellows from New Brunswick and Gaspé and the Madeleine Islands up there. *Maudit Chris'*, they had a funny way to talk. We used to have a lamp at each end of the camp; some guys would have a fiddle, a bit of singing, playing poker. There were good times, too. We didn't know any better. That was the life, eh?

"The first power saw I seen was 1940. That was a big one, it took two men to handle it. Later, when I started using the power saw, I couldn't go back and use the Swede saw again. Instead of cutting two or three cords a day you might cut five or six with the power saw."

Although the first power saw appeared about 1855, they were a rare sight in the bush until after World War Two. The Dolmar and Stihl companies of Germany first marketed a gasoline-powered saw on a wide scale in 1939, with results which were not encouraging.

"In the first six months of the so-called operation of the machine," wrote J. W. Challenger, a British Columbia lumberman, "I think we may, between breakdowns, have operated it a total of five or six weeks. The rest of the time was spent in repairing and rebuilding it. The reaction of the rest of our crews was a mixture of well-concealed interest and ill-concealed scorn. I well remember one of our old-timers who wandered through one day to where the power saw was working, and having the usual difficulties. He watched the performance for a while, then, as he turned away, 'Pfui,' he said. 'I could cut more timber with a crosscut saw in half a day, with one hand tied behind my back, than that rig can cut in a week. "[17] Challenger kept tinkering and rebuilding and within three years was using 22 power saws although at first they were awkward and heavy. "When they first started using power chain saws two men would go out to the bush with the Swede saw and two with the power saw and the Swede saw men produced twice as much pulpwood as those with the chain saw."[18] Old-timers scoffed, as old-timers will, that three chain saws were needed for each man: "One being repaired, one coming back from the repair shop, and one being sent to the repair shop."

By 1947 a 28-pound one-man power saw had replaced the two-man monster which had weighed 130 pounds. A tree which two men

Canadian Pulp and Paper Association

When power saws appeared in the 1930s they were so heavy and awkward that two men were needed to operate them. The development of the light one-man saw after World War II revolutionized logging.

cut with a crosscut saw in one hour might take a power saw man one-quarter of that time. Since power saws could be used for notching as well as for felling and bucking, they not only replaced the crosscut saw and bucksaw but also did away with the last of the axe work. The power saw also marked the end of old attitudes. "Before the power saw came in, when we had men working in gangs, some fellow would be the leader and every man was working as part of a team. But once the power saw came in it was more individual, every man for himself. So it changed the lumbering."[19]

THE SEASONS: FALL
THE SKIDDERS
6

Once the trees were felled and the logs cut, skidding gangs hauled them out of the bush on rocky, muddy trails. In the beginning oxen were the only draft animals most lumbermen owned. Oxen could live on coarser food than horses, withstand harsher treatment, were less excitable, and their cloven hoofs could carry them through swamps which would spook a horse. Wooden yokes or ox-bows for the teams, whittled out in camp, were cheaper than horse harness and did not break. An ox pulled more than a horse although he was only half as fast and, moreover, needed much more time to chew his cud than a horse needed to eat his oats. Caravans of ox teams returning from the shanties in the spring, red-flannel banners flying from poles on their sleds, were gala sights in the woodland hamlets.

Oxen were used much later down east, particularly in Nova Scotia, but horses began to appear on the Ottawa in the 1830s, and by 1850 John Egan had 2000, 10 for every ox. It was on the west coast with its giant timber that oxen reached their greatest glory.

Where eastern bull whackers drove two oxen or four, a west coast "bull puncher" might need a team of 10 or 12 to haul a great Douglas fir log two miles down a skid road. The most experienced yoke, the leaders of the long team, were followed by several yoke of "swingers," and at the rear there were the wheelers, the two heaviest oxen

Oxen skidding logs in New Brunswick. Decked out with bells on their necks, copper caps on their horns, and copper hearts sewn into the leather of their head gear, oxen bore names like "Buck" or "Bright." They wore iron shoes, one on each side of their cloven hoofs, and hauled logs, plodding along at one mile an hour.

Courtesy of The New Brunswick Museum

This photograph tells the whole story, at a glance, of a British Columbia logging operation in the early 1890s. Eight oxen prepare to haul a Douglas fir log, which might weigh 20 tons or more, down the well-worn skidway from Fraser's camp near Vancouver. The gang includes two fallers notching undercuts into the trees at far right and left. The stumps they left were taller than a man's head.

Provincial Archives, Victoria, B.C.

of the team. Armed with a nail-studded five-foot prod and language that was guaranteed to wither man or beast, a good bull whacker such as Stub Dillon of Vancouver was paid three times more than an axeman. Unlike farm oxen the logging bulls were shod, two half shoes on each cloven hoof, because of the rough trails. They suffered little from cold or wet but did suffer from sunburn and could die from careless handling. Some were killed by falling trees. In British Columbia they were replaced by horses around the turn of the century. During the industrial revolution in the west coast woods in the early 1900s, steam skidding with donkey engines replaced the horses.

In the pine forests of the east, skidding a log out of the woods was rough work and the trail hacked out by the swampers with their double-bitted axes was full of holes, stumps, and rocks. The horse was not as strong as the ox but he was more easily managed.

"Some of those old skidding horses were as wise as the men who drove them," recalled Jim MacDonald of Thessalon, Ontario. "Once over a skidding trail they could take a log out with little or no direction. I well remember my first experience at skidding as a young lad of about 13. I had cut some white birch poles for firewood and borrowed an old bush horse to snake them out. He was a monstrous, patient bay animal and was very wise in the ways of the woods. I began by hooking the chain too far back on the birch pole and too far away from the single tree. My next error was to jerk the horse too sharply on the first bend in the trail and fouled the pole up solidly in the base of a tree. That's when the horse and I came to a better understanding. He turned his big bay face around to me and the look in his eyes unmistakedly conveyed the thought, 'Well, you are a green one, aren't you?'

"... I felt pretty good about getting a job skidding so I went down to the brush shelter where they kept the horses to have a look at the one I was going to drive. When I got there I saw Billie Ring sifting some light-looking powder into some oats for one of the horses. I think the horse's name was 'Sandy.' Billy looked up when I came into the shelter and asked me, 'Are you going to drive this horse, Kid?' I said, 'Yes, I guess so.'

" 'Do you know what I'm mixing with these oats for him?'

" 'It looks like dynamite,' I said.

" 'You're right it is,' he says. 'So don't ever hit this horse and make him stumble.'

"The next day I was skidding up on the hill above the camp and a log got hung up on a cross-haul. Joe Castinette was working on the skidway near there. He was rolling. When he saw me hung up he came over and said, 'Take a brawla to that horse and he'll take that log outta there.'

"I said pretty quick, 'No siree, you can't lick Sandy. If you did he might stumble.'

"Joe laughed at me, then he grabbed a big limb . . . Before he had time to swing at Sandy I took off down the cross-haul. I looked back as I broke over the hill and saw him take a swipe at Sandy's rump. When I was quite a ways away and didn't hear anything I turned around and went back. Joe had got the log to the skidway all right and Sandy was standing there all in one piece . . . I said, 'Billie Ring told me if I beat that horse and made him stumble, he'd blow up!' "[1]

Because of the rough bush, reins were rarely used once a teamster attached a 12-foot chain from the harness to a log. "A good skidder, or yarder, as we called them in New Brunswick, he would work only by word of mouth. 'All right, Barney, pick it up.' 'Come back, Barney, come back.' Horses have good hearing so a yarder would speak in a low voice. If you changed a horse's name it would take him time to learn the new one and they do know their names. Any man who could not train his horse by word of mouth was not counted for much."[2]

— "What makes a good skidder? You have to have the patience of Job. One old Belgian horse we had, she didn't like to back up, no sir. She'd do everything else. But back up? That was ridiculous. I remember I got out in front of her with a little twig and I just kept tapping her on the nose and she got madder and madder, but she kept backing up. That cured her. But they know just where you are and what you are doing and if you are going to hook a chain on a log, why, some of them know to the split second when it is hooked. We had one horse who did more work than the others and he'd give you about six seconds to hook your chain on the log and then he was off and going and you'd better be hooked up by the end of that time and out of the way. They are just like people. If a horse will draw for me, if I knew he'd give a good draw, I'd put up with a few other faults. But we never had a horse that wouldn't give you everything he had in him. Of course you have to have a harness that fits so it's comfortable. You take a big raw spot on his shoulder, you can't expect he'll be very happy working."[3] Horse collars were fitted by experts and a horse with straight shoulders and a wide neck needed a moulded collar called a "full sweeney," in reference to the horse's sweeney bone. There were half-sweeneys and quarter-sweeneys. "The old horse skinners would worry more about the fit of a collar than about their wife, if they had one. A sore shoulder was a disgrace."[4]

The skidding gang worked a day behind the axemen but if the cutters were slow the swampers cutting the trails and the skidders with the horses might overtake them. That could be dangerous for man and horse although the skidding horses wore harness bells to signal their whereabouts and the cutters called a warning: "Timber-r-r-r!" or "Watch out!" when a tree began to fall.

That cry has disappeared in the gasoline fumes of mechanization but once it was hammered into the impressionable minds of young cutters. "We had a young New Zealand boy there about 1917. The foreman warned him to holler 'Timber' when he cut a tree down but the guy had never handled an axe before and when he started chopping he wasn't getting any notch into it, just hacking at the tree. But he would start hollering 'Timber-r-r!' from the first stroke and kept hollering all the time he was chopping. The foreman came along and asked, 'Why are you hollering all the time?' And the boy said, 'You told me to holler 'Timber-r-r' and I'm sure not going to risk killing anybody.' "[5]

In horse skidding the most frequent accidents were broken legs suffered when a log, slewing along at five miles an hour, hit a teamster. "They put me skidding once in snow six feet deep. The logs had been felled every which way so I put a long chain around them and hitched them to a big team which was slow but strong — like bulldozers. I'd take maybe six or eight logs at one time and there was a swamper there, an old fellow, and I called out, 'Hey, Mister, you'd better get out of the road. If those logs hit you they'll kill you.' And Gee Whizz those logs hit the tree he was hiding behind and knocked him right under the snow. I had a heck of a time to find him. We had to dig that swamper out of five feet of snow. I feared he'd been killed but he was all right, the logs hit the tree he was behind and the snow came down and covered him right over. I'd just tied the reins up on the harness, on the hames, you see, and yelled, 'Get up!' and away they'd gone. There's nothing I could have done."[6]

Widow-makers, branches broken in storms and accidentally dislodged in the cutting or skidding, were dangerous — a widow-maker killed Harry Dunn from New Brunswick. Young Harry was a common enough type in the 1880s, for according to the ballad he was "a wild Canadian boy who leaves his happy home, and longing for excitement to Michigan will roam." He was swamping out a trail one day with his friend, Charlie, when a hanging limb fell down and "crushed him into clay."

In the 1920s teamsters as well as cutters were put on piece-work, but, unlike the earlier days, by that time there were often men in the booming camps who had not grown up with horses. In the early 1920s there were 90 000 loggers in the camps across Canada.

"Fellas would come in who didn't know even how to harness a horse. Boys oh boys, they butchered them. It was all money. For when you were on piece-work," said Bob Smith, of Renfrew, Ontario, "you had to pay for board, saw, and axe. I piece-worked one time for 10 cents a log. Oh, sure, I had to work like a fool but our gang put up 130 logs a day. There were gangs that winter going into the hole or just barely earning their board, foreigners who had never

The Public Archives of Canada   C 19883

"Big wheels," or "arches," hauled by horses were sometimes used to skid big logs, chained up off the ground to the axle. Some of them were 12 feet high and since they had no brakes they were used on level terrain.

Ont. Ministry of Natural Resources

Foreman James Monet, right, and teamster skidding a 16-foot white pine log out of the bush on the Little White River in northern Ontario in 1923.

The "go-devil." At first the go-devil was just the crotch of a hardwood tree with the end of a log resting on it, chained to an ox. In time the blacksmiths developed more sophisticated sleds to skid logs out of the bush.

The Public Archives of Canada C 10702

Two cant-hook men build a skidway, or storage pile, of logs, rolling a log up a pair of "piling skids," which are two stout poles. Occasionally accidents occurred when a heavy log rolled back and crushed a man.

Ontario Archives

The average skidway, or storage pile of logs, was 25 feet wide and 70 feet long, containing 350 logs. Two cant-hook men formed the bottom layers of logs, placing them athwart the two large timbers which served as a foundation. As the pile grew, special rigging was necessary: a block chained to the top of a pole with a long decking chain running through it. One end of the chain contained a sharp hook which was driven into the log lying below the space where a new log was to be fitted. The other end of the line was fastened to a "bitch hook," a grab hook on the doubletree of the horse which then pulled the log quickly and easily up onto the growing pile once the cant-hook men had placed it in proper position by rolling it up a little ramp. The skidway might be 10 or 20 feet high.

Canadian Forest Industries, Toronto

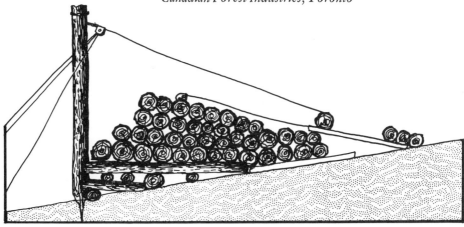

worked in the bush before. Two of them would cut and a third would skid. Maybe he'd never seen a horse in his life before. It was pitiful. My brother, he was working with two Danes, two great big Danes. They wanted to cut logs and needed a good man who knew how to skid. They said they could cut logs but really they didn't know how. One day the foreman came over to me and said, 'You ought to see those fellas with your brother Jack. They cut two or three trails all right but now they've managed to fell a log across every one of those trails.' They were getting no logs out at all and they had Jack covered up all the time and he could do nothing."

For heavy logs a "go-devil" might be used. In the oxen days the go-devil was just a crotch of a hardwood tree, sometimes called a "school marm," which was dragged along the ground with the end of a log resting in the crotch. Later, go-devils were built by a blacksmith and were small sleds with runners. If distances were more than a few hundred feet "big wheels," an arch between two 10-foot wheels, was sometimes used to haul heavy logs.

There were few places a horse could not go, and in deep snow, in Newfoundland or in the Rocky Mountains, horses were even fitted with their own snowshoes, rounded pieces of two-inch birch with grooves for the horseshoe and straps to buckle to the hoof.

Dog teams were sometimes hitched to small loads for short distances, and in the ravines on the north shore of the St. Lawrence logs were sometimes hauled by men — "chienning," or "dogging," as they called it. The hand sleighs looked like dog sleds. On steep hills they let them down with a rope snubbed around a stump, while on more gentle ground one man would pull in the shafts while another pushed. They might haul 20 sticks of four-foot pulpwood in a load.

All logs, except for the short bolts of pulpwood which were piled in "cord cradles," were hauled to skidways along the "main road," the artery which linked the skidding trails which were like ribs attached to the backbone of the main road. The men who stacked logs on the skidways were "rollers." Some of the skidways, built up across two big logs which formed the foundation, might contain 350 logs and if the pile was badly built the whole thing could collapse, maiming men and horses.

The log pile was also where the culler, or scaler, worked. With his measuring stick and a small tallyboard strapped to his left arm with a rubber band, he would go to one end of a log and his helper to the other and both would measure the diameter and the scaler would write down the smaller diameter and mark the log with blue crayon. Their main problem was to be sure they were both measuring the same log at the same time in the big pile. "New Brunswick mothers used to say, 'Don't ever grow up to be a scaler.' When he came in to scale, no matter how likable he was, he wasn't popular

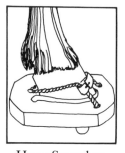

Horse Snowshoe

CANADIAN PULP AND
PAPER ASSOCIATION

Abitibi Paper Co. Ltd.

The measurement of logs was originally called culling, and then scaling. Each inch mark on the scale stick also shows the contents in board feet of a log of that diameter. For measuring the length of a log a wheel, consisting of 10 spokes tipped with spikes, was run along the log. Each revolution measured five feet.

The Public Archives of Canada   PA 60622

A skidway of logs awaits the winter sleigh haul. After the cutting and skidding, late in the fall, logs were piled at intervals both as a handy work place for the scalers, or log measurers, and as a pick-up point for the teamsters who hauled the logs to the river.

with the men because he worked for head office direct. The contractors feared he was cutting down on their profits, but he had his responsibilities. If he scaled three million feet in the woods they had to get three million feet out of it when they sawed it in the mill."[7] The company reported the scaler's tally to the government and once a year government scalers came in to check that proper dues were paid on Crown land timber.

Thus throughout the October days of Indian summer and the chill November rain, day after day, six days a week, from dawn to dark, the whole camp worked to pile up the logs and the "buck beaver" and his swampers hurried to finish the main road for the winter sleigh haul. "You wouldn't generally go out and work if it was storming when you got up but if it started snowing when you were out there, if it wasn't too bad you'd tough it out. In eastern Canada, at least, if it started to rain out there they'd wait an hour or so to see if it would ease but if she settled in an all-dayer they'd stop. In the cold fall rain — 'the water running down the crack of my ass,' they'd say — you couldn't work. They'd get miserable and cold and completely soaked and put neck covers on the horses and it would take a long time to dry their clothes. The first snowstorm they used to call the 'pacemaker' because a lot of men quit at first snow although with snow on the ground yarding was easier."[8]

But no matter the weather, rain or snow, the buck beaver kept his swampers hurrying to build the main road for the climax of the autumn's work — the sleigh haul.

And through November and early December the men and horses grew thinner and tougher, the days grew shorter, and the skidways of logs grew higher, and soon the snow came, and Christmas, and the iron-cold days of the sleigh haul.

THE SEASONS: WINTER
THE TEAMSTERS 7

At four o'clock each morning,
the boss begins to shout,
"Heave out, my jolly teamsters,
It's time to start the route."

The teamsters they all jump up,
in a most fretful way,
"Where is me boots? Where is me pants?
"Me socks is gone astray."

THE SHANTYBOY'S SONG

There is music in the deep woods when the wind rolls through the pine and spruce, but the music the old foreman loved was the shout of his horseman and the ringing of trace chains as the lead teams creaked out of camp on a frosty, starlit morning. The winter sleigh haul was lively work.

Eastern logging camps were horse camps and from Christmas until spring thaw the teamsters hauled great loads to the lakes and frozen rivers. The pace of the camp was the pace of the horse and the death of the horse in the 1950s changed logging camps more than any other thing.

It took a week or more to build the momentum of the sleigh haul but once the logs were moving in January there was a thunder of rolling timber and a rasp and whine of sleigh runners on frozen snow until late March. "The teamsters used to shout. On a cold, frosty morning I'd hear the sleighs comin' from a long distance and screeching away and I'd hear the teamsters shout. The teams would come along one after the other and at the skidways the torches would be flickerin' away there in the dark. The team of horses would come, the frost all over them, and you'd hear them comin'. Some of those

99

Prince Albert Pulp Co. Ltd., Saskatchewan, Historical Society

A lumber camp at Bannock, northern Saskatchewan. Until the mechanization of the 1950s, most camps east of the British Columbia rain forests, where steam power was used, were horse camps. Old-timers claim the disappearance of the horses changed the camps more than anything else in lumbering history.

Abitibi Paper Co. Ltd.

Tony Starbuck hauling pulpwood near Auden, northern
Ontario, in the winter of 1951, the whiskers of teamster
and horses frozen white. Within a few years the horses
were gone, replaced by trucks and tracked vehicles.

teamsters were jolly, you'd hear them sittin' up there on their loads in the morning singin'."[1]

"Build her up and get to loggin'," the foreman said, and to be chosen lead teamster was an honour. A teamster was up and out an hour or two before dawn, his breath standing straight in the frozen air like smoke from the shadowy cook-house. "The cook knew where you slept and would shake you so as not to wake the rest of the camp. It would be cold as hell. We'd harness the horses by lantern light and feed them oats. If the teamsters were late getting started the foreman would come and say, 'All right, Daylight in the Swamp!' and Jeeze would we get out of there!"[2] The eastern horizon was still dim when the lead sleigh slid through the dark woods. The sleighs carried no lights but at the skidways where they loaded they made "canned daylight" from tins of coal oil on poles stuck in a snowbank or nailed to a tree. The sleighs left camp at 30-minute intervals, the time it took to take on a load at the skidway, and a team might haul 20 or 25 miles in one day. The lead teamster would usually return to camp by sunset but the tail teamster, the last man out in the morning, was rarely in time for supper and sometimes the lights were out and the camp asleep when he got back.

The horses were big: Clydesdales, Percherons, Belgians, each 1700 pounds or so, although smaller *habitant* horses working singly instead of in teams were used in the Quebec pulp camps. Each of the big companies kept enough horses in the bush to mount an army of Cossacks. Even in 1950, when trucks and tracked vehicles were replacing horses in the east and horses had long gone from the west coast woods, there were 35 000 horses in the logging industry. Sleighs consisted of two bob-sleds with nine-foot birch runners shod with iron, coupled one behind the other and topped off with timber "bunks" on which the logs were piled. A sleigh loaded with 25 or 30 logs might weigh 20 tons.

The teamsters risked their necks day after day down the steep hills, standing atop a shaking load with the running horses straining out ahead at the end of the sleigh pole. "It was a scary thing coming down those steep hills. Old 'Gentleman Charlie' Sproule, he wore a belted trench coat and a hat and always looked like a bank manager even when he was driving his roan team, Duke and Jerry. When he came to a bad hill he'd say, 'Get up Duke,' and he'd begin to sing 'Jesus Saviour, Pilot Me.' He was sort of religious. When he was hauling off Duck Mountain he was always frightened. So was I."[3]

"Sand hill men" scattered hay or sand on steep grades to keep the sleighs under control. "You had to have a real good man tending a sand hill. His job was not as simple as it sounds. You could bring the sleigh down so slow it would get stuck on the hill or on the other hand you might not have enough sand on and the sleigh would get a run on and maybe pile up. I saw it happen. The horses would break

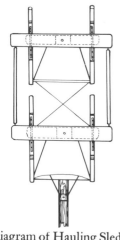

Diagram of Hauling Sleds
CANADIAN FOREST INDUSTRIES, TORONTO

their legs or get killed. No two teams are alike on a sand hill. Some want to hit it at speed. I remember one team of rather light horses full of go and lively and they always hit a sand hill fast. A sand hill man should know each team. A 'run' means getting out of control and then there's no use trying to hold back on a hill with a big load of logs like that. A horse has to get right out on the end of the sleigh pole so he can control the steering. If a teamster started to hold her back . . . she's gone."[4]

The sand hill men lit bonfires along the "sidehill," as loggers always called a hillside, to keep their sand hot. If a team came too fast the sand hill man would throw more sand on but if it came too slow the man would throw snow on.

Some of the best teamsters were Ottawa Valley farm boys such as Bob Smith of Renfrew who worked in the bush for 16 winters in the Ottawa Valley and north to Chapleau, Ontario.

Bob Smith's Story

"I saw a horse killed and another get piled up and I don't know how he come out of it. I was for Taylor up at Whitney, around Algonquin Park. It was rainin' and they couldn't get the sand to work and they'd switched a lot of lead horses around and this lad got on a load and started down and, Oh Pshaw! he was only a wee piece when the whole load started to go. One horse had fallen down and the other pulled off sideways and got away out of it. The sleigh ran off the road and hit a stump and the logs sluiced out ahead. The foreman and I walked down and here was the horse lying in front of the sleigh. 'Well, it's too bad,' said the foreman. 'It's killed him.' 'God,' I said, 'He's movin'.' I hitched my team to that horse and pulled him out of the hole he was lyin' in. He didn't have a strap of harness left on him. I went to unhook the chain and that horse kicked and jumped up on his feet and away he went down the hill and he never was hurt a damn bit. The logs had come fallin' out but hit on the big stump and the horse had fallen into a hole four feet wide and three feet deep and the logs hadn't hit him. At Chapleau a sleigh got away and there was a big skidway at the bottom of the hill and the horse was driven right up on top of it by the sleigh and it killed him. The other horse was hurt a bit but come out of it.

"The sand man always gave the teamster a wave whether it was okay to come down and the teamster wouldn't face down the hill until he knew whether the first team was down over the hill. There were lots of times going down when she'd get stuck on the sand. Your sleigh starts bouncing around a bit and, whoa! you want to stop it or it will shake your logs right off. If it's a steep enough hill it don't matter, for it will only be a second or two and as soon as the runners cool off she'll start off again by herself. You have to use

103

Courtesy of the New Brunswick Museum

Sleigh haul on the Miramichi in New Brunswick in the late 1800s. "On a cold, frosty morning I'd hear the sleighs comin' from a long distance.... Some of the teamsters were jolly. You'd hear them sittin' up there in the morning singin'." BOB TAYLOR

Metropolitan Toronto Library Board

The skeleton of an unloaded logging sleigh, on the Opeongo River, Algonquin Park, 1924. Sleighs were two sleds coupled together, called a "two sled" in New Brunswick. The bunks on which a load of logs normally rested have been slewed fore and aft for easy travelling but normally spanned the sled from side to side. The chains were for binding the two outside logs of the bottom layer of the load.

the whip driving downhill or the horses would want to hold back.
If they start holding back they'll maybe pull the sand off with their
feet. A horse, once he's had a bad run, will get frightened and won't
want to go. You have to tup him up a little. A good teamster never
uses a whip unless he's going downhill and the horses want to hang
back. The French were good with the 12-foot blacksnake whip and
you'd hear them crack it and think a gun went off.

"Coming down those hills, if there was a team coming back up
empty you'd shout, 'Whoo! Whoo!' and they'd hear you roarin' and
know to get off the road. The loaded team had the right of way. A
loaded team, if it goes off the ice road, you're stuck and you can't
move it. I've been in places where it took two teams to draw even
an empty sleigh, which may weigh two tons, up a hill.

"You would haul logs when it was snowin' but you'd have to
know yourself and your sand man. A straw or hay hill is not as good
as sand. If there is any snow at all mixed with the hay and straw it
can be pretty slippery and if the horse hangs back at all he'll pile the
sleigh up on you, but you'd see them go through some awful things
and not get hurt. Tony Roulett was coming down with too big a
load for the amount of sand on the road and the horse must have
jumped and got right on top of a skidway of logs five or six feet
higher than your head. Once we had him unhooked the horse came
crawling and pawing and stumbling down himself.

"I've seen us going down so fast you could play cards on your
coat-tail — it was standing straight out behind you. It was bad if you
struck a long hill and it was 60 degrees below zero and you just had
to stand up there and hang on and the old frost would hit your nose
— whoo boy! It was cold! You'd be eight feet up in the air on top
of the load. One time I was so high up — they had put 175 logs on
my sleigh — that I had only about six inches of reins up there to
hang onto.

"I always figured you talked as little as possible and the horse
always knew what was goin' on. Some people talked all the time and
the horse didn't pay any attention. Of course a horse has got to
understand you. If you were drivin' a good team they just knew your
humour. The horse has terrific hearing.

"I was 15 when I first went to work in the bush, in from Mattawa
on the Ottawa River. I cut roads, big timber, and didn't know a
soul. They were all Frenchmen. I spoke very little French. When I
worked up near Chapleau, at first they were all French or Indians,
then a majority of them got to be Finnlanders. I was cutting white
pine.

"In 1930 I went up to the 'Moccasin Line,' as we called it, to
Beauchène near Timiskaming and on into Quebec there, and it was a
'muzzle loadin'' camp, cookery and everything all together under

one roof. They were all Frenchmen from Maniwaki. I was a teamster and we drew logs up a hill with a steam hoist that winter. Holy
Jumpin', it was quite a hill. You'd take the horses off the sleigh and
the hoist would draw the sleigh up the hill, and the horses would
be hooked on again at the top.

"I worked with a 'crazy wheel' on the Black River on the Quebec
side of the Ottawa but I didn't like it at all. Maybe you'd get halfway
down and there would be another lad coming halfway up the same
hill before turning off on what we called a 'go-back road.' By Jingo,
the man running the crazy wheel would have to snub you there and
let this fella get up out of the road. When they hit you with that
snub the old cable on the crazy wheel would just sing, and down
below you was the hill — a straight stretch right down. Oh my God
I didn't like that. I didn't like workin' on that Quebec side atall, atall,
atall. The Quebec side wasn't near as good as Ontario. Accommodation wasn't as good, nuthin' was as good. Not up on the Black
River Section atall, atall, atall."

The "crazy wheel" was one of the many devices the teamsters
used to brake a descent on a steep and snowy hill. Other methods
included wrapping a "bridle," or brake, chain around the rear runners or dragging a "packsack" of logs behind the sleigh, but the most
elaborate invention was the Barienger Brake, or crazy wheel. It consisted of an endless loop of cable, perhaps half a mile long, threaded
through six wheels of a patent braking device anchored to a tree at
the top of a hill. Its complexities gave rise to its name, because it took
an expert to thread steel cable through the various wheels. A wire
sling was wrapped around both the sleigh and its load of logs and
hooked to the cable of the crazy wheel. When the brakeman wanted
to stop the sleigh on a hill he pushed a lever and compressed the
moving wheels of the brake onto a hardwood block until it smoked
with the friction. On a frosty morning the "queek, queek, queek" of
the crazy wheel could be heard for miles. "You could hang a whole
load of logs, horses and all, right in the air with them once the horses
got to know them. At first they were a little nervous taking the hill,
but you could stop the sleigh any place."[5] "Most of the lumberjacks
thought it was invented to make them crazy," said Harold Burk of
Espanola, Ontario. "One of the popular pastimes in the camps
after supper would be to try to thread a miniature crazy wheel.
The men would whittle out little models and they'd get string and
try to thread the wheels. It was a complicated process and there'd
be betting on the outcome. They'd worry so much and spend
hours and hours trying to get the thing threaded properly and everyone said it was making the lumberjacks crazy. So it picked up the
name crazy wheel. That's true."

Horses at full gallop to keep ahead of a sleigh load of pulpwood running down a small hill. The loads were too heavy for a team of horses to hold back, and the skill of the teamster lay in keeping the horses moving fast to steer the sleigh. On steep hills horses were sometimes crushed to death when sleighs got out of control.

Abitibi Paper Co. Ltd.

The Barienger brake, named for its American inventor, eased sleighs loaded with logs down long, steep hills. The brake, consisting of four or more heavy steel drums threaded with cable which was attached to the sleigh load, was anchored to a stump and operated by one man with a lever. Because of its complexity, it was also known as a "crazy wheel."

Dan Hill of Bruce Mines, Ontario, six feet three and as rangy in his 70s as when he started hauling wood at the age of 16, marvelled that more teamsters did not get killed on the sidehills.

Dan Hill's Story

"When we were up at Camp One, up on the west branch of the Thessalon River, we hauled logs from 'way back — rough country. Holy Mackinaw, off mountains! We had a crazy wheel and I didn't like them because if the cable broke good-bye me and everything else. O Lord, yes. The outfit I was working for cut logs 'way up on the hills and then after they got them all ready, gosh, they didn't know how they were going to get them down off those hills. So they finally came down a cliff right into a marsh. I was lead teamster and had to go up and haul the logs off this mountain. I knew I'd be the one up there because I didn't fear anything. Really, I didn't. That's the pure truth. That winter I was 20 years old and got top wages. I went up there and we had to go away around, a heck of a place, to get up there. When we finally got our loads on they had this crazy wheel there. We would come to the edge of that steep hill where they had a big cedar to block the road and mark the turn, and then the road turned and plunged straight down. Right down. There'd be some slack when they hitched the crazy wheel on and when you broke over the brow of that hill the cable would catch and you had the lines in one hand and gripped the chain around the load with the other and all you could see was sparks from the cable snapping and you going like mad, clean over that darn mountainside. The other two teamsters, were they ever scared! But I never did care. I thought if I was to be killed I couldn't avoid it. That's it. The last day I went up there one fella said to me, 'You know, Dan, I wish I was never born. I'm just terrified but I hate like anything to quit.' 'Forget about it,' I said, 'you're all right.' So anyway, we went up there and I said to the loaders, 'How many logs have you got there?' It was either going to be one terrible big load or me and the other fella would have to make two small loads. So I said to the loaders, 'If you can put them all on my sleigh put them on.' They put them all on. There I was, 'way up there in the tree-tops, and down we went. They put 87 logs on it and I took them off that mountain.

"There was another hill, a sand hill, three-quarters of a mile long and we had 28 sand hill men working on it. One fella behind me got a run on and he got scared and jumped and the sleigh went right over the top of the horses and killed them. Sometimes those horses would be running wide open down a hill. You had to put the whip right to them. I had some dirty old runs. I had a run when the chain wrapper around the logs broke and when I landed at the bottom there was only three logs left and I was on one of them. Forty or 50 logs came off, all spread over the hill. Ira Mills said, 'I never knew you could step dance so well.' Boy was I jumping around on those logs. The horses would be going at top speed and sometimes those sleighs would just go like chain lightning. Just flyin'. I used to tell them I was going 100 miles an hour but that was exaggeration. Nobody ever timed it. It depends on how much sand was on the hill. I had one horse, the right hand one, fall once and I just put the whip to the other fella and he just put the load right into the bank. When I stopped, all the side of the harness was wore clean off but the horse wasn't hurt. They told my bother, Doc, 'You'd better go over and see Dan because he's going to be killed.' I said, 'No, I've no feeling like that at all. So long as I don't have that feeling it's okay.' It's surprising, wonderful, more men and horses didn't get killed.

"I like to use a horse the way I like to be used myself. When I'm tired I like a shot of whiskey, so I sent to Thessalon and got some horse dope — there is all sorts of dope, Spanish fly is one — but you have to know how to use it. If you use it right you'll never hurt the horse a bit but if you didn't start them out and end them up right on it then they'd die. It's just like giving a man a drink. You'd give them just a drop on their tongue, then up would go their ears. I used to carry sugar too and they'd get their nose in my pocket."

Sometimes harness would break, a horse would slip and fall, and the whole thing would "sluice," or crash. "I remember one time a fellow needed a team of horses so I bought a team from a farmer and I said, 'That's your team, go ahead and draw logs with them.' Well, he killed them the first day and I said, 'There's no use buying you horses.' He drove them right out of sight into the frozen ground. He had not stopped at the top of the hill to put on the crazy wheel and there was a turn at the bottom. He jumped off. He wasn't hurt but he killed those two horses. The sleigh went right down on them and drove them into the side of the hill. They were buried there. They are there yet."[6]

Old teamsters swore it was a disgrace to leap off a runaway sleigh and leave the horses to their fate but most foremen urged new men to kneel, not sit, atop their loads so they could jump if they had to. "One fella he jumped to the side and there was a crowbar standing in the snow and it went right into him. I saw that happen back on Blue Lake."[7]

In 1906 Billie Breen met his death on the sand hill near Willan's camp behind Thessalon. "As the heavy load started down, the sleigh runners began alternately to grab the sanded surface of the road and to shoot ahead rapidly on the slippery spots. This set up a jerking motion that increased in violence as the enormous weight of the logs urged the sleigh down the steep slope. The team was helpless to steady it. The logs began to shift dangerously with each jerk. Then the load broke into a threshing tangle of logs. Billie tried to jump clear, but he was thrown off balance by the careening logs. As he fell he was brutally crushed between the logs. He died several hours later."[8]

Loading a sleigh with 15 or 20 big logs, any one of which could crush man and horse, required skill. A greenhorn might end up with a haphazard pile of logs on a sleigh rather than a proper load. The expert "top loader" stood on the pile with a cant-hook, or a peavey, a four- or five-foot stock with a hook on the end like one-half of a pair of ice tongs, and fitted the logs together in a balanced load almost as wide at the top as at the bottom. The main thing was to build a solid base and they would use a crowbar to wedge the bottom logs in firmly. The top loader would select each log in the order he wanted it.

From the skidway two "rollers" sent the logs bounding down to two "senders" who steadied the logs with their cant-hooks, looped a decking line around them, and the decking line, pulled by a horse, rolled the logs up to the top of the load.

"The men were wonderfully expert with their cant-hooks. They used them with so little effort it looked as if anyone could easily handle them but the amateur soon found out that this idea was entirely wrong; the hook would swing around and fall into every position except the right one."[9] The decking line was 100 feet of light chain which ran from the horse up through a block rigged to a pole or a tree and was looped down over a log and back to the top of the growing pile of logs, where it was anchored by a sharp "swamp hook." Loading could be dangerous work.

Peter Emberley was crushed by rolling logs near Boiestown, New Brunswick, in 1882. He had just arrived from Prince Edward Island and hired on with McLellan's on the Southwest Miramichi River. When his work-mate, John Calhoun, carried the dying boy to McLellan's farm he heard Peter speak deliriously of his home, his harsh father, and his loving mother. They buried him in the Catholic cemetery at Boiestown in a blizzard so fierce the priest could not reach the graveside. *Peter Emberley*, written by Calhoun, became the best-loved ballad on the river.

> I hired to work in the lumber woods,
> Where they cut the tall spruce down,
> While loading sleds with yarded logs,
> I received my own death wound....
> Adieu unto my dearest friend,

I mean my mother dear,
She raised a son who fell as soon,
as he left her tender care . . .

Lumberjacks considered it unlucky to sing *Peter Emberley* in the bush. "You'd think people was pretty rough in them days. People wasn't so rough. They feared the woods. The lumber woods was a dangerous place at all times."[10]

The old skills and dangers of the cant-hook men began to wane with the introduction of such methods as the jammer, a primitive, horse-powered crane which hoisted logs up onto a pile and was invented before the First World War by Peter Wallace at Blind River, Ontario. Unloading logs from a sleigh on the river bank onto the ice far below, however, continued to call for skill. "I never saw guys who could use cant-hooks like Frappier's men. The logs were just literally flying through the air. They'd let go the chains around the logs and the whole pile would fly out and come down those skids and start bounding onto the ice. The guys with cant-hooks would grab any log bouncing off the skids and just give it a flick with their wrist to get it straight again."[11]

Binding for a Load of Logs
CANADIAN FOREST INDUSTRIES,
TORONTO

Sometimes, for the fun of it, they built "brag loads" of more than 200 logs and one Sunday in 1916 Dan Shanahan, the best loader at Big Ed Hoover's camp at Webbwood, Ontario, accepted a challenge from the Foley brothers. Loggers came from all over the north shore of Lake Huron to watch. The Foleys loaded 275 logs and then stood back to see what Shanahan, Johnny Ryan, Martin Lang, and Denny Shea could do. By noon Shanahan's men had loaded 306 logs and the Foleys had gone home crestfallen to Sault Ste. Marie. The best teamster in Hoover's camp was chosen to drive the brag load three miles to the log dump and he had almost reached it when he was ordered to jump off. As the sleigh came to a halt there was a loud crack and the whole thing flew to pieces like the wonderful one-hoss shay.

That they had been able to move such a load at all was due to the "ice road." As soon as the frost and snow came each December, level stretches were plowed and flooded to a glassy surface with two deep ruts so the sleighs would not slide off. On roads like that the sleighs ran along almost like horse-drawn railway cars. The men who built the ice roads were the drivers of the water tank sleighs who worked all night to make a fresh ice surface for the next day's haul; their jobs were the coldest and loneliest in camp, their only diversion the howling of the wolves. "You had to be quick, you know. If your tank leaked you'd freeze, sleigh and all, right to the blasted ground and you'd have to hammer the runners loose."[12]

"We used a line and tackle and a barrel with a little door in it to load water in the tank and when you let the 45-gallon barrel, always

111

A record "brag load" of 306 logs at foreman Ed Hoover's Webbwood, Ontario, camp in 1916. The driver is standing at the base of the load between the horses. On roads polished to glare ice smoothness two horses could haul 20 or 30 tons once the load was started.

Courtesy of Larry Elger,
of Feric, Montreal

New Brunswick Archives

Landing logs on a "brow," or river bank, during the sleigh haul season. Great piles of logs were stacked to await the spring thaw and the river drive to the mill.

Sam Gagné, a top loader, placing logs on a sleigh with the help of two bull rope men who steady the ends of the logs as they are rolled up a skid onto the load. The logs are being hoisted by a horse jammer; the horse, out of the picture to the right, hauling the log up the skid by means of a chain running through a block and tackle atop the A-frame at right.

Abitibi Paper Co. Ltd.

covered with ice, down into the hole in the lake the door would open and when you pulled up the barrel the door would close. The water would not be in the tank long, and that and the shaking would keep it from freezing solid. There were two plug holes in the back of the tank for the water to come out. Oh, that was cold! But the grub we ate, we were so fat the cold couldn't hurt us."[13] Occasionally the tank men would find a muskrat in the barrel when they hauled it up. "I'm paying you to ice the roads, not to trap," the foreman used to say. By spring an ice road might be 12 inches thick.

"Road monkeys" kept it clean of bark and branches during the day and because they swept off the horse manure as well they were also known as "chickadees." By January, when the sleigh haul started, the blacksmiths had changed the blunt skidding shoes to sharp toe calks to grip the ice. When, despite their winter shoes, a horse's hooves got "all balled up" with snow and ice the teamster used a small ball hammer to knock it out. Some horses, when they saw their teamster coming with a ball hammer, would automatically lift a foot.

"Before horse stocks — the wooden frames to hold the horses — came into use the horses were very difficult to shoe," said Maurice Lavoie of Dolbeau, Quebec. "We had to wrestle with them and some were dangerous. I remember when Savard died from a kick in the stomach, and another time I was shoeing one when he broke the rope and jumped right out through the window."

The leather-aproned blacksmith and his handyman, pumping forge coal with a hand-blower in their clanging, smoky shop, shoed horses, built sleighs, made cant-hooks, peaveys, and pike poles and chains, and fashioned bunkhouse stoves from 45-gallon oil drums.

"I worked seven days a week from six in the morning sometimes to nearly midnight," said Tony Shushack at Mattawa on the upper Ottawa. "I worked 57 years and I never was fired off a job. My family was Polish and I worked on their farm at Wilno near Barry's Bay and went to school only about a year. I was working as a handyman for Jack Macrae in Algonquin Park when he said, 'I want you to go and be a blacksmith.' I learned to use the fire.

"Horseshoes came in barrels, ready-made, with eight nail holes in the sides but you shaped each shoe in the forge and anvil because horses are like people, their feet are different sizes. If you put the wrong shoe on, it would bother his feet. You had to weld the calks on, blunt for skidding in autumn and sharp for the ice roads. When you picked up a foot to put the shoe on you'd trim the hoof and rasp it off and if it was an inch too narrow for the shoe you'd shape the shoe to fit. Some blacksmiths left the shoe sticking out too far and the horse would catch his front foot with his hind foot and pull a shoe off. Those wild broncs from the west, Holy Jeeze, you know what I did? Before they got horse stocks I put a collar and a set of hames on him and I got a rope between his legs and laid him down and a man held his head so he couldn't get up. I put the front and hind right shoes on him, then we grabbed him, two men, and rolled him over — he weighed 1600 pounds — and put the other shoes on because, Christ, you could get killed with a horse like that. In all my 57 years, though, I only got hurt twice — my thumb was broken and my left arm. I never wore gloves. I've shoed thousands of horses and if the horse wasn't all right it wasn't the animal's fault but the man's. I always said don't abuse an animal, because he can't talk. I'd sooner use them good, pet them, and after that the animal knows what's going on. It's better for the animal. You know that yourself. Sometimes the teamsters didn't have much experience and there were horses flattened down and bushed from overwork. But this fellow, Charlie, he really knew horses. He got some of this Dr. Bell's syrup and put it on the horse's tongue and the horse just lapped it up. A few days later Charlie said, 'Look at that horse. He sticks out his tongue now to get that syrup. Just like for communion.' "

The bush life of a horse was not long. "They worked them too hard and they fed them too much. A horse will get kidney trouble if he's fed too heavily and left standing too long. But horses are like people, some are old at 12, or even 10, and others don't know when to quit. We fed them according to what they were doing. If they were standing in the barn we'd feed them maybe a quart of oats three times a day, but when they were working we'd feed a horse about a gallon of oats an hour and a half before he started work and then some at noon although maybe for only half an hour because they get cold feeding outside. Then you'd give them a good gallon at night. I've seen distemper get into a camp. It's very contagious, and there was swamp fever, a blood disease like leukemia. If we didn't know what was wrong we'd give it Dr. Bell's medicine, 30 drops on its tongue and it seems to warm them up."[14]

"Maybe when you were taking your team out of the barn in the morning you'd see one of them staggering and maybe by noon he'll be right down and can't get up. We'd send out for a vet and he would give the horse shots and that's the only thing would bring him around. Any sick horse, you'd have to put his medicine in a brandy bottle and push it down his throat until he swallows. The bot fly — the gadfly — will sting a horse and lay eggs in his fetlocks. The horse bites the stung parts and gets eggs in his stomach where the worms hatch and the flies attach themselves. Really painful. Good, strong, cold tea was good because it would make the flies let go."[15]

"Any teamster who went away from camp for the day took a bottle of colic cure in his pocket. There was laudanum in it and something else to kill the gas, or if a horse got colic — severe pains in the belly — you could give it a good shot of whiskey to warm it up.

John Kelly with his horses, Dick and Spot, in a snowstorm at Kelly's camp on the Puskaskwa in the 1920s.

115

But a horse seldom got colic if the teamster knew how to feed him. The heaves was a lung disease, no cure for that. In the spring you had to watch out for black-water fever which paralyses horses and was caused when a horse worked hard all winter and then was put in a stable and stopped dead but still fed the same. It was death."[16]

"My team," said John Kelly who came from Buckingham, Quebec, and hauled wood at Pukaskwa on the eastern shores of Lake Superior, "were always Dick and Spot, a bay team. I drove them for six years and they were small for bush horses, about 1500 compared to the usual 1600 or 1700 pounds. You always tried to mate your horses; you couldn't put a slow horse with a fast horse or a heavy horse with a light horse because one of them would do all the work and they would kill each other. One of my horses got pneumonia and died. The other got pretty old and they had to shoot him. If a horse couldn't work any more they took him up on a hill far from camp and shot him. I wouldn't shoot a horse myself, that's one thing I certainly would not do. They'd always get somebody else, some old fellow who was not a teamster but who knew what had to be done. The horse would be old or hurt and he'd do it as a favour. But you never would ask a teamster to shoot a horse."

On the St. Maurice they told the story of how an ailing old horse had to be killed. "Since they were not permitted guns in camp, someone decided to tie dynamite to the horse's head, blindfold it, and tether it to a stump. But the horse smelled the smoke and broke the tether and went running down the trail after the lumberjack."[17]

Although there were always teamsters who would rather play poker at night than tend their horses, there were many, too, like Mike Scorback who had come to Thunder Bay from Slovakia. "They were my chums, those horses. There were some horses in camp with raw necks. Guys didn't clean them. I used my own water to heal them with urine and I cured them in two weeks and stole oats from the barn boss to give the horses more blood."[18]

" . . . But there was a fella had a nice team of bays, he was good to them, babied them when he was skidding, and they were fat and looked good, but when the sleigh haul started I was loading across the lake from him and he got his load on and by golly they wouldn't start. To hear him crackin' that whip and beating those horses you'd think it was the 4th of July. He would have got a jail term for that today."[19]

In late March teamsters often started "hot logging," which meant hauling logs right from stump to river in order to fill their quotas before the ice roads thawed. "We used to get up at three A.M. with the moon shining bright and the stars snapping and we never got back until one A.M. We'd leave the harness right on them in the stable and we did that for a week."[20]

116

Abitibi Paper Co. Ltd.

Pulpwood teamster shovelling out a "cord cradle" in northern Ontario in order to load eight-foot wood onto the sleigh bound for a riverside log dump.

Abitibi Paper Co. Ltd.

Before the Second World War, tractors began to appear at some camps although it was well into the 1950s before the horses were finally displaced by internal combustion engines. Here the two meet, the old and the new.

117

With the spring sun melting the ice, horses sometimes were drowned crossing a lake. "On Radford Lake in northern Ontario I saw four horses drowned through the ice. Two were hooked onto the drowning ones to haul them out but they were all drowned. Another time I saw one horse go through the ice at Camp 18. They got a heavy pole between the horse's front legs and lifted him a bit and the old barn boss, Drew, put his foot on the horse's buttocks and started shoving down, bouncing him, and another guy at his head shut off the horse's wind with a rope and as soon as the wind was shut off the horse started pawing and came up out of that hole just like that. If you choke them they'll fill up with air. Once you got the horse bouncing up and down in the water he just popped out of the ice to safety."[21]

—"You would get them to shelter pretty quick for they wouldn't live long in the cold. Some horses were easy to get out and some just seemed to . . . well, a fellow said they just stick their head under the water and drowned. They didn't have too much to look forward to and that was the easy way out."[22]

— "Sometimes they floated up again and you could see their backs out there. It was kind of sad."[23]

As the sun warmed the southern slopes and turned the snow to slush the teams had to be taken off the roads at midday and hauling was done only in morning and evening when the ice roads were firm. By the end of March the haul would be over, the teamsters paid off, and the foreman would wait for the ice on the lakes and rivers to melt and release the logs for the most dangerous job of all — the spring log drive. The teamsters went home to their farms.

"In the old days," said Lee Fletcher, of Sault Ste. Marie, "teamsters were the élite of the camp, often with sleeping quarters of their own. That was for two reasons: they'd have to get up an hour before breakfast to feed and harness the horses, and also, after a month of being with the horses, and no washing to speak of, they'd smell pretty horsy. In the evening the teamsters all used to go down to the barn and curry and water the horses and I can still see them — each had a hand lantern going down the yard, their legs scissoring and casting shadows against the snow. I used to go down there at night. It was like a club. The smell of the horses and the sound of them, I remember it yet. In the late 1930s there were very few real teamsters left . . . just people who steered horses around."

Deep in the woods behind Poplar Dale, Ontario, east of Sault Ste. Marie, Shannon Assam, 70, and his brother, Paul, 65, were still logging with horses in the 1970s and looked as strong and tough as men 20 years younger. They ran their own old-fashioned sawmill and obviously loved the life.

"When you are driving horses it's a hard day's job," said Paul

Assam. "Once you've lost a generation of teamsters it's gone, hey?"
But in the days of cant-hook men, the crash of rolling logs, and hell-
for-leather teamsters flying down the hills, an eastern lumber camp
was a horse camp.

8 THE SEASONS:SPRING RIVER DRIVERS

Come all ye jolly river boys,
I'll have ye all draw near,
And listen to the dangers,
Which ye will quickly hear.

THE JAM ON GERRY'S ROCKS

— TRADITIONAL

When the ice broke up on the lakes in April or May and rain and melting snow filled the woods with the sounds of tumbling water, the river drivers came with their pike poles, peaveys, and spiked boots.

Some say there have been river drivers on the St. Lawrence since the French intendant Jean Talon introduced the practice on streams near Quebec City in the 17th century.

Unlike the raftsmen, who banded timber into solid rafts and navigated the Ottawa and the St. Lawrence with sails and oars like mariners, the river drivers herded loose logs. They stamped logs with the owner's brand, drove timber over falls, rode the logs down rapids, chased strays into flooded swamps and corralled them finally in holding booms at the mouths of rivers. They slept beneath the stars beside the cook-boat, or "wangan boat," and roistered like cowboys in bar-rooms at the end of the long drive.

Every spring from high up the rivers they sent tall piles of logs crashing and splashing into streams swollen by melting snow and ice. "Watering the wood" was dangerous work when a 50-foot "brow" of logs began to topple. A "river hog," wading chest deep after a maverick log, was prone to chilblains, arthritic "black leg," and rheumatism when he rolled up at nine o'clock in damp blankets by the fire and slept until the foreman shouted, "Daylight on the creek! The water's not hot, it won't scald you this morning!" "They some-

With peaveys and calked boots, lumberjacks rode stubborn logs with great skill and, by running on the rounded surface, could spin, or birl, them through still water.

Northeast Archives of Folklore and Oral History, University of Maine, Orono

"Watering the wood." When the ice disappeared from the rivers, lumberjacks armed with peaveys and pike poles pushed the logs into the fast water and the drive got into full swing. The first logs down would usually "grease" the stream, that is, fill up little bays and backwaters and form harmless "side jams" so that the logs coming behind would continue running down the natural channel. At the end of the drive, men would come down to clean up the logs which had stuck. This operation was called the "sweep," the "sack," or "picking the rear."

Archives Nationales du Québec

times didn't get their tents up but they made roaring big fires and put up sticks to dry their clothes. Their feet would get 'scalded' from the icy water in their woollen socks and they used to buy Gall Fluid, used for horses, to cure the chafing."[1]

"I got sent to one camp north of Thunder Bay," recalled Frank Moran, "and it was an awful cold early spring morning with about a quarter of an inch of ice on this little lake. There was a line of us walking behind a big old Finn foreman, Gus Hill. We were up to our knees in water along the tote road because they had opened the dams to flood the river. Nobody said a word, but I thought, 'Good Heavens, we aren't going into that lake!' They were watering the wood and the men were wading into the water breaking the ice and all. The wood was all in piles on the shore and we had to get it into the lake. The tremendous art to river driving, nowadays people know nothing about."

To make use of every glint of daylight they worked 15 hours a day and ate four meals; breakfast by 4 A.M., first lunch 9:30, second lunch 2:30, and supper at 7:30. Some old-timers had a trick of stepping on a log and sinking it deep in the water to wet their feet and legs to the knees. They claimed they had better balance after their feet were wet. A "runner of the loose," a river driver herding logs, could run along a log which barely supported his weight, leaping to another when it started to sink. "White water men" were skilled at riding logs through rapids or breaking log jams. "Black water men" rafted logs across lakes and tended booms. Often one man did both jobs.

The pride of a river driver was his shin-high boots, studded with sharp quarter-inch steel calks, pronounced "corks," which anchored him to a floating log like the claws of a cat. Those boots were a logger's caste mark, his weapon in high-kicking bar-room brawls where their wounds were called "logger's smallpox," and his memorial in the days when a river driver was buried where he drowned and his boots nailed to a tree to mark his grave. "In New Brunswick they carved a cross on a tree and hung his boots up on a limb. When a man drowned in Quebec they sent for a priest and he blessed the land and we built a cross there. The Wessenneau River, up the St. Maurice Valley, which I drove, was lined with crosses."[2]

"This fella up the North Pole Stream on the Miramichi in New Brunswick, they found him in a pool standing up, his feet anchored in the sand, his long hair waving in the current. They buried him right there and nailed his boots to a spruce tree. It happened around the turn of the century and they tell me the little curled-up pieces of leather and rusty calks are still there."[3]

"The year I drove the Dumoine River, up the Ottawa, pine and

Calked Drive Boots

Far up the Ottawa River, where it broadens into Lake Timiskaming, a crew of river drivers, pike men, and peavey men gather to round up the white pine logs for the spring drive downriver. At right is a capstan, or "headworks," used to kedge and warp logs across a lake.

Ontario Archives

Foreman Bob Carpenter, the bearded man leaning on his peavey stock between the two figures in the foreground, starting the river drive on Aumond Creek in the Ottawa Valley in May 1902. This was cold work. "As long as the water did not rise above the top of their legs," wrote Charles Macnamara, "the men did not mind it much, but when it came up on the body they suffered. They seldom had dry clothes to change into and often had to sleep in wet garments. They have told me that when they threw off the blankets in the morning steam would rise into the cold air from their still damp clothing. Only strong, young men could stand such work. A few rare cases of inflammatory rheumatism were known."

Charles Macnamara Collection, Ontario Archives, Courtesy of Mrs. Jean Cunningham, Arnprior, Ont.

pulpwood, spruce and balsam, there were 35 graves right there at Ryan's Chute. When Peltier got drowned they put his boots on the cross and a fellow working with us there, he looked at them boots and he said, 'Peltier, you don't need them and I do — mine are pretty near worn out.' As honest as I'm tellin' you that fellow picked the calk boots right off the cross, put them on, and switched."[4]

Before calk boots appeared on the Ottawa, in the 1860s, shanty-men wore slippery, knee-high beef-hide moccasins, called moccasin boots, larrigans, shoe packs, or *bottes sauvages*.[5] After World War One, "lumbermen's rubbers," with rubber bottoms and high leather tops and bellow tongues to keep out the water, made their appearance. They had no calks, but since they were mostly used on the pulpwood drives and most pulpwood was too small to ride, the calks were not missed.

The rest of a river driver's outfit consisted of an old felt hat, perhaps a red and black mackinaw shirt flapping outside his "stagged" pants, which were slashed off at his calf, and a peavey or a pike pole. At first his tools for canting and lifting logs were primitive: a hand spike, which was simply a five-foot pole with a spike in the end, or a "swing dog," a stout pole with a hook fixed so loosely to the stock it might swing erratically as the man was canting a log and throw him into the river. Joseph Peavey was watching just such a contre-temps near his forge on the Penobscot River at Stillwater, Maine, in 1858 when he got the idea for the tool which bears his name. On a five-foot ironwood stock Joe Peavey fashioned a spike to steady a rolling log and attached a pointed, thumb-like hook to move up and down but not, like the swing dog, sideways. It resembled the earlier skidway cant-hook except it was bigger and had a spike instead of a blunt toe. The peavey revolutionized river driving and men said it was a shame and a wonder it had not been thought of before. The driver's other tool was the pike pole to prod the logs along, 12 feet or more of seasoned black spruce or ash with either a blunt toe or a gaff like a sharpened boat hook.

By the time the drivers had rolled the logs off the winter dumps into holding booms — timbers chained to encircle the logs in a compact mass — it might be early May and time to start the drive. On a lake the boomed logs were towed to an outlet stream by "head-works," a raft mounted with a camp-made wooden capstan which, like sailors on a wind-jammer, the men pushed around, "winding her up." They kedged the boom across a lake by dropping anchor a few hundred feet ahead of the raft, winding raft and boom toward the anchor, and repeating the slow process until they reached the stream they meant to drive. When they built bigger rafts, 20 feet by 40 feet, they used a horse to wind the capstan.

When head winds pushed the logs backwards and a drive might

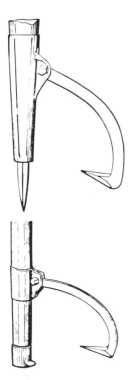

The cant-hook differed from the peavey in that it had a blunt toe on the end and was used mostly on the skidways. The peavey had a sharp spike and was used mostly on the river drives and sometimes on the skidways. Both had hardwood handles.

Northeast Archives of Folklore and Oral History, University of Maine, Orono

Headworks raft, 1890. Three lumberjacks turn a home-made capstan on a raft to haul a timber boom across a lake. An anchor would be dropped a few hundred yards ahead of the raft and the men would "wind her in," pulling raft and towed logs up to the anchor, and then the whole kedging operation would be repeated until the logs were hauled across the lake. The capstan moved a boom of logs at the rate of 1000 feet an hour.

125

Photograph by MALAK, *Ottawa*

In the white water rapids of Rivière Tomasine in Quebec a river driver
cants a log into the water with his peavey to keep a jam from building.
The invention of the peavey in 1858 improved river drive techniques
immensely. With its hook swinging in a fixed orbit, the peavey could
move logs more quickly and safely than the primitive handspikes or
spruce poles which had been used before.

126

be held up for weeks, the men lay idle and the foreman puffed furiously on his pipe and eyed the sky for a change of weather. When the head winds died at last the crews worked all night to get the logs across. "I remember being called at midnight, the wind had changed on a lake up the Montmorency in Quebec. I went to the bunkhouse and routed everybody out. 'Up and at 'em, boys! Get your boots!' And up we got a mile and a half to the lake and put guys on the capstan, walking around it pushing three-foot poles. You had a terrible time when the wind was blowing against you for days."[6]

Those were red-eyed nights with sleepy lumberjacks stumbling around the capstan, winching logs across the dark lake, beacon fires burning ashore, the wooden capstan creaking and groaning like a torture chamber until someone put a five-pound chunk of fat pork into the spindle hole to cut the racket. Occasionally a man fell into the water, and in the days before ratchet-brakes a capstan-bar might fly back and break a man's arm. It was a blessing, they said, when in the 1870s John West of Simcoe, Ontario, designed a scow with a steam winch to replace the headworks. He called it an alligator because once it had hauled the boom across a lake it could winch itself overland on skids from lake to lake. "On some rivers you'd get out to the front, to the mouth, in a month or six weeks, but on the Serpent River in northern Ontario it could take two years because of the succession of big lakes."[7]

When the logs were launched in a river and were scrambling down-country, rearing crews boarded drive boats to sweep, or "sack," the shore and shallows, refloating stranded logs, a mobile force to break sudden jams. "I remember the rear of the drive coming down the St. Maurice River in 1928 with maybe 200 men, cook scows, boats, the whole works, coming down and taking out stranded logs and they moved like crazy, very fast, and when they reached La Tuque all the mothers pulled their daughters in off the streets and storekeepers barricaded their front doors."[8] Like a travelling circus, the white water men pitched their tents for a night or two on the outskirts of a river town and then were gone with the dawn. By 1880, 234 eastern Canadian rivers were being driven. The drivers came shouting down the rivers, sometimes fighting with other drive crews who contested their right of way or tried to hog the spring freshets which kept the logs moving. That was in the days before government regulations and before lumber companies formed their own cooperatives to make the drives more orderly. In 1870 the federal government decreed that all logs be butt-stamped with their owner's registered mark. A lumberman might use a different device each year to tell the age of his logs. Stamping hammers bore designs of crow's feet, diamonds, arrows, stars, turtles, swastikas, and initials. Some operators cut bark marks into the sides of a log or daubed on

A steam winchboat, or "alligator," invented at Simcoe, Ontario, in the late 1800s for drawing booms of logs, weighing thousands of tons, across lakes and down rivers. Like real alligators they could crawl, or winch themselves, across land from one lake to another.

As the drivers swept downriver behind the logs, working from dawn to dusk and sometimes all night as well, eating four meals a day, they were never far from a cookery, mounted on a pointer in rough water or on a scow on a lake. This drive gang on Lake Timiskaming up the Ottawa were enjoying a Sunday visit from some lady friends, in second boat from right.

Ontario Archives

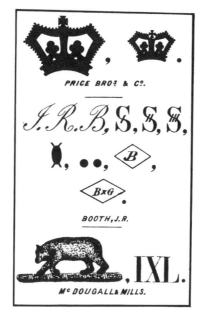

From The Lumberman's Timber Mark Guide, *by J. Barnwall Jackson*

Brands stamped on the butts of river driven logs. These came from the 1870s when the practice began. Price Bros. Co. stamped the likeness of a crown, J. R. Booth used initials and symbols, including J.R.B., and McDougall & Mills used the likeness of a bear.

128

paint spots to guard against theft or confusion at the booming grounds at the end of a drive.

The 250-mile St. Maurice, which shares headwaters with the Ottawa, did not become a great drive river until the 1850s when men began to tame it a bit with dams and improvements. Since then half a dozen dams and the work of the St. Maurice Drive Company, founded in 1904, have smoothed out the river and opened up the Valley, but in the rough old days the greatest rivermen east of the Ottawa and west of the Miramichi were the 1500 *draveurs de la Mauricie*.

There were usually six to a boat: four *rameurs*, two on each side with long pike poles, a *derrière-de-barge* steering with a nine-foot paddle, and a *devant-de-barge*, or foreman, braced in the bow with a 12-foot pole to help the stern man steer through the rocks and shoals in the speeding current. Never taking his eyes off the river, the *devant-de-barge* guided his crew with hand signals or shouts of "Ho!" — for sustained all-together effort, three or four shouts — which were about the only human sound the men could hear above the roar of the white water. But it was often in utter silence, the river blocked by logs and ominously still, that they met their greatest test: a log jam a mile or two long, logs piled atop each other like a wall. It was then they left their drive boat and crawled in on the logs to find the timbers, usually one called the "key log," holding the whole drive back.

Drive boats, or *bateaux*, were often built locally to suit a particular river but the best known was the "pointer" devised for J. R. Booth in the 1850s by an Ottawa wood carver, John Cockburn. Pointed bow and stern, sturdy as an east coast fishing dory, and as skittish as a Venetian gondola, Cockburn's pointer had such a shallow, flat-bottomed draft that loggers boasted it could "float on heavy dew." Shorn of lumberjack exaggeration, that meant a pointer carrying eight men was once made to float in five inches of water. In a small workshop at Pembroke, beside the Ottawa River, three generations of Cockburns crafted V-bottomed pointers with pine tongue-in-groove planking, white cedar ribs, and a preservative of oil and jeweller's rouge which gave the pointers a distinctive brick-red colour. The Cockburns made their pointers to last at least 10 years, but many never lasted a season — smashed in rough water on sharp rocks.

Early in the century seven men were killed on the Quince River near the headwaters of the Ottawa, swept over Devil's Chute Falls while attempting to reach a small log jam. "The most desperate struggle with the oars and the most expert wielding of the 9-foot paddle by the steersman held them for a few minutes against the awful current," wrote a witness to the tragedy, "but soon realizing the futilities of further effort they all stopped rowing and passed

The Flying Rear. A four-man pointer rushing down the rapids in the wake of a log drive, the bowman poised to fend the light boat off the rocks below, the rowers ready to ship their oars at a command from the steersman kneeling in the stern. After the drive had gone through, boat crews and pike pole men on the bank "swept the rear" to collect stray logs left behind.

Photograph by MALAK, *Ottawa*

A 40-foot pointer boat, carrying food and supplies, plunging over the "Graveyard" rapids on the Spanish River, north of Lake Huron, in Ontario. The man guiding the boat is Leo Restoule. The boat got through safely, but it took skilled men to manoeuvre the precious cook boats and supply boats down the white water on a river drive.

Courtesy of Harry Colborn, Espanola, Ont.

calmly to their doom before the eyes of their comrades on shore."[9]

As a drive sped downstream, filling a river for miles with a sliding brown carpet, men were posted two by two to fend off logs at the river bends and to "tend out" the rapids where a crooked log caught on a rock could jam the drive higher than a house. At McLean Chute, on the upper Lièvre River, the logs rushed down at 40 miles an hour. The tip-off to a pikeman that a jam was starting somewhere upriver was the sudden disappearance of the log flow. "There was a big one out there on Stuart Rapids, pine logs coming into Rock Lake on the Thessalon. I was only a kid and it would make your hair curl, pretty near, to see it. Twelve feet high, the width of the river, and 300 yards long. When I got there quite a few logs had jammed up; one must have got up on a rock and the jam built out from shore. As it got higher one log would get on top of the other and weigh it down and there'd be hardly any water flowing downstream. You have no idea how much power there is to water on a thing like that. Four of us kept prying away at one log and the foreman said, 'You fellows get up on shore there and I'll finish this.' When that thing broke and started there were logs going end over end and everything else. They would come down on one log and break it right in two. The noise of that thing! And the power behind it! It sounded like a couple of freight trains or one of those big jet planes."[10] A log jam on a river, like a shipwreck at sea, was the worst thing that could happen.

There were three kinds of jam: a centre jam which started in the middle of a river, a side jam which built out from a log snagged on shore, and a full jam right across the river. "We used to drive the Wolf, which was a fast river, all the way down. There were bad jams there and you'd have to pick them from the sides and corners. We'd use water control — water released suddenly from dams on the side streams — but when that water hit the back of a jam sometimes the jam wouldn't move. The water would just squeeze it tighter. So you'd just have to pick the sides and get enough of it out to get it to move and pull. Sometimes it would pull and the whole works would go as slick as a whistle. Other times it would pull for maybe 150 feet and then back up and you'd have to do the same doggone thing all over again. Sometimes it would take four or five days to get 10 000 jammed cords of pulpwood out of the river, which meant you were flooding, stopping, flooding, day and night. Guys out there up to their armpits in water. It was the only way you could do it. I never saw anything tougher than drivin' that Wolf River."[11]

The job of the jam busters was to pry off logs, one by one, until they found the key log which had started the jam and which held the others. Working down in the gap in front of a shaking wall of logs was a job for volunteers. "Take that spruce!" the foreman

Ont. Ministry of Natural Resources

River drivers try to stop a log jam from building at Pig Pen Chute on the Mississagi River north of Lake Huron. "In a spring drive," said Wes McNutt, "the level of excitement was such that you could extract the ultimate juice from it. All around you would hear the roar of water, the big and little streams, and the river itself. There was excitement in the air."

Log drivers were more often wet than dry. When a log slewed around in the river and threatened to hang up the drive, a "river hog" would leap bodily into the icy river to wrestle it free. "I've fallen off logs," said Harold Green, "when there were chunks of ice floating all around you."

Ont. Ministry of Natural Resources

would shout, and peaveys, the stout hooked poles used to grab logs, would rattle and clank as a log was canted out of the tumble of giant jackstraws. The foreman, down on the logs along with his men, would watch and listen. Sometimes the mess would shift and groan and every eye would turn to the foreman for a signal. He would study for a moment and shake his head and the work would resume. "Take that jack pine!" They prodded a log here, lifted one there, cut this, pulled that, until there was a sudden shudder through the whole mass. "Leave her boys!" the foreman would call, and the jam would "break and go." Sometimes one or two men went with it. If a jam buster was fast he would be out of the gap and off over the logs to shore like a scalded cat, his peavey held high across his chest for balance. If he moved too late the best he might hope for was a rough ride to quiet water on one of the tumbling logs. "See the bravado of yonder Frenchman. There is 20 feet of water between him and the shore . . . If he goes another hundred feet over the next pitch he shoots and is lost. Look! There comes a log just outside the mass. He jumps upon it, swings his pole quicker than lightning, steers the log toward the shores."[12] The river drivers of Quebec and the Miramichi in New Brunswick were the best in the business.

Harding Smith's Story

"The Little Southeast Miramichi was one of the roughest streams that ever laid outdoors. There were rocks in the middle three feet high. On Rocky Brook, a very rough stream, here was a jam in a place they called 'The Jaws' and there must have been 100 men there and no one would dare go out on the jam. But you could hear Miles Hunter — whistling. Always when he was going out onto a bad place you'd hear him start to whistle. He took off his coat and went out on the jam. One mis-step would have meant certain death . . . They would put six men on a center jam and they would work until the center was about to go. I've seen Billy Johnson run those logs down through canyons in Rocky Brook when they were doing everything. He had no fear at all. He was a wonderful white water man. You couldn't shoot him off a log. Bill MacPherson had perfect balance, he could walk on any small log that would carry him, walk right down to the end of it, turn around, and walk back, just like a crow on a limb. Billy Griffin of Boiestown, here would be water cascading through the jam, all lashed to a foam, you couldn't hear anything for the roar of that stream. He was perched right down in front of that and there was logs going for him all the time. He was just as sure-footed as a goat. He never missed a step and when the jam went out . . . those logs, after they started you never could tell what they would do.

At every bend or rough stretch on a river, men were stationed with long pike poles to fend off logs and keep a jam from building. Log jams, the worst things that could happen on a drive, were caused by logs grounding in low water or by piling up on rocks, curves, or narrow stretches of a river.

Photograph by MALAK, *Ottawa*

Courtesy of the New Brunswick Museum

Log jam. When logs jammed on rocks or a bend of the river the whole drive would choke and back up for miles behind the jam. "The log jam would be always quivering, a hell of a pile of water and pressure backing up behind it. The men would be out working on it, trying to pick the logs loose with their peaveys. Sometimes she'd go, all together, and someone would suddenly shout to us to get ashore fast. Sometimes she'd only go a little bit and stop. When she'd go altogether you should see them cheer. They'd throw their hats in the air. Oh, yeah, a helluva time."

"They used to bury men right where they took them out of the water. There was one fellow, Fred, he had no relatives so they buried him there in two flour barrels. They shoved one flour barrel over his head and another over his feet. He wasn't a tall man. That was the casket he had. There were three men lost at Priestly Rapids right up this river I drove when I was 17. They had to be sure-footed. One mis-step meant certain death."[13]

Sad songs retold those river tragedies, like the ballad describing the drowning of young Anthony Barrett of Belleville, Ontario, on June 2, 1860. " 'Twas on the Napanee," they sang, "while driving sawlogs down. He fell into the water there, and there, alas, was drowned . . . " On 20 rough tributaries of the Ottawa, 130 men were drowned in 1846. Jimmy Judd was drowned on the Bonnechère.

> He went forth to break the jam, and
> with it he went through,
> In spite of his activity,
> his precious life to save,
> In vain was his exertion, for he met a watery grave.

In 1878 Jimmy Phalen drowned trying to carry out his foreman's orders to break a jam below Cross Lake on the Mississippi, off the Ottawa, when two rafts collided. It took an hour to find his body.

> Now here, now there, his body went, a-tumbling o'er and o'er
> One fearful cry for Mercy,
> "O Lord look down on me,"
> His soul got free from early care,
> Gone to Eternity.

No less than 14 verses celebrated the watery death of Guy Reed in New Brunswick but of all those river threnodies *The Jam on Gerry's Rocks* was the favourite. Since place names were usually changed to please local audiences, shantymen still argue its origin. "I was in the State of Washington one time sitting in a third-rate hotel, a lumberjack's hotel. Some lumberjacks were sitting around there and they got to talking about that and one fellow said it was in Minnesota and another argued it was from the State of Maine. Some even thought it might have been on the Ottawa or the Gatineau."[14] There is some evidence that *The Jam on Gerry's Rocks* originated on the Penobscot in Maine, perhaps written, since it concerns Cana-

135

dians, by a New Brunswick or Prince Edward Island "Province-man," as Maine lumberjacks called the men who crossed the border in their thousands.

> It was on a Sunday morning, as you will quickly hear,
> Our logs were piled up mountains high, we could not
>   keep them clear,
> Our foreman said, "Turn out, brave boys, with hearts
>   devoid of fear,
> We'll break the jam on Gerry's Rocks and to Bangor
>   we will steer,"
> Now some of them were willing and some of them were not,
> For to work on jams on Sunday, they did not think we ought,
> But six of our Canadian boys did volunteer to go,
> And break the jam on Gerry's Rocks, with their foreman,
>   Young Munro.
> They had not rolled off many logs when they heard his
>   clear voice say,
> "I'll have you men be on your guard for the jam will
>   soon give 'way"
> These words were hardly spoken, when the mass did
>   break and go,
> And carried off those six brave youths, and their foreman,
>   Jack Munro.

Many died unsung; many were simply maimed. "My brother, Louis, lost his arm in a jam, his right arm, on the Mississagi River in 1909. He had been a violin player and was going to get married. He never got married after that but he went into the bush and cooked in the camps. There was no compensation then, nothing then."[15]

If a jam did not respond to peavey and pike the foreman might try a "jam dog," two strong hooks in the middle of a rope stretched across the stream. The hooks were driven into the key log and pulled by men on opposite banks or hitched to horses. A foreman tried to avoid blasting so as not to splinter the logs but when all else failed a powder monkey such as Rory McBain, "Dynamite King of the Thessalon," would saunter in with his caps and fuses, bind sticks of explosive to a long pole, shove pole and fuse into a hole in the jam, yell "Fire," and retreat with well-timed nonchalance to the shore. When a sodden explosion heaved the logs up in a burst of spray and splinters the men on the banks would throw their hats in the air and cheer.

The dynamite, packed like soft brown sugar in a paraffin-coated cartridge, came in wooden boxes padded with sawdust. The fuse came in 50-foot coils and the charge was ignited with a copper cap containing fulminate of mercury. "The dynamite men weren't afraid of dynamite. They'd just throw the box right on the road and break it loose. But they wouldn't use an old fuse. You take a new piece of fuse and it will burn 30 seconds to the foot and they always wanted a new roll of fuse because they wanted to know that when they had a foot of fuse they were going to get 30 seconds. With an old fuse they never knew what they were going to get. Of course they had respect for the caps."[16] To make a primer, a fuse was stuck into a cap, the end was crimped, and the cap was stuffed into one of the cartridges of dynamite. "You would use five or six sticks of dynamite, depending on the way they'd blow. You'd take a cartridge of dynamite and poke holes through it and put a cap on it. Some fellows would put the cap in their mouth to bite it and put a crimp in it. I once put the cap in my mouth and bit it and Murdoch MacDonald — it's the only time I ever heard him swear — said, 'You Goddamn fool!' He was afraid I'd blow my head off. It would have, too, if I'd bit it too close to the end. You put soap on it so the water wouldn't get in. You'd light the fuse and have a couple of minutes to run behind a tree. Bud Hart was blowing a jam on the Goulais River and was bending down behind a tree when the thing blew up and a piece of log came down and broke his back."[17]

In a rocky gorge they sometimes let the dynamite man down on a rope. "When the dynamite was placed you'd light the fuse and when the man hanging over the rail saw the smoke start from the fuse he would start pulling . . . and finally before the fuse got through to the explosive you would be in the cave with your two buddies. And sometimes it wouldn't be long until the report came, and it was a deafener, for the steep side of the gorge through which the river rushed was a perfect sounding board. Then you would look over the low wall that you had been hiding behind and see the jam go tearing along, breaking logs, and you would feel thankful you didn't happen to be among them."[18] When 18 million feet of logs jammed at Grand Falls on the Nepisiguit River near Bathurst, New Brunswick, they made an electric detonator with a battery and two wires 250 feet long, placed two kegs of dynamite under the foot of the jam "which mounted 30 feet above the top of the cliffs," and carefully floated two kegs of dynamite down on the rear of the jam. "The roar of that explosion could be heard miles away but it lifted the logs out and threw them in all directions with such force that a broken end of a log was found in the woods 400 feet from the jam. As they fell the whole jam rushed through the gorge in a wild tumbling of logs, ice and water, like nails in a keg."[19]

There were hair-raising accounts of dynamite on the rivers. "A man was standing on a dam talking to his brother who was coming

137

Photograph by MALAK, *Ottawa*

Courtesy of the New Brunswick Museum

Dynamiting a jam of pulpwood on the southern reaches of Quebec's La Vérendrye Park country, some 200 miles north of Ottawa, in the spring of 1950. In order to save wood, the foreman usually resorted to blasting only if all else failed to break the jam.

Sometimes the only way to break a log jam in a chasm was on the end of a rope. Down there a cant-hook was no good and there was no place to stand. "But you might," said Fleetwood Pride, "get a toehold with one foot on the ledge and another on the log ... I have had the log break that I was boring and the jam start with me dangling on the rope ..."

138

toward him up the creek. He sees a column of smoke curling up behind his brother and supposes he is smoking a cigarette. All of a sudden, whammo, his brother was literally blown to him because his brother was carrying dynamite behind him." Wes McNutt of North Bay also remembered another accident on the Montmorency River in Quebec where he worked on drives in the early 1930s: "We once lost seven men at one crack in a flatboat. They were dropping out sticks of dynamite after igniting the fuse with a match, throwing it out just like flowers. Spring was coming, the sun was nice, but there was still ice and they had to break it up to get the drive going. In the midst of this the whole boat blew up. One fellow was rowing with his feet braced on a dynamite box which was half full, a tremendous amount of explosive, and all he got was perforated ear-drums. Others were transfixed with hunks of pulpwood — real carnage." The man who had been rowing with his feet against the box of dynamite suffered only from shock and temporarily crippled feet, in addition to pierced ear-drums. The man hunched between his legs was killed.

Jack Hughes of Chicoutimi was witness to a tale with a happier ending. "In 1946 on the Mississagi River in the pine country north of Lake Huron this boat full of Indian drivers from Manitoulin Island was in the middle of the river and the top driver in the boat placed a dynamite charge under a centre jam. Then they rowed away, a boatload of master-drivers, very solemnly rowing with much style down the river. They had four or five sticks of dynamite tied around an eight-foot alder pole and a 30-inch fuse tied to the dynamite. The rest of the drive crew were on top of a hill 300 feet away. What the men in the boat did not see was that the dynamite wasn't hooked under the logs properly but had got caught in the backwater of the boat as they rowed away and it started to follow them downstream. As they rowed away, the dynamite kept following them and we could see the smoke from the fuse as the dynamite bobbed along behind them. We all started to holler and as there was a lot of water going by, it was noisy and they couldn't understand what we were saying. Eventually the captain of the boat lowered himself to look under the stern where we were pointing and saw this dynamite following him and everybody started rowing fast. The faster they went the faster the dynamite went — until they went so fast they broke contact with the dynamite. They were 100 feet away from the dynamite when it finally went off."

On small streams there was usually a struggle to get enough water to float the logs and in a bad year, they used to joke, a foreman would have to wring the sweat out of his shirt to raise the water level. They counted on spring freshets and "splash dams" to raise water on streams which in high summer could hardly float a fence post. The foreman would have sent in crews the previous summer,

New Brunswick Provincial Archives

If the water level fell in the streams before the drive was out a whole winter's log harvest might be "hung up" until the following spring. On this Miramichi stream bed, drivers with peaveys wait for splash dams to be opened up on the tributaries to try to flush the logs loose.

Photograph by MALAK, *Ottawa*

Breaking up a pulpwood jam with horse power in the shallows of Rivière Tomasine, Quebec, some 200 miles north of Ottawa, in 1948.

when water was low, to grub out boulders and sunken logs and the constant stooping and lifting of rocks from the cold water all day long was the meanest job in the bush.

Sometimes, as Fred Kinnehan at Sault Ste. Marie, Ontario, recalled, it might take years to get out a drive. "On the Thessalon they started a drive in 1913 and even in 1914 they couldn't get it out because they didn't have enough water. The next spring, 1915, when the ice left the lakes and the water started running down, why they had more than 200 men along the banks right from the log dumps down to Thessalon to get those logs out. That was the year the timber slide washed out. There was nobody watching it and it was full of water and the flood took the whole thing out and the dams below it and that was a mess. We had been all winter building that timber slide."

Timber slides, either the dry type or those half filled with water diverted from a stream, were log or plank chutes for sliding logs, one by one, down a hillside. Some of these, called flumes, were like viaducts, built on trestles 50 feet high to cross ravines — one built on the Shipshaw River near Lac St. Jean, Quebec, in 1925 was 10 miles long.

Loggers cut their wood in lengths that would fit the stream they happened to be driving. With the advent of the pulpwood saw, lumberjacks could more readily cut four-foot lengths than the 8-, 12- and 16-foot logs cut with the crosscut saw. "Jams of four-foot wood, a helluva nuisance, because the stuff, when the jam is broken, runs all over the country and overflows the bank following the water."[20] "We used to have a bunch of fellas down there with pulp hooks and they'd throw the four-foot wood into the stream all along the water course, from piles of pulpwood hauled there in winter. The idea was to very quickly pull out the stop-logs of the splash dam, which was a good, descriptive name, and discharge the water. The dam was loaded with just that amount of water the stream bed could carry. If you made the mistake of overloading it with too much water it would overflow and cause the damndest jam and you would have to pick it all up by hand. You would load the bottom of the creek, which would be virtually dry, and flush the wood out like a toilet."[21]

In the 1940s, with bulldozers cutting roads deep into the bush for trucks to haul direct from stump to mill, river drives were on the wane. "I built the first road ever built by bulldozer in eastern Canada," recalled J. A. McNally of Montreal. "That was up the Montmorency River northeast of Quebec City in 1934. In those days Anglo-Canadian Pulp and Paper of Quebec City — later part of the Reed Group — was the first in eastern Canada to follow the practice of cutting wood all summer." Year 'round cutting, however, had

The loggers made gravity work for them and "downhill logging" was the rule. Logs cut on the hills were dragged down to the rivers by sleigh in the winter and driven down streams to the valleys in the spring. Sometimes they built wooden flumes to float logs downhill where there was no natural stream. One of the longest was the 10-mile Shipshaw Flume in the Lac St. Jean region of Quebec. In this 1928 photo of a flume in British Columbia, a logger is riding the wooden trough filled with water diverted from a nearby stream.

British Columbia Forest Service

Splash dams, to furnish a reservoir of water to drive logs down streams after the spring run-offs had ended, were the key to river driving. The dams could be opened and closed like a faucet to "splash," or flush, logs down rocky river beds where the water level had sunk too low. "You'd have to send a runner away six or seven miles through the bush to open the Henessy Dam in the Michipocoten River country of northern Ontario," said Frank Moran. "It was a big, V-shaped valley, fast water all the way, seven miles, and when they started sluicing the wood down you could hear the whole river like a steady roar, echoed by the ridges."

always been practised in the milder climate of the British Columbia coast.

On the west coast, although not in the British Columbia interior, river drives were rare because of the small size of the streams and the large size of the trees. When, in 1906, loggers tried to drive 10 million feet of logs north of Courtney on Vancouver Island, the wood jammed so badly they had to straighten out the stream by dynamiting the banks before they could get the wood out. But from the timber berths of interior British Columbia eastward, including Saskatchewan's Little Red River which was crammed with 40 miles of logs most springs until 1918, the river drives flourished.

In the east, log drives have lingered on, since river driving is still the cheapest method of moving wood on more than half a dozen rivers — on the Coulonge in the Ottawa Valley, for example, or on Long Lac in northwestern Ontario, and on the St. Maurice where hundreds of thousands of cords of pulpwood flow, as on a conveyor belt, down a cunning path of guide booms, glance booms, and fin booms, rarely touched by pike or peavey, to the sorting booms of the St. Maurice Drive Company at Trois-Rivières. The last drive on the Main Southwest Miramichi was in 1955. On most other rivers there are few reminders of the white water men: a few scraps of boot leather nailed to a tree, a rusted peavey hook in a stream bed, the memories of aging men.

"I like to remember," said Fleetwood Pride from the Saint John River, "that along all those rivers I worked with men who were men. They smoked pipes and wore braces and didn't spend half their time hitching up their pants . . . Driving logs was always a dangerous job and I think the danger and the many thrills had a lot to do with keeping those thousands of men seeking the work each spring . . ."[22]

9 TALES OF THE TIMBERBEASTS: THE DUNGARVON WHOOPER

There are many versions, in song and story, of the whooping ghost of the Miramichi River country but the best I heard was told by Tom Pond of Fredericton, who heard it from the old-timers when he went to work in the camps at the age of 15 after the First World War.

"The Dungarvon Whooper, the way I heard it, happened on the log drive in the spring. On the Dungarvon River which feeds into the Miramichi there's a place they call Whooper Springs and Whooper Landing. I've seen it, there's a big spring there and a big high landing, I suppose all overgrown with trees now. That's where the Dungarvon Whooper is supposed to have put in an appearance. There must have been *something* because some of those old fellas — look, they weren't scared of *nuthin'*. Bad old bastards, some of them, if the Devil himself come along they'd go and pull his tail. They didn't scare easy, but by jeeze after that drive they got so they wouldn't even go in there!

"The story I heard they were coming down on the drive. The spring before they'd had hard drivin' and had left some landings — logs piled high on the shore — so this time they had orders to put those logs into the water. But by this time the logs had all settled together and tipped over onto each other, a helluva mess. They tented on the flats there, just above, and went to work on those

144

landings, and it was a hard, slow drag because the logs were so tangled and so dangerous.

"Anyhow there was this one fellow in the crew who was notorious for his blasphemy. Now to the old-timers there was swearin' and cussin' — and there was blasphemy, which was a different thing. With blasphemy you cursed the Lord and you defied him and all this kind of stuff. Blasphemy, you had to be a pretty bad character to do that, but this fella was an awful wicked man in this way, a lot of people didn't want to work with him. He was awful cranky and ugly and hard to get along with.

"They were having breakfast in the morning and finally he threw down his plate. They had been working on that landing and it was so bad the foreman had said, 'Watch it.' Anyway this fella said, 'I'll break that Jesus landin' this morning or I'll eat my breakfast in Hell.' He grabbed his peavey and away he went. The foreman called to him but he didn't pay any attention and had just rolled off a few logs when the whole thing caved and of course four or five brows, or piles of logs, were all tangled in together and when one started, it tore all the rest of them out. Twenty-two-foot logs. The thing had stood there the whole year and when an old landing like that tumbled there'd be a cloud of dust come up. When the dust began to settle they looked out and saw the logs had filled the whole Dungarvon Stream and this animal, or creature, had come out on those logs from the landing side. A long, brown animal, with a great long tail and a round head like a man and short horns. So it was the Devil. When he got to the other bank in terrific leaps, 20 feet or more, he disappeared into the woods and they heard this awful, blood curdling screech — which was this fellow's death whoop, you see. The Devil was taking him away. They never did find him. So the Devil had come and got him to have his breakfast in Hell.

"This creature was seen afterwards and heard many times and it got so a lot of those old fellows would not go in there. I remember old Bob Ross, he had three or four teams and used to portage stuff to the camps. He was a great horseman — well-trained teams — and one time he went in and his horses ran away and broke his waggon all up. His story was, he came down into this brook and stopped his horses to have a drink and all at once the horses lifted their heads and started snortin', jumpin', and threshin', and he looked up and laying on a log was the Whooper. It took a great long jump up into the woods and let out this screech and Bob couldn't do anything with his horses, they went right crazy. So he never would portage in there again. Well, that old jeezler saw *something*, boy, or they never would have stopped *him* for he had a good thing goin' for him and he didn't scare easy."

Perhaps, suggested Tom Pond, it had been an eastern panther, also known as cougars, or mountain lions, which were rare in the New Brunswick woods and unfamiliar to the old woodsmen. They grow seven feet long, are known for their chilling screams, and at least four were sighted around the Dungarvon in the years 1908–1923.

In another version, the Dungarvon Whooper was the wandering ghost of a young camp cook who had been murdered for his savings. But whatever the cause of the ghastly screams, people were so frightened that Father Edward Murdoch of Renous village came in and read a service of exorcism and, it was said, the unearthly whoops were heard no more.

THE BULL
OF THE WOODS 10

*The old-time foremen were self-made men, worked up from the axe,
never asked a man to do something they couldn't do themselves.
They didn't mix with the men much, they were like regimental
sergeant-majors."*

GEOFF RANDOLPH, ST. MAURICE RIVER WALKING BOSS

When a 19th century "fighting foreman" such as Larry Frost of
Pontiac came driving down the Ottawa, it paid to get out of his
way. Frost was hired not only because he could fell trees, break
jams, and blaze roads better than the next fellow but also because
his fists could cow a bunkhouse trouble-maker or a rival gang intent
on beating him out to market in the spring log drive. Foremen in
those days had to "run faster, jump higher, and spit further than any
son of a bitch in camp" and Larry Frost in a playful mood was a
sight to behold, jumping up to imprint the spikes of his calk boots
in the ceiling of the Lanark tavern.

The old-time foreman was a man who had started work as a boy,
had done practically every job, and whose style and energy set the
pace of the camp. In a remote logging shanty a week from anywhere a foreman's word was law, like a captain's word at sea, and
his badge of office was the light axe he carried. Years after a camp
had mouldered into the ground, grizzled lumberjacks in some skid
road tavern would remember "The Push" or the "Walking Boss"
with fond profanity and invent unlikely legends to make him twice
the size of life — or perhaps to cut him down to more comfortable
size.

"This American logger came into camp. The Push, tired of men
kicking about the grub or jumping camp before the work was done,

147

New Brunswick Archives, Fredericton

Bull of the Woods. Like a sea captain, the shanty foreman's word was law. This photograph was taken at Peter Loggie's Miramichi lumber camp in 1898, the foreman seated in the centre of the first row, his dignity enhanced with watch chain, necktie, and salt and pepper whiskers.

148

Ont. Ministry of Natural Resources

*Courtesy of J. E. MacDonald,
Thessalon, Ont.*

Old-time foreman George "Cockeye" McNee.

"The Push," or foreman, came in all shapes and sizes, but none worked harder than old "Mike," a boat foreman on the Mississagi River drive in June 1949.

149

looked up and growled, 'What are ye, a Michigan Jumper, a Wisconsin Kicker, or a Minnesota Stayer?' The fella, he didn't like his tone, and said, 'No, I'm a North Dakota blizzard. I just blew in and I'm gonna blow right out again.'" Or there was that heavy-handed foreman up a tributary of the Ottawa. "The Dumoine was one of the first rivers in the country to be drove. It was a long time on the go when I first saw it. The story is, the 'Lord of the Dumoine' had a camp there and he just hired and fired at will and pretty much had his own way. A fella came in and chewed the rag about something and the Lord of the Dumoine said, 'Do you know who you're talking to? The Lord of the Dumoine!' And the fella said, 'Do you know who *you* are talking to? The Devil of Canada!' And he turned around and knocked hell out of him."[1]

It was a pretty poor "logging chance" that could not boast its own famous foreman. On the Miramichi it was "Fighting Fint Brophy" who worked for Jabez Snowball. On Vancouver Island few forgot the red-wigged Hank Phelan who weighed 220 pounds and could empty a riotous Saturday night saloon single-handed just for fun. Or there were the strong silent foremen like Jim Boyd. "I knew Jim Boyd. He worked on Lake Témiscouata in eastern Quebec and the *bûcherons* called him 'Bonne Homme Jim' and he came to fame because he kicked a bear to death. He was doing the drive one spring for Frasers and was walking down the Touladi River which is between Rivière-du-Loup and Edmundston, New Brunswick. The bear was asleep on the other side of a windfall and Jim jumped over the log and landed right on the bear, with calk boots, too. I don't suppose it made the bear feel very good and the bear reared up and they had it out right there. The Old Man just kicked and beat and thrashed and killed the bear. Of course I wasn't there and it gets — you know — stories. It tore his drive boots to pieces and he had to walk 41 miles in his stocking feet and he called on Archie Fraser and said, 'Mr. Archie, you owe me a pair of $14 Palmer-McLellan drive boots.' That's how Jim Boyd came into the limelight."[2]

Most foremen had nicknames and in the pine woods north of Blind River Bob Smith was always "Moonlight Smith" because he kept his men out working so late. There were camps where the hours worked depended on how little sleep a foreman needed and some foremen were accused of deliberately "mistaking" bright moonlight for daylight and waking up the crew for breakfast in the middle of the night in the days before clocks were introduced to the shanties.

"Cockeye" George McNee of Arnprior and the Ottawa Valley won his name through calling anything he did not like "cockeyed." Tom Smith was "Sidehill Smith" since the days when, as a green,

150

young foreman he built a camp on a hillside so steep "that when the men went out at night to pee it was back in the camp before they were." Some nicknames persisted long after their origins were forgotten. " 'Cruel Face' McKinnon, they said he'd swear and throw his hat on the ground and defy the Lord to come down and pick it up. He used to work as a teamster and then he got to taking contracts, jobbing, and then he was a foreman. He wasn't good lookin', but he was a pleasant fella and always chewed tobacco and had some tricklin' down each side of his face. I don't know where 'Cruel Face' came from but by God it stuck."[3]

As the logging industry mellowed with the years so did the foremen, or most of them, although even such a kind and jovial Push as Jack Bell on Vancouver Island allowed that "there were always some problems with the crew and you had to show them you were the boss and get in a few fist fights. Once a guy went berserk in the bunkhouse and he was going to carve a bunch up and they all ran out and I had to go in and take the knife off him. Once I found the cooks drunk. I went over to the cookhouse and told them, 'Get your time and get out of here!' But then what were we to do? There were men coming in to feed that night so I said to the men who were left around camp, 'Well, you guys get the cold meats out and I'll cook bacon and eggs.' So I put on the cook's whites and high hat and when the crew came in they saw me standing there flippin' eggs. They laughed and ate bacon and eggs and loved it but any other time you served them bacon and eggs for supper they would have walked off the job."

Perhaps the foreman's trickiest job was to lay out the sleigh haul road for the winter haul in eastern Canada. That road was the key to the whole logging chance, and a poor road through a swamp which might flood before the haul was finished in late March was a nightmare. In the flash thaw in the spring of 1916 Charlie McGrath had to leave 6000 logs stranded in the bush to rot when his road washed out on the north shore of Lake Huron. With something like that an outfit could go broke. A foreman had to have his wits about him.

Far from towns and hardware stores, lumberjacks had to improvise and no one was more inventive than a foreman. He could dream up half a dozen ways to fix a sleigh with a birch pole and a hunk of scrap iron or to fix harness or peavey with a twist of hay wire which was the lumber camp equivalent to a housewife's safety pins. The foreman was up at dawn to roust his crew with the time-honoured cry of "Daylight in the Swamp!" or "All aboard!" and was usually the last to turn in at night.

The old-time foreman began, slowly, to fade away by the 1930s when men from the forestry schools began to run camps as well as

The office and foreman's quarters at the Klock depot camp on the Ottawa. As well as serving as a work place for camp boss, timber cruisers, and clerks, it was headquarters for the log scaler who measured the timber.

The Public Archives of Canada PA 8391

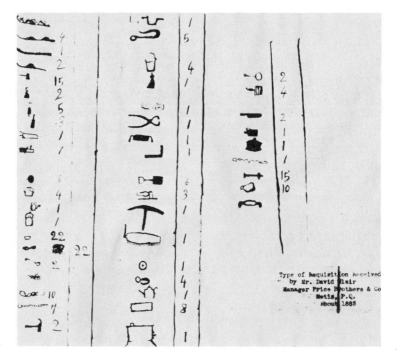

In 1885, when schooling was sparse and few foremen could read and write, this was a requisition for supplies received from a lumber camp foreman by David Blair, a Price Brothers & Co. manager at Métis, Quebec. The pictograph for the articles required — hammers, saws, dishes, a stove — was followed by a figure for the number wanted.

The Price Co. Ltd.

cruise for timber. "I graduated from the University of Toronto Forestry School in 1926 and although there had been contractors' camps up at Kapuskasing before that, they put a company-run camp in there as a trial," recalled G. W. Phipps. "I was camp foreman there in 1928, a company camp of 150 men, a board-and-tarpaper camp. In those days the boss of a camp was a real boss. He hired and fired."

As the years went by the "Bull of the Woods" had come to mean the Walking Boss, who was more than a foreman since he had three or four camps to run. Before company-run camps became general 30 or 40 years ago, he supervised the contractors' camps. "They called us Walking Boss and they weren't kidding," said Buzz Lein. "It was nothing to walk 25 miles a day. I never walked so many miles in my life. At the end of the season I was so bad in the morning I used to have to walk for about an hour before the pain and stiffness would go away."

Contractors, or "jobbers," had appeared early. In 1819 Philemon Wright used them on the Ottawa and they reached "the top of their bounce," as the loggers would say, in the pulp camps of the 1920s. A jobber, who was often, in effect, a foreman who supplied his own men, horses, and camps, was financed by the company which possessed the timber rights. He might be a small "packsack" jobber with a handful of men, perhaps relatives, who cut a few hundred cords, and he roamed from job to job, like a gypsy, with his wife, children, brothers, and nephews. On the west coast a jobber was called a "gyppo," a term of pride. Or he might be a "Grand Jobber" who cut 100 000 cords and engaged sub-contractors.

Edouard Lacroix of St. Georges, Quebec, employed 6500 lumberjacks in an operation which straddled the international border and had camps in Quebec and Maine. A hard-driving man who, like so many of the early boss loggers, became a member of parliament, he built one of the first gravel roads (50 miles of it) ever constructed to truck pulp in the 1920s. He boasted a logging railway which "started nowhere and ran nowhere" as so many of them seemed to do.

Grand Jobbers became almost as big as the companies they serviced. John Murdock of Chicoutimi, Quebec, as French as his name was Scotch, started as a scaler, or log measurer, and became the biggest contractor on the Saguenay. Henri Perron founded a lumber dynasty at La Sarre in northwest Quebec. Henry Selin, a Swedish immigrant whose 50 000-cord contracts made him one of the most successful pulpwood jobbers in northern Ontario, had worked his way up from axeman.

Jean Crête, "*le roi de la Mauricie*," employed 5000 lumberjacks in Quebec's St. Maurice River Valley. Crête was in his teens when his father died and he took over the family business of toting supplies to the lumber camps. There were no roads and Crête ran a flotilla of 50-foot *chalands*, or barges, hauled upriver by horses on tow paths. Crête's first big logging chance came in 1928 when the Maclarens of Buckingham asked him to take on an unusually large contract on the Lièvre River north of Mont Laurier. Crête tackled the assignment with the flair he brought to all his operations. He hired a small army of 800 men from around the St. Maurice and a Canadian Pacific Railway train to transport them 300 miles to Mont Laurier 90 miles north of Ottawa. Faced with the usual festive boozing of lumberjacks on their way to camp, he had his friend the Chief of Police in Trois-Rivières lock up the noisier ones until train time in the morning. To help two special constables keep order on the train he sought out the toughest, noisiest man in each carriage. "I know you are the best man in the gang," Crête told the potential trouble-maker, "and I charge you to keep order here." There was no more trouble and when the train arrived at Mont Laurier at six o'clock next morning in a cold November drizzle Crête mounted a horse and, as proud as any general, led his bleary-eyed men on the lengthy march to camp. By the time he had finished the contract his work force totalled 1200 men and 400 horses on the Lièvre. Crête was a successful contractor in the St. Maurice Valley until 1954 when the big companies took over their own logging operations. "I think," said his son Paul, "that we got better output from our men than the companies would get in those days because we knew the men personally. We had sub-contractors and their men coming from all over Quebec, from Matane in the Gaspé, from the Beauce and Lac St. Jean. Some sub-contractors were about the same as foremen; we paid their men and bought food and horses for them."

Jobbing could be risky. A miscalculated bid, an exceptionally snowy winter, an unexpected early spring, and the loss of his ice roads could all threaten a jobber with ruin. He had to know his business.

Paul Provencher recalled a conversation with his uncle, a small but successful jobber from the north shore of the St. Lawrence.

"I said, 'Do you think you'll be interested in taking a contract here?'

"He said, 'What's the wood like?'

"I said, 'Oh, it might be all right . . . in certain places.'

"He said, 'You don't have to tell me all this. I don't even have to go out and look to know what it's like. All these buildings, like this one we're sitting in, have been built of local wood. Look at those planks, you can't see three inches without a bloody knot. I don't have to go out to the woods to see there are knots in those trees out there and a contractor won't make money here cutting wood be-

Le Nouvelliste, Trois-Rivières, *Que.*

Jean Crête, right, whose logging enterprises on the St. Maurice River won him the title *"le roi de la Mauricie,"* inspects a camp with a friend, Sorel, Quebec, industrialist Edouard Simard.

Nova Scotia Provincial Archives

A jobber's camp in Nova Scotia in the early 1900s. Farmers often logged their own land with 10 or 12 men and sometimes, if the camp was not too remote, they would bring wife and children along. The food in a Nova Scotia camp was apt to consist of salt meat, salt herring and codfish, potatoes, turnips, carrots and sauerkraut, baked beans, bread, molasses, and ginger cookies.

cause he'll have to spend most of his time chopping limbs off trees.' "

Jobbers camps came in all sizes and conditions and a typical medium-sized moderately successful northern Ontario operation was one located on Spruce Creek in the Agawa district above Sault Ste. Marie in the mid-1930s. The jobber had contracted with a pulp company to produce 4000 cords of spruce pulpwood delivered to a nearby lake. He began work in September with a crew of 36 men, half of them French Canadian and the other half Finns and Anglo-Saxons. He paid his camp clerk, cook, and blacksmith $60 each per month, his teamsters $45, and the choreboy $35. The cutters, on piece-work, received $2 per cord. When the cutting ended in December he reduced his camp force by 10 men and finished the winter hauling season with 26 men and eight horses. His camp, which cost about $700 to build, consisted of a bunkhouse with an adjoining wash-room and a drying room for clothes, a separate cookery, a camp office where jobber and clerk also slept, a stable, a blacksmith shop, a separate bathhouse or sauna, and a cabin for the wash-woman who laundered clothes for 20 cents per man per week.

His total cost for the season was about $23 000 and his profit was nearly $5000. His profits included $200 from the cookery, since each of the piece-workers paid 75 cents a day for meals, and about $150 from the "van," or camp store. In the same area there were small camps of sub-jobbers or "shackers" — four or five men, mostly Finnish.

There was great variety in jobber camps right across the country, but nowhere more than in Quebec, a generation ago.

— "One year on the South Kénogami near Lac St. Jean I had 49 jobber camps and we cut 229 000 cords over an area which extended one way for 25 miles and another way for 30 miles. I was the Walking Boss and could never get around them all in one winter. The French jobbers, for a long time they brought their wives in. The wife used to be the cook and the daughter the cookee but then it got to the point where we started discouraging that. Men were better cooks . . . I've seen shanties in Quebec with no windows in them at all. Up on the Dolbeau River I came down a hill one winter's day and walked over this thing. I thought it was a hump in the snow but it was a jobber's camp. He had a great big stove in the middle. No floor. He lived there with his wife and a couple of men and his horse in there and they all lived in the same place."[4]

— "In winter the Walking Boss travelled by snowshoes and one night there was a storm brewing so we put up with a jobber in his small camp. We found five men who were the jobber's relatives, plus his daughter, all sleeping in the same bed, a 'muzzle loader' which you had to climb into from the end. The daughter was about 16. It was big enough for the eight of us. Everybody peeled off their clothes down to their long underwear although they may leave their shirt on. They'd hang their clothes on a home-made clothes hanger by the stove. It was not a big room, perhaps 12 by 14, and you could see the horses through the partitions. They had two teams which were producing a lot of animal heat in the camp. But here's the jobber, he's sitting here and I'm sitting next to him on the bench, and the stove is there with a pot of beans or pea soup and above the stove were clothes and socks and felt harness pads drying. The jobber reaches under the seat and takes a flake of hay, part of a bale, and passes it across the stove to the horses. The girl was cousin of the men and daughter of the jobber. There was no hanky-panky. She was the cook. She had this great long underwear too. I swear some of them got into that underwear in the fall and didn't get out of it until the spring."[5]

By the 1940s cooperative jobbers had appeared in Quebec. Farmers who went into the bush to cut pulp elected a camp council and a foreman and shared equally in the profits. The cooperative camps were organized, according to La Fédération Régionale des Chantiers Coopératifs, "for the purpose of solving the personal problems of farmers who are forced by circumstances to augment their earnings by working in the bush . . . the earnings of each member of the cooperative camp depend directly upon the success of that camp, thus the group that commences an operation sees it through to the end." During the years when perhaps 60 per cent of the pulpwood cutters were farmers, there was less manpower turnover in the cooperative jobber camps than in traditional camps where, in good times if not in depression, it was said there was usually "one man coming, one man working, and one man going."

By the 1950s the overhead costs of logging mechanization in the east became too heavy for the jobbers and many companies took to running their own camps. "When they put those big machines in the bush," said Charlie Lampi, a Finnish jobber, "well, that's the time I quit and retired."

11 LOGGERS OF THE RAINCOAST

The logging industry, like colonization itself, came late to British Columbia. The Fraser River gold rush in the 1850s helped get the industry started and some of the 30 000 prospectors stayed on to cut logs in the sparsely populated colony which was as isolated from eastern Canada as if it had been another country.

By the early 1860s, half a century after logging had become a major industry in the east, professional lumbermen had begun to trickle into British Columbia, some around the Horn in sailing ships and some by way of the Great Lakes pine camps and the Washington Territory. Sewell Prescott Moody and William P. Sayward, who founded lumber mills, came from Maine. From England came the bluff sea captain Edward Stamp with his schooner, *Meg Merrilies*, to log on Vancouver Island and build a sawmill in the forests where Vancouver now stands.

Some, such as Jeremiah Rogers, came from New Brunswick. On Vancouver's English Bay, near what is now known as Jericho Beach, Rogers established one of the first real lumber camps on the Canadian west coast in 1865. He cut 150-foot Douglas fir masts for the navies of France, Russia, and Holland — a Rogers mast was one of the best in the world. By the time he died in 1879 at the age of 61, Rogers had, like Philemon Wright on the Ottawa before him, set a pattern for those who followed.

BRITISH COLUMBIA RAINCOAST

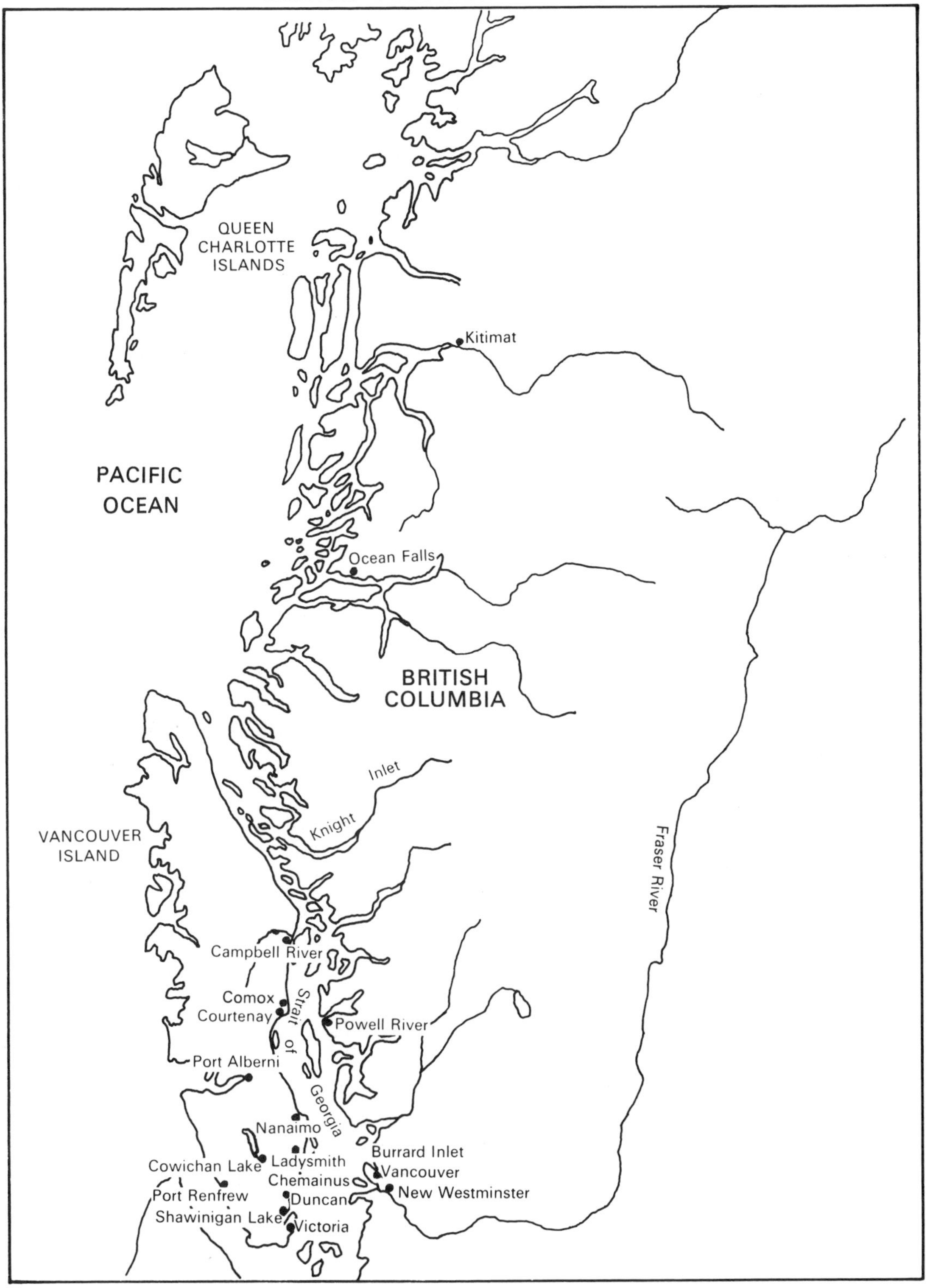

QUEEN
CHARLOTTE
ISLANDS

Kitimat

PACIFIC
OCEAN

Ocean Falls

BRITISH
COLUMBIA

Inlet

Knight

VANCOUVER
ISLAND

Fraser River

Campbell River

Comox
Courtenay

Powell River

Strait of

Port Alberni

Georgia

Nanaimo

Cowichan Lake

Ladysmith

Burrard Inlet
Vancouver
New Westminster

Chemainus

Port Renfrew

Duncan

Shawinigan Lake

Victoria

On the coast the easterners found a logger's paradise, trees of a size they had never seen, crowding down to the Pacific from the misty slopes of the rain forest. What timber! Douglas fir, the biggest tree in Canada, 200 feet high with a trunk like an elephant's belly. Men claimed to have seen Douglas firs which grew as high as 300 feet, 15 feet around at the base, twice as high as even the biggest pine they had seen in the east. There was fragrant red cedar 150 feet tall, Sitka spruce 10 feet around. Even hemlock and balsam fir, scorned as weed trees in the days before the pulpwood trade, were almost as big as the white pines of the east. And thick! "Holy Old Mackinaw," they said, there were stands of Douglas fir which sawed out at 10 times more wood to the acre than the choicest pineries on the Miramichi or the Ottawa. The moist and temperate climate, particularly on Vancouver Island, grew the thickest softwood stands in the world.

Such timber called for heroic logging. Being easterners they set to work with the methods they knew, with ropes and oxen and poll axes. Being lumbermen, and therefore inventive, they adapted their ways to the giant trees and mountainous terrain. Where four oxen might serve in the east, 10 or 12 were needed here. Since coastal winters were too mild for ice roads they fashioned wooden skid roads from poles, like trackless railways, and greased them with oil to give the bull teams a fighting chance. Some, like the four DeBeck brothers from New Brunswick who settled on Burrard Inlet in 1867, took to hand logging like the Haida Indians before them and cut trees to topple down a mountain and into the sea.

In the east they had chopped the pine a foot or two above the ground to get above the swell of the root. Here the trees were so big they took to chopping much higher and learned to fashion springboards to stand on while they chopped. They tired of the puny eastern poll axe and developed the double-bitted west coast axe with a narrow, one-foot blade and a long handle so they could bite deeper into the wood. For 20 years and more they swung those axes, three and a half pounds of double-edged steel on the end of a three-and-a-half-foot hickory handle, day after day, while the man with the crosscut down in the underbrush dodged the falling trees and cut them into lengths of 32 or 40 feet for the mills or 110 feet for construction timber. When, by the 1880s, crosscut saws came equipped with rakers to pull the sawdust out, they began to saw the great trees down — in one-half or one-third the time taken by the axemen. For two generations the "rat-scratch, rat-scratch" song of the two-man crosscut saw and the cry of "Timber-r-r-r! Timber Down the Hill!" echoed through the salty fog of the west coast woods.

"Even in the 1920s," said Jack Bell, who went to work in the woods as a teenager and worked his way up to Bull of the Woods,

160

Provincial Archives, Victoria, B.C.

Making the undercut in a west coast red cedar, probably at
Myrtle Point on the coast, northwest of Vancouver, in 1924.
The photographers of the time, still marvelling at the size
of the trees, often got a young logger to pose, safely enough,
in the notch.

B.C. Timber Museum, Duncan, B.C.

The woodcutters' basic tools in British Columbia up to World War II. At bottom is the iron-shod
springboard the cutters jammed into the trunk to stand on while they falled a Douglas fir. Flanking
the double-bitted west coast faller's axe are two versions of the crosscut saw, or "Swedish fiddle."
Between every four cutting teeth there were rakers to pull out the sawdust.

161

"there were lots of six-foot-thick trees and it would take 30 or 40 minutes to fall one if it didn't have conk or twists or pitch seams. However, your normal tree by then would be three or four feet thick and you might fall 15 or 20 a day. You and your partner got on each side and chopped the undercut with an axe and then went around to the other side and sawed the backcut with the crosscut saw. To clean the sticky pitch off your saw you carried an old whiskey bottle with a hook tied to the neck. It was filled with kerosene to cut the pitch. When piece-work came in during the 1920s the fallers would work eight or nine hours and wouldn't stop much for lunch. Some of the hand loggers had their own system of cutting. Along the Alberni Inlet on Vancouver Island there was a big Swede, 'Hand Logger' Johnson, and he always bought a little patch of timber on a real steep pitch and he'd go there and work by himself. He'd chop the undercut and then, on the other side of the tree, he'd take a sapling and bend it back and tie one end of a crosscut saw to it and he'd pull the saw toward him and the pole would pull it back so he didn't need a second man to help him saw. He would fall one or two trees a day and if they had enough momentum they would slide into the water. If they didn't, he'd fall saplings in front of them and he had a Gilchrist jack and he'd roll the log over and get behind it and push it and wiggle it until it would finally crash down. All by himself."

Hand logging was the method used by Captain James Cook's sailors to cut masts on Vancouver Island in 1778 and there were still a few hand loggers operating on the coast in the 1950s, but the great days of hand logging were from 1890 to around 1912. Their best pitches were the steep mountains up the mainland north of Vancouver and in 1900 they were pushing up the coast, to the annoyance of the local Indians, to Knight Inlet, 200 miles up the broken shoreline.

Hand loggers usually worked in two-man partnerships but they also worked alone and lived for months like hermits and if they injured themselves with axe or saw they might die before anyone got around to looking for them. Like prospectors — a calling some of them also followed — they were a motley crew and there were thousands of them on the coast: lumberjacks from the Maritimes, sailors who had jumped ship at Seattle or Vancouver, adventurers from San Francisco, remittance men from England, Scandinavians, a few French from Quebec, men who had seen better days, and men who had seen worse. There were characters like the "Sockless Swede" who wore no stockings summer or winter and "Dirty Dan McClusky" whose indifference to soap and water was offset by a ruthless reputation for honesty.

A hand logger would load a small boat with a few hundred dollars

162

British Columbia Forest Service

Hand logger at Tekearn Arm near Powell River, on the coast of British Columbia, hoists a half-peeled Douglas fir log with a Gilchrist jack to slide it down the mountainside and into the sea.

Provincial Archives, Victoria, B.C.

Skid road loggers sit down to dine. The bull punchers did not bother to doff their hats but the rule of silence at mealtimes prevailed, as it did across the country. Many of the cook's helpers, or "flunkies," as they were called on the west coast, were Asians.

163

worth of grub, boom chains, a couple of axes and saws and Gilchrist jacks, and cruise the coast until he found a sheltered inlet where he could hang a log boom to collect the timber he slid off the cliffs. He was up before daybreak in all weather, for the rain is a way of life on that coast, scrambling up the slippery mountains with his treacherous tools, falling, stripping bark, coaxing tree trunks down the slopes, and cutting them into 60-foot logs down in the salt water. Oxen and horses would have been useless on such slopes so he always tried to cut a "stumper," a tree which "would leap clean over the side" and down into the water. Just as often he would have to pry it free to start it sliding, wary that a sudden lurch did not plunge him over the cliff along with the tree. In the evening he climbed into his rowboat and towed his day's work, perhaps only three or four logs, into the boom and went home to his shack to take off his wet clothes, cook a sketchy supper, and fall into his blankets. He was, at least, his own master and every once in a while the company sent up a tug to haul his wood to the mill. His overhead was small and there was the hope he could save enough cash to set himself up with a proper camp in the valley, with men and oxen. Hand logging, by its nature, was confined to a few hundred feet from tidewater but it was a way to make a stake.

Down in the valley with a team of oxen to pull logs down a skid road a man could push a mile or two back from the ocean and in camps like those the ox team driver, or "bull puncher," set the pace. No one who met the "bull whacker" was likely to forget him. He carried his nail-studded, four-foot goad like a badge of office, cultivated a blasphemous roar, and at the end of the day his voice was a croak. He fitted the horns of his red, white, and black bulls with copper caps, taught them to answer to their names, and for 40 years was the highest paid hand in a west coast camp. On a skid road you could hear him long before you saw him, his yells, entreaties, and general profanity drowning the rattle of chains and the thumping of logs. "Gee, Buck! Hump, you, Lion! By the Holy Moses Mackinaw God I'm a-comin'!" He wore a sweaty slouch hat, was up before anyone else in camp to feed his bulls with mash, and for some reason was usually a Scotchman.

"The bull puncher was an artist in his work. They had a long rod with a half-inch or three-eighths-of-an-inch-long brad in the end that was used in an emergency but it was very seldom used. It was altogether by voice . . . The wheelers were generally the good big-headed ones (oxen), and the most intelligent if you can get them because they had to be able to respond quickly and they had to start a turn of logs. A turn is a line chained together, probably six or seven, eight logs, as much as that, and they had to start the first log in the chain and the other logs would start. Then they'd get the whole team going and by the time they'd taken up the slack in the chain between the logs there'd be enough jerk to start a log and so on down the line until they got them all started. Once they got them all started they had to keep them going."[1]

Just ahead of the moving logs skittered the skid greaser, a boy with a swab and a bucket of rancid dogfish oil, though even with the oil the skids smoked from the friction. The greaser was so spattered and stinking the other men complained when he entered the bunkhouse at night. At the end of the yawing, sliding turn of logs rode the "P.F.," euphemistically referred to, outside the camps, as the "pig man." The "pig," or small log, he rode in was hollowed like a dugout and contained tools to unhook the logs at the end of the haul. It took most of a morning to pull a turn of logs, perhaps 50 tons or more, a mile or two down the skid road to the mill if you didn't get hung up on a stump and could keep the oxen moving. "I remember one time an old white ox laid down, wouldn't get up, and Dad built a fire under him."[2]

The skid roads were laid with care to follow a gentle slope if possible so a five-ton log would not lunge ahead and crush the legs of the rear oxen. After the trail had been swamped out by axemen, short logs, a foot and a half thick, were half buried crosswise a few feet apart like railway ties and a notch, or "saddle," adzed along the middle for the logs to slide along. The townsite of Vancouver was bisected with skid roads from camps in what is now Stanley Park or from Jeremiah Rogers' camps on English Bay, False Creek, or down on the north arm of the Fraser River. It was a handy arrangement for Bill Barbrick who, his bull whacking done for the day, could cross False Creek in the early 1880s for a drink at Gassy Jack Deighton's tavern in what is now called Gastown.

Once a log was hauled from the bush to the skid road the "sniper" would smooth the butt so the log would not catch on a cross skid and the "ride man" would figure how the log would "settle and ride" down the skids once it got moving and would then peel that side smooth. The "hook tender" and his men would drive "dogs," short iron spikes with an eye in one end, into the logs so they could be roped or chained together. Then all hands would pick up iron bars and bend to the task of helping the bull whacker and his bulls heave the whole thing into motion.

By the 1890s horses were replacing the bulls because they were smarter and faster though they could not pull as much weight. There was a need for speed because the mills were working overtime to fill orders from South America, Australia, and China, where B.C. wood was used to build much of Shanghai and the Imperial Palace outside Peking. Horses replaced oxen for a dozen years or more although a few camps did try mules and it is said that Jeremiah Rogers, for some

Provincial Archives, Victoria, B.C.

A team of ten oxen hauling a "turn" of four logs down a skidroad in 1890 from a Ross Maclaren camp in what is now suburban Vancouver. The bull puncher with his goad stands in the background. Seated before him are the pig man, on the left holding the maul, and the skid greaser in the white shirt. A Boker screw jack, used for lifting logs, stands between them.

Provincial Archives, Victoria, B.C.

In the days before donkey engines and steam logging, the slow oxen were replaced for a few years by 10-horse teams on the skid roads. A piercing whistle from the photographer not only got the horses' attention but got their ears up as well.

LOGGERS OF THE RAINCOAST

reason known only to himself, experimented with camels but what they did and how they did it remains obscure. Some of the horses were smart enough to work without supervision.

"They always had a lead horse. There was one called Pat. They'd speak to him. He was the one spoken to. Pat was a big black horse. They seemed to have had it figured out just like a man would, a horse understands so many things . . . A horse can like you or not like you. He'll work for you or he won't. He'll pull for one man and pretend to pull for another. They do a little thinking as well as we do. On skid roads nobody drove 'em. A horse can count and they made six trips a day."[3]

J. L. Henslowe of Shawnigan Lake on Vancouver Island, a teamster and logging contractor in the 1920s, remembered John Alexander, a black whose family had fled to Canada "in the early days" to escape slavery.

"John was grey-haired, bow-legged, been around horses all his life, in a saddle of one kind or another, face lined and seamed like a coconut. He got horses to a state where they all knew his voice and knew him and he was practically uncle to them all. Horses were his life and he taught me — I was 15 then — to study their personalities. He worked with, rather than drove, a 16-horse team, and I can still see him bringing them together for the initial heave that would start the logs clinking and bumping down the road to the mill.

"When he stopped for a smoke he'd walk down along his team and talk to them in his slow, southern drawl, and gentle them, soothing one, encouraging another, easing them forward to feel the load. This was 'roading' and they'd have to start a turn of eight to 10 logs. The skid road was practically level so it meant breaking the inertia in one big heave. Old John, he carried a long, long stock whip, always had it coiled in his hand. He'd climb stiffly down out of his saddle when he was all hooked up and ready to go. He'd walk slowly down the line and he talked to Polly and he talked to Bess and he talked to Jim and he talked to all the horses and rubbed their ears and said, 'Okay boys, move up in the collar. It's going to be a big pull, come on Jess, get up in the collar there a little, take the strain now, lean forward.' And those great big beasts of horses — huge things — they would lean into the collars just like that! Then he would walk back — and it would take a while to walk back the length of all those horses — and he'd light his pipe and these horses were lying up in their collars waiting for him. He climbed into his saddle, the sparks flying out of his pipe, undo his whip, and let out a blast of invective which would scare anyone, and crack his whip. But he never touched a horse with it and they all gave this heave and once they'd done that it wasn't too bad. He would haul up to two miles and he would stop somewhere along and give them a breather.

Never would his whip find a mark on horse flesh, save to check ill temper or mischief . . . God knows they worked for him."

Although horses were used in the smaller camps on the coast through the 1920s, they began to go the way of the oxen in the early 1900s when a new source of power, which the loggers called "the donkey," began to appear. The completion of the Canadian Pacific Railway in 1886 had opened a lumber market to the east on the prairies and although logging camps were opening in the B.C. interior, where trees were smaller and logging was done by the old sleigh haul and river drive methods of the east, there was great pressure on the coastal camps to produce more wood. It was taking too many horses to keep the mills supplied with logs. Steam power logging, born among the giant redwoods south of the border, was introduced.

"My dad had a bit of a ranch just outside Nanaimo at East Wellington on Vancouver Island," said Bob Swanson. "We were right on the edge of the primeval forest. They had a sawmill in there, logging with horses, and although they weren't logging with locomotives in the way they did later they did have a little locomotive to haul lumber from the mill and it ran past our door.

"Then one day, right past my bedroom window, along came a flatcar carrying a great, marvellous thing. It was a 'donkey' they told me. It looked to me like a big can of stove polish because it had a round thing on top, a little cone. They told me 'the Chinamen' were going to work on it and — I was pretty little then — I thought the Chinamen *lived* in it." Bob Swanson, a logger who became one of the best known steam engineers on the west coast, was witnessing the early days of steam logging.

"When I was a little older they took me up to see it and by golly the thing was hauling logs. Out at the end of the skid road was this little donkey engine with a boiler and two revolving drums and this thing would haul logs four or five hundred feet out of the woods and dump them on the skid road to be hauled to the mill by horses. The Chinamen carried water to it in buckets balanced on a yoke and it was fired with bark."

The donkey engine brought industrial revolution to logging in the Pacific northwest 50 years before eastern camps found it necessary to mechanize anything on the same scale. One of the first donkey engines seen in British Columbia was brought in by McIntyre Brothers of Moodyville in 1897.

In the tangle of islands, bays, fiords, and channels, west coast loggers had always worked with one foot, so to speak, in the sea and the other in the forest. It was hardly surprising that the engine which revolutionized coastal logging came out of a ship. In the early 1880s Captain Stewart pulled an old steam winch off a ship's fore-

By 1905 two-spool steam donkeys, with horizontal spools or drums, which were more efficient than vertical capstans, were in use — not only to yank logs out of the bush but to "road" them down the skid roads to the sea. This was a 9 by 10 Washington donkey operating on Shawnigan Lake, Vancouver Island. The figures referred to the size of the cylinders. On long "roading" hauls there might be four or five donkeys spaced out at intervals along the skid road.

Provincial Archives, Victoria, B.C.

One of the first donkey engines, flat-geared, with vertical spool or capstan, used to haul logs at Chemainus Lake, Vancouver Island, in 1902. The boilers took a steam pressure of 150 pounds. By the time the engine hauled a log a few hundred yards into the machine, the men would have to wait for a short time until enough steam was built up to haul in another log.

British Columbia Forest Service

castle, where it had been used to sling cargo and weigh anchor, and put it to hauling logs into Burrard Inlet.

Down among the redwoods at Eureka, California, John Dolbeer, who logged with his partner William Carson from New Brunswick, had been trying since the 1870s to hitch steam power to his logs. Since he was a former marine engineer, he transformed a ship's donkey, a small steam engine with an upright boiler, into "Dolbeer's Patent Steam Logging Machine" in 1882. On ships it had been called a donkey because it lacked the hauling power of a full-grown horse and Dolbeer's little donkey suffered at first from the same anaemia. It had a horizontal shaft with a spool, or "gypsy," on each end. A rope was attached to a log, led back to the machine through a series of seven or eight snatch blocks, and wound around the spool of the donkey which then pulled the log in. To generate more power he evolved an upright capstan system to replace the side spools and soon the Dolbeer donkey was doing the work of 10 bulls at less expense, pulling a log 500 feet which was the practical limit for Manila rope. Within a few years David Evans had invented a more powerful version, called a Bull donkey, bolted to great sled-like logs and powered with a 10-foot boiler topped with an iron smoke-stack and with gears and drums. They reeled in logs like whales on a harpoon line while the donkey bucked and shuddered and belched steam and blue smoke among the trees. The things looked somewhat fearsome and a blown cylinder head could take off a man's legs. The "donkey puncher," or engineer, spent half his time, it seemed, tightening bolts with a monkey wrench. One end of rope was wrapped three or four times around the spool and a "chokerman" looped, or "choked," the other end around the butt of a log out in the woods. Halfway into the bush was a man with a flag who re-layed signals from the chokerman to the donkey puncher and the "spool tender" who coiled the rope as the capstan wound it in.

The first donkey engines had merely yanked logs to the head of the skidway for the bulls and horses to haul down to the mill. They were slow and cumbersome and the rope stretched in the rain and often broke. Improvements made to iron and steel rope about that time added an important new ingredient to the logging process and with good wire rope they were able to speed up the skidding. Two or three donkeys could haul logs right down the skidway, 40 logs a day, and do away with bulls and horses. For a while only one horse was left, the "line horse," plodding back and forth between the donkey and the woods, without benefit of teamster, dragging the heavy cable. When a second drum and several hundred feet of haul-back line were added the donkey could reel the cable back and forth itself and even the line horse disappeared from the woods. So the donkey engines replaced horses and the last of the oxen in

A patent sketch of the Dolbeer donkey engine, dated 1882. This version had a horizontal shaft with gypsies, or spools, at both ends and a fair lead at the right-hand corner of the frame to guide the hauling line to the spool behind it. The spools were run by the steam boiler at the back of the frame.

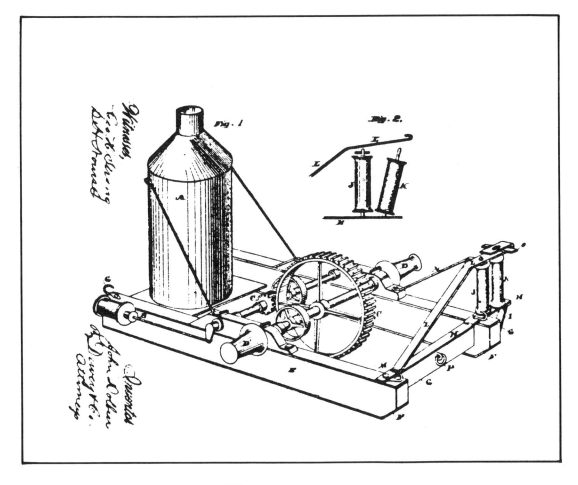

the early years of this century and due to a lack of suitable log drive streams logging railways appeared and spread quickly. A typical west coast logging show combined the donkey engine to skid the logs out of the bush and a little railway to carry the logs to mill or "salt-chuck," which was the logger's word for the Pacific. They took the Chinook word for water and tacked on the word salt.

Hauling, or "yarding," a log along the ground with a steam donkey was "ground leading," which meant logs caught on stumps, tore up underbrush, and picked up stones which fouled the mill saws. A writer in 1906 described how ground leading worked: "The area was littered with windfalls, tall butts, sawed-off tops and branches, upturned roots 15 feet in the air. Huge logs loomed amid this woodland wreckage like the backs of a school of whales in a sea . . . The engine clattered, the drums began to revolve, and a wire cable which seemed to wind off to nowhere in particular grew taut. The 'donkey' surged against its moorings; its massive spread began to rear and pitch as if striving to bury its nose in the earth. There was a startling uproar in the forest, wholly beyond seeing distance, mind you. In a moment a log came hurtling out of the underbrush nearly 1000 feet away. It burst into sight as if it had wings, smashing and tearing its own pathway . . . so fast that when it fetched athwart a stump it pitched over it as if it were taking a hurdle. It is an awesome sight to see a log six feet through and 40 feet long bounding toward you as if the devil were in it, breaking off some trees as if they were twigs."[4]

By 1910 British Columbia had surpassed Quebec in lumber production and was second only to Ontario. To speed production the coastal loggers had taken to anchoring their ground lead cable high up a tree on a pulley to lift one end of a log off the ground as they hauled it out of the forest. Whereas the ground lead had yanked the log out with brute strength, like a wild boar, the "high lead" brought the log hopping out like a kangaroo with its tail dragging.

High leading had first been tried in the 1880s by Horace Butters of Ludington, Michigan, to haul white pine. Then it was used, with somewhat more success, in the cypress swamps of Louisiana with a powerful and complicated donkey engine called the Lidgerwood Skidder, or "flying machine." After the turn of the century high leading appeared in British Columbia. H. B. Gardner installed a Lidgerwood and a high lead system at Discovery Bay in 1906. Along with high leading came the daring young man called the high rigger.

The high rigger, like a steeple jack, was a specialist and hung the blocks and lines of the high lead system 175 feet or more up a Douglas fir, which he called the spar tree. With axe and saw swinging at his belt and climbing irons strapped to his boots, he twitched his way up a Douglas fir, lopping off branches as he climbed. His

Ground leading, introduced at the turn of the century to skid logs short distances out of the bush to the head of the skidway, at first consisted of a primitive "spool donkey" which hauled a log over the ground, bucking rocks and fallen trees and stumps. A horse pulled the Manila rope back into the bush for another log. By about 1905 this system had been improved with a horizontal drum replacing the upright spool and an endless iron rope feeding through blocks mounted on stumps to haul in the log and get the line back out to the bush without the use of a horse.

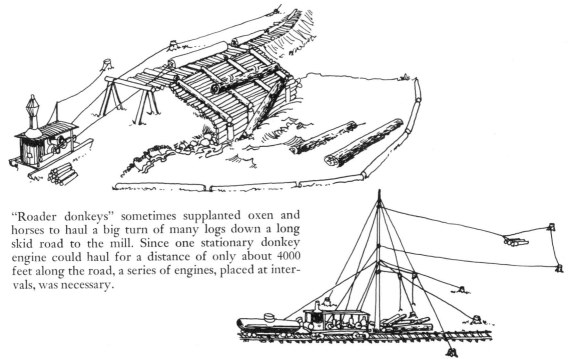

"Roader donkeys" sometimes supplanted oxen and horses to haul a big turn of many logs down a long skid road to the mill. Since one stationary donkey engine could haul for a distance of only about 4000 feet along the road, a series of engines, placed at intervals, was necessary.

The high lead system became popular after the First World War. The main line was hung up on the spar tree by a high rigger to lift a log over obstacles. This doubled the production obtained by the old ground lead system.

From Rhymes of a Lumberjack, *courtesy of Robert Swanson, Vancouver, B.C.*

173

safety rope was fitted with a steel core so he could not cut it by accident. At a point where the tree was still thick and strong, perhaps a foot and a half thick at 175 feet, he notched in an undercut with his axe and sawed off the top. The reaction was terrific. The jolt of 20 or 30 feet of heavy tree-top breaking off would shake him back and forth like a rag doll in a hurricane. J. L. Henslowe on Vancouver Island tried it only once. "I never lost so much sweat. As the tree-top goes it gives a kick and, hanging onto your rope, back you go and look down over your shoulder and swear you are never going to stop. The next thing you know it's going the other way and you are looking down on the little white faces below. The biggest danger was if the tree split open when you topped it. It would squash you with the steel core belt right up against the tree."

Once the tossing and the turmoil ceased and his stomach settled down, the high rigger leaped down the tree like a monkey, his life line and spurs braking his descent every 10 feet or so. He climbed back up and secured a 15-pound pulley and a coil of light steel cable called the "pass line" and with those in place a small rigging donkey at the foot of the tree began hauling up the "jewelry," the two-ton "bull block," also called a "Tommy Moore," for the man who had invented it, and the secondary blocks and lines and the guy lines to guy the spar tree.

Jack Bell, who did about every job there was to do in the Vancouver Island woods, high rigged for 10 years.

"I was 21 when I began. Before you became a high rigger you usually worked up from the rigging crew which helped him. You'd borrow his belt and spurs and learn how to climb, shinny up a tree and skin your nose and hands. The best test was when you topped your first tree. You had a 25-foot rope and you dug your spurs in and threw the rope up and around the trunk. You couldn't just lift it up like they climb a telephone pole because the tree was too thick. The worst hazard was topping in a high wind.

"I fell 90 feet out of a tree once, broke my leg, but I was back riggin' in four months. I had been up the tree, in a hurry, and had untied my rope so I could work above the guy lines. I was giving instructions to my ground crew down below and I was pulling a rope through the pulley, pulling it out and wasn't watching what I was doing and I pulled the end right out and let it go. I saw it going and made a lunge for it and my spurs came out of the heavy bark. I grabbed the guy line with my hands. Normally you'd be able to hang on but it was snowing and there was sleet and I had leather gloves on and they were sopping wet and I had to let go. There was a large log lying at the bottom of the tree and I hit with my foot on the log and cart-wheeled through the air and came down across another log. It didn't take long to come down, you didn't have time to think. Boom, and you were there. I still have a bit of a limp."

Even chokermen and "chasers," who risked death themselves among hurtling logs on the ground, spoke with awe of the high climbers.

"At Comox," said J. L. Henslowe, "on Vancouver Island, there was a high rigger who used to show off standing on top of the tree. As a matter of fact he would often relieve himself standing up there in a high wind, with everyone below running for cover. This one time as he climbed up on top he flipped his rope and it flipped too high and he went over backwards. He landed on the railway track below and we picked him up in a basket."

"I saw two bad accidents," said Watson "Waddy" Weeks, a Vancouver Island logger who did everything from setting chokers in the 1930s to driving logging railway engines and finally logging trucks before retiring in 1974. "They were riggers falling out of trees. Jim Atchison fell 75 or 80 feet and nearly hit me, but he lived. Another fella fell about 20 feet away from me up at Cowichan Lake and broke his back, all crippled."

Spar trees and high leads tripled log production. As well as yarding direct to fill the cars of a logging railway the crews, or "skidding sides," would store logs in "cold decks" 50 feet high. A good crew "high balling" logs fast to a spar tree could drag in 200 a day.

More spectacular than the simple high lead system was the skyline. Whereas the high lead stretched from the top of a spar tree down to a distant stump, a skyline stretched between the tops of two spar trees like a giant's clothes-line. The spar trees were usually 750 feet apart although on mountain slopes they might run 5200 feet. The skyline was straddled by a wheel carriage, or "bicycle," which could lift a 20-ton log right off the ground and whizz it at 20 miles an hour to the "home tree." By World War One 200-ton Lidgerwood Skidders mounted on giant sledges or railway flat cars were replacing the simpler donkey engines all along the coast. The first Lidgerwoods often had Finnish crews brought up from Louisiana.

"The Americans came up here and taught the Canadians how to log," said Bob Swanson. "Logging with cables, it all came from the States, the whole damn lot of it. The Americans built the best machines.

"You had as many as 13 drums on them, miles of cable all over the place, and they would load 50 railway cars a day. You'd be sitting on a sort of mower machine seat with both feet going and both hands. You had six levers and kept pulling them. You didn't worry too much about your steam valves, you'd know by the feel of it what it was doing. I've had them pull spar trees down all around me and had to dive underneath the machine. It makes a

175

The high rigger. With climbing irons strapped to ▷ his boots and falling axe swinging from his belt, the high rigger climbed a tall Douglas fir, twitching his safety rope up the trunk, to lop the top off a spar tree.

Photograph by JACK CASH, *Canadian Pulp and Paper Association*

◁ Logs were often stored in a "cold deck" to await transportation, the equivalent of a log skidway back east. A cold deck pile of Douglas fir might contain as much as a million feet of timber.
Provincial Archives, Victoria, B.C.

One hundred and eighty feet above the ground a high rigger hangs on for dear life as the top of a spar tree tumbles off. The recoil when the tree-top fell could set the spar tree lashing back and forth in a 20-foot arc. "The worst hazard," said Jack Bell, "was topping in a high wind because you could chop your undercut in and then start from the back to saw and the wind would hit it and split ▽ the tree — with you tied to it."

Rigging crew on Vancouver Island in 1926, clustered around the spar, or "home," tree with a length of the miles of cable that went into a sky-line "setting." "A tree-rigged skidder would take you maybe three days to rig up," said Jack Bell. "There would be 18 guy lines on it.... One skidder we had, we figured that with the spare line there were 22 miles of cable..."

Provincial Archives, Victoria, B.C.

Some of the high riggers, such as Big Bill Moraski, who weighed 240 pounds, liked to show off a bit, standing atop a spar tree with outstretched arms once they had sawn off the top and rigged it with the "jewels," heavy pulleys, and more than a dozen guy wires. Few of them fell off.

▽ *Provincial Archives, Victoria, B.C.*

kind of creaking and when you see things start to shake you dive. But a good donkey puncher always knew what was going on out in the woods — every minute. Phil Lamare was one of the best donkey men on the coast. He sent the rigging back kind of tidy and when you wanted slack let down he didn't drop it in a great bloody big heap. He was watchin' all the time. He was only 16 when he started."

By the time Phil Lamare got into the woods the skylines were running full blast. One "setting," swung progressively around the points of a compass on the fulcrum of the spar tree as each quarter or section was logged off, could clean out 20 to 40 acres of heavy timber in three or four weeks. They called easy logging slopes the "candy side" and hard ones a "suicide show."

"From a skidder engine," recalled Lamare, white-haired now and living in Duncan, B.C., "you couldn't see what was going on. It was all done with signals. The rigging slinger, or the hook tender, either one, would give the whistle punk his signals. When you were yarding you were back 1200 feet from the bush and when a log got hung up halfway in on a stump or something they would fight it clear just by giving the right signals — back the turn of logs and go ahead on her again. The rigging slinger would shout the signals to the whistle punk. 'Ho, ho!' meant back her up, or 'Ho, ho, ho!' meant go ahead easy. With the high lead you'd have one end of the log dragging but with a skidder system on the skyline you'd take the logs right up to the skyline most of the time. It depends where you are working. You can take them up to the skyline or just halfway up or just drag them along the ground. There was always danger you'd start the line before the chokermen were in the clear. I always used to start out quite slowly and if no whistle come in you knew you were all right and you'd tighten up and away you'd go. You can see back perhaps five or six or seven hundred feet and then they'll get back over a knoll or something and you can't see them and then you've got to be careful. You could put four or five logs on the line. She'd handle quite a load. We'd work in all sorts of weather, snow and everything.

"Sometimes a spar tree would break and everything would come crashing down all around you. There's two sets of guys on her, buckle guys about halfway up and then your top guys. She'd usually break 20 or 30 feet from the top and when she comes down she goes right out over those buckle guys and throws everything away from the machine. When you felt her go you just opened that old rig wide open and the line pulled the falling tree-top right away out so she would not fall on the men below. Usually when she broke you were hung up on something and pulling pretty hard. All you had over your head was that tin roof to keep off the rain. Nothing.

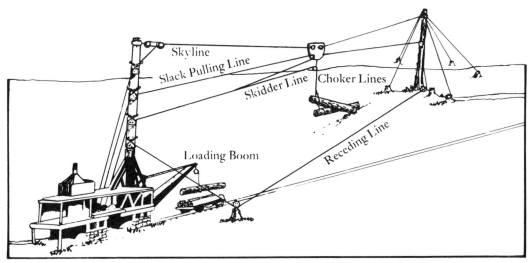

Skyline

Slack Pulling Line

Skidder Line   Choker Lines

Receding Line

Loading Boom

From Rhymes of a Lumberjack, *courtesy of*
Robert Swanson, Vancouver, B.C.

Skyline, or cableway, logging reached its height in the early 1920s. All skyline systems, tight line, slack line, Northbend, Tyler, had two things in common: a "flying machine," or super donkey engine, often a Lidgerwood, to power them; and a layout which consisted of a heavy wire rope threaded through a massive pulley — a "Tommy Moore," or "bull block," on the "head spar tree" at the log landing. It led back to the "tail spar" where it went through another pulley at the edge of the "setting" where the wood was being harvested.

The Flying Machine, or skyline skidder. The ultimate in donkey-powered log yarding, some weighed 200 tons and were equipped with a dozen drums for hauling logs and loading them on flat cars. This monster tamed the forests near Campbell River, Vancouver Island, in 1926.

Provincial Archives, Victoria, B.C.

The debris would come clatterin' down. I've left the rig and gone underneath her! In those days, in the 1930s, you were logging larger areas with much heavier equipment than what they are using today. The trees were bigger. Steam is huge stuff when it's working, compared to diesel and gas. A skidder crew might total 22 men."

The skidding crews had not only grown larger but they had changed a good deal. The donkey puncher was a licensed engineer and the spool tender had been retired by the automatic haul-back line and had been replaced by a "chaser" who unhooked the swinging logs with the nimble timing of a ballet dancer. The signal man had thrown away his flag, tied a clothes-line to the steam whistle on the boiler to transmit his signals, and was known as the "whistle punk." The chokermen out in the bush lassoed the logs with chokers or lengths of wire which hooked them to the high lead or the skyline and there was a boss chokerman, or "rigging slinger," to keep them out of trouble. Over the whole banging, rattling, whistling show reigned the "hook tender," or "hooker," who bestrode a battered stump halfway down the line and directed traffic when he wasn't down in the slash wrestling with some ornery turn of logs.

"If I was to draw a picture of a hook tender of the old days," said "Waddy" Weeks, "I'd say he would be about five feet eight, half bald, and usually had a chew of snoose, Copenhagen chewing tobacco, in his mouth. He was barrel-chested and could lift a ton, it seemed. Holler, swear, and curse like hell and solid, bloody gold from the bottom of his heart. Some of the old-timers couldn't read or write, hardly, but they were very smart men. If a boy was willin' and wanted to learn, God, he would do anything in the world to help you." A lot of them sported gold teeth, their natural teeth knocked out by swinging rigging or in bar-room fights of long ago. The hook tender's title had come down from the man who used to hook the logs together in the bull team skid road days but his heart was the heart of the fearsome old bull whacker.

"In those days," said Arne Bergland, who worked up from horse logger in the interior and rigging slinger on the coast to camp foreman and Bull of the Woods, "there was not too much thought of safety. The biggest concern was to get the logs out. There were a lot of accidents, a lot of people were hurt, and there was no union at all when I started. As rigging slinger I was responsible for picking out what logs we were to hook. Whether you wanted to take one, or two, or how many, and I told the chokermen where to place a choker cable around a log. There was a terrific turnover in camp with men coming and going. It was hard work. These people today wouldn't even consider workin' like that. You wouldn't have anybody in the woods today if you asked them to work as we did."

The poet of the skidder crews, Peter Trower of Gibson, B.C., a

W. H. Gold

"We wrestled with their steel ropes and swore and grumbled," wrote the west coast logger-poet Peter Trower. "It was very like a war..." A "rigging up crew," November 1942.

A whistle punk stands on a stump at Buckley Bay transmitting orders from hook tender out in the bush to the donkey puncher operating the skidding engine.

Vancouver Public Library

logger himself, has compared those high ball, high lead "settings" to a battlefield.

> No bombs explode, no khaki regiments tramp
> to battle in a coastal logging camp
> yet blood can spill upon the forest floor
> and logging can be very like a war . . .
> The savage cables rattle through the mist,
> The boxing chokers curse the men they missed,
> We wrestled with their steel ropes and swore
> and grumbled. It was very like a war . . . [5]

"Someone," recalled Waddy Weeks, "might step in the bight of a cable, not watching, and the line would smear them. One place I was working, three guys got killed in four days. There was a Chinaman got killed, a faller got killed, and an old guy who was slinging riggin' on a donkey. The first one killed was the Chinaman. He was cutting wood for the steam engine when a line hit him on top of the head. You get a break in a skyline, 1000 feet long and it strung up there like a fiddle string, and when that breaks, Lord God, *something* goes. That thing just wipes everything right out, a big steel line like that. Woosh! You could hear the thing starting to go and guys were off at the bloody gallop.

"Well, the next day old Charlie, a big old Finn, was standing in the bight of a cable and when the donkey started up it got him. That man weighed 240 pounds and it up-ended him 20 feet away and busted his neck. Never knew what hit him, killed him instantly. Then they missed a day and the next day a faller chopped down a tree right along the hill. A big fir. The bucker came along but his saw kept hitting this limb so he took his axe and chopped the limb off, but it was the only bloody thing holdin' that tree on the sidehill. It got him, and there was three of them in four days. There was this guy from Ontario and he said, 'Oh my God, is this the way they work out here? I'm gettin' the hell out of here.' The 30s were bad, and the late 20s, they were high balling like hell in those days. We always used to knock off, you know, go home for the afternoon, if anybody got killed. It was always the custom. One a day was enough, they'd say, let's get the hell out of here.

"When I was loadin' there was always a helluva racket all the time, roaring, screaming whistles — but one *foreign* sound and boy you understood it instantly. Something was coming. A line was breaking or something. You could hear the spar tree vibrating and the engine working harder and harder, chuga, chuga, chuga, and look out! All that stuff was going over your head all the time. I was settin' chokers with Ken Halberg one day. He was over on the other side of the log and I didn't know he was there. I hit him on the head with a choker and knocked him flat. He was over on the other side of the log with his head split open. I didn't know he was there. He's got a big scar on top of his head yet. With two choker-men, there was one on each side of the big log. Choker lines would swing back on the skyline and you'd grab them and slide the bell coupling back and over to the other guy to take the nob and put it in and then you'd get the hell out. You'd run! One time on a land-ing I got caught under a pile of logs. They all rolled down on top of me. I was down among some logs setting a choker and there was a hell of a roar of logs and dirt and dust and down they come, but I was lucky. A chaser I was with one day, he had 10 small logs on the skyline and was crawling in amongst them unhookin' and he had only half of them undone. There were logs rolling all around him. He would duck under one, put his hand on another, and jump over a third. Those logs were comin' all around him. I don't know how he made it. He was on the move, boy, duckin' and runnin'. A chaser's job could be more dangerous than a chokerman's. You had to use your noodle. Look over a situation. Don't pull the hooks off that — she's liable to roll and get ya. They always wore calked boots. Go? Oh my God. Eleven hours a day. I was a punk kid then, and there were four chokermen, a rigging slinger and a hook tender, a donkey engineer, fireman, whistle punk. Nine men on that side."

"The first time I went into the woods," said Jack Bell, "the hook tender was killed right in front of my eyes. The logs were coming in and they tangled into a 100-foot sapling standing there and pulled it with them, sticking out at an angle. A 'sidewinder' they called that. They hollered at him and he saw it coming and he ducked behind another sapling and just before the thing got there he stuck his head around to see where it was and it hit him.

"I blew whistle for two years and then I went settin' chokers. We didn't think it was hard work in the old days because we made a fun game out of it. You had to move pretty fast because in those days it was what they called a high-ball system and you'd either produce or you 'went down the road.' The riggin' slinger went right into the bush with you and made sure you hooked the logs up right and then came out with you and the cardinal rule was that the chokerman always stood behind the riggin' slinger. Periodically you'd have a careless type and he wouldn't worry and then you'd have somebody hurt or a fatality. I've seen quite a few people killed. Six long blasts on the whistle meant a man injured and seven meant a fatality.

"There were a lot killed on the old duplex loaders on a skidder, loading logs on railway cars. The 'second loader' would throw out a pair of tongs to grip a log and if you got up on the load you could throw the tongs — which weighed 80 pounds — out 30 feet and catch a log. You'd throw it out and spin it and the donkey operator would let out slack until the tongs reached the log — like casting for a fish. If the tongs came off they would come back and hit you. Eighty pounds on a swinging cable like a pendulum.

"In the 1930s and 1940s the skyline was your main method of logging although the small contractors, or gyppos, as they called them, would still be using the old methods down below among the smaller timber. The idea of the skyline was to get up two or three thousand feet on the mountain slopes. One big skidder we had, we figured that with the spare line there was 22 miles of cable, four skylines at 3000 feet each, 7000-foot receding lines, guy lines, and everything. Others might just use seven miles of cable with a portable steel spar rather than a wooden spar tree. One of the largest camps ever, in its heyday, was Franklin River, a railway show on Vancouver Island, where I worked. There were 550 men. As superintendent, if anybody was short, I'd run the locomotives and I'd run the skidders. You had to do everything. Franklin River was one of the first camps to get tractors, around 1935, the first diesel tractors, although there had been gas tractors before which were just used for odd jobs."

The Lidgerwood Skidders and their like had turned the coastal timber limits into outdoor factories, without walls or roof but with as much steel and steam as you were apt to find in a mill. Everything on the coast was bigger, faster, mechanized, and even their lingo was strange to the ears of an eastern lumberjack. Lumberjacks, they said on the west coast, were those fellows in funny tuques and red sashes who drove on the sleigh hauls back east and balanced on logs in the river. On the west coast they were not lumberjacks, but *loggers*. Even their clothes were different — canvas hats and "tin pants" so daubed with waterproofing and grease they could stand up by themselves. They wore calk boots not for driving rivers but to keep their footing on the thick logs in the bush. Some dressed like mill hands, in greasy overalls, and carried a monkey wrench in one pocket and an oil can in the other but they were all "loggers" and, unlike their counterparts, the lumberjacks of the east or the B.C. mainland interior, they rarely switched to farming in the summer. Except perhaps for times of deep snow on the high slopes or extreme fire hazard in summer, coastal logging went on all year. When they wanted work they hung around hiring agencies like Captain Bill Black's in Vancouver or they could be found in Cordova Street saloons and skid-road hotels. The best of them were hired direct by a foreman who knew them, and some were picked up by the "man-catchers" who made a career, like baseball scouts, picking good, well-balanced crews to high ball for a high-production outfit.

With hundreds of camps tucked away on islands and inlets up on "Kissmeass" Lagoon on Drury Inlet, or up around Ocean Falls or even north of Kitimat, their only transport was the coastal steamers. The red, white, and black steamers, like the famous *Cassiar* of the Union Steamship Line, tramped the coast on vague schedule and dumped them, sometimes hung-over, often in the middle of a rainy night, on a rocking, slippery float lit by a dim lantern and moored beneath some mountain-slope camp. They slept down in the steerage "bull pen" and a typical passenger list in those days might read "15 passengers and 50 loggers." The mates were expected to man-handle drunks as well as navigate, especially when the likes of "Rough-house" Pete Ohlsen were aboard, for the voyages were traditionally times to throw a final party before the long, dry months of logging began.

"I ran into Rough-house Pete," said Bob Swanson, "up at Stillwater on the mainland. He was a hook tender. He used to kick the bejesus out of the boats when he went up north. He'd get drunk and kick all the banisters out of the stairs and he'd be put in the brig. He got a reputation. Once you got a reputation you had to live up to it. When the grub wasn't right Rough-house would jump on the table and clean all the stuff off with his feet. He did that more than once in the camps. One time they brought stew out to lunch at the spar tree and there were alder leaves in it. Rough-house Pete saw that and said, 'I'll show you,' and put both his bloody feet in the stew pot.

"I was 14 when I got a job punkin' whistle and I got to know all the loggers pretty young. I was 15 when I started firing donkey and by the time I was 16 I was running the machine. I became government inspector of railways and locomotives and donkeys and boilers and I got into the various camps and I got to know everybody. My older brother was 'Seattle Red.' He'd do nothing but work on the riggin', riggin' slinger and chokerman. He was quite a logger. He worked out of Seattle and he worked out of Vancouver and he died in '68 and I've often thought I should get a big stump made for a tombstone. He worked for 25 years for Comox Logging, steady, but in his young years he'd go to work in a camp for a few weeks and then move on to another. He kind of got rheumatism but he worked up to two or three years before he died at the age of 68.

"Bill Barbrick, the old bull puncher, I knew him when he worked at Camp Five, the beach camp. Red Morrison, he was another old-time logger. I started under him. In the camps where production was big there were younger guys; you had to have stamina to get out in the bush on a sidehill and 40 or 50 was getting old for that.

185

But in the smaller camps where production sometimes was at a slower pace there were older men — the 'home guard,' they called them. There was one story at Rock Bay: They kept their men until they could hardly walk any more and were very good that way. Some new foreman came up and took over and when the big boss came up, I think it was Saul Reamy, he said, 'Where's old Charlie?'

" 'Well,' said the foreman, 'we sent him into town. He couldn't do anything any more. He was just hanging around here.'

" 'Well,' said Saul, 'could he not draw himself up to the table any more. Could he eat?'

" 'Oh, he could eat!'

" 'Well,' Reamy says, 'bring him back. As long as he can eat he can stay here.'

"It was home guard, you see. As far as I know Saul Reamy came from down east. A lot of those guys came from the Maritimes. The Lambs came from Nova Scotia, Daddy Lamb and Tom Lamb. And loggers on the coast ran heavy to Swedes, Norwegians, and Danes. They were hard-working men in the old days and you could leave 10 or 15 dollars in your clothes in the bunkhouse and nobody would touch it."

Loggers delight in the tales of characters like "Eight-Day" Wilson, a big hook tender, whose claim to fame was that he would never stay in any camp more than eight days. There were "boomers," or "drifters," who used to see how many camps they could work in during a year from Oregon to the Queen Charlottes. They would spend a couple of weeks in each camp and one "Camp Inspector," as the loggers fondly called them, claimed a record of 36 camps.

They never had quite the same traditions of music, dancing, and story-telling that they had back east although there were accordions and mouth organs and Saturday night dances with the girls in nearby towns on Vancouver Island. Those who had money, the high riggers and hook tenders, played "high-ball" poker for big stakes and those who had little contented themselves with a bit of modest "haywire" poker.

"They played poker all the time and one end of the bunkhouse was known as the poker shack," said Jack Bell. "Every once in a while a card sharp like 'Seven Draw Pete' would come in. He didn't want to work but the idea was to get a job in camp so he could get into a card game and clean up. He might stay two weeks to a month before he made his pile and quit and went back to town. Some of them caught cheatin' were run out of camp. There were some wild poker games. The biggest game I ever saw was one in which more than $25 000 was exchanged over a Saturday night and into Sunday."

When they got a chance to go to town there were always spots like "Pecker Point" up the coast from Ocean Falls or the "Goat Pasture" near Port Alberni for a sinful weekend. For those who felt their sin a burden, there were visits from the Reverend George Pringle of the Logger's Mission in his gas boat "Sky Pilot."

On the west coast a contractor was not called a jobber, as in the east, but a "gyppo," and like the gypsy he was often on the move. Most gyppos were mechanized, after a fashion, although their machinery might run only to a second-hand $5000 donkey engine and a few hundred feet of cable on an A-frame rigged to haul timber down the mountain into a bay. They built camps on log floats in a bay or inlet, not only because level ground was hard to come by on that mountainous coast, but also because a float camp could be towed from one job to another. Many gyppos prospered: P. B. Anderson, for example, came from Sweden by way of Minnesota in 1910, bought cheap timber limits, and seven years later was running six donkey engines, a 55-ton locomotive on his logging railway, and had money in the bank.

The first successful gyppo might be said to be Jeremiah Rogers in his pioneer logging camp of split-cedar shacks on English Bay. It was Rogers who brought an early form of steam power to the western woods in 1875: two second-hand steam traction engines, which resembled steam rollers and drew logs along tracks made of flattened logs laid lengthwise. Those early models were not successful, but later versions, adapted from the traction engines employed for prairie harvests, were used in logging across the country. They waddled through the bush like dinosaurs. Some had two high wheels in back and a steering wheel, or, in winter, a ski out under the nose. They were navigated by a driver who sat out forward clutching a tiller like a dry-land yachtsman, unprotected from rain and cold and with sparks from the smoke-stack forever scorching his hair and stinging his neck. Sometimes the engines were fitted with flanged wheels, like bells laid on their sides, to run on tracks of peeled logs. In Nova Scotia at Emile Stehelin's camp at Silver River, 20 miles from Weymouth, even an eight-ton locomotive designed for a steel rail was tried out on a pole railway but the wood twisted and sprung and the project was abandoned.

The first steel railway logging was tried in Michigan, the birth place of so many logging innovations, in the 1870s, when snow was too scarce for the usual sleigh haul. It did not become common in British Columbia until the turn of the century. Although the Ross-Mclaren Company at New Westminster had developed plans for a steel railway show in 1892, the first successful logging railway was introduced only about 1900, probably around Chemainus on Vancouver Island, although soon after that Saul Reamy was using "locies" on Quadra Island and Thurlow Inlet in the Strait of

Ont. Ministry of Natural Resources

Before the First World War a few steam crawler tractors were brought into the woods to haul sleigh trains of logs. This one was used near Lac St. Jean in Quebec in 1920. It was mounted with a steering wheel on a sled in front of the engine, its headlight an oil lantern. By the 1930s crawler tractors were being made with internal combustion engines.

British Columbia Forest Service

Steam tractor of late 19th century, forerunner of the logging railway. The first machine used in the Gillies camp in B.C. in 1876 drew 40-foot logs, each weighing five tons or more, and collapsed after two trips. The steam tractors fared better at their original work of hauling harvests on the level prairies.

Georgia some 150 miles northwest of Vancouver. At first the loco-motives hauled logs, big turns of 20 or more, along rails spiked to the skidways just as the bull teams had done. By 1910 Reamy's camp had 50 flat cars and five locomotives as well as 26 donkey engines. There was nothing but handbrakes on those early logging cars and when the engineer whistled for brakes on a mountain slope the brakeman had to climb out on the logs with an axe handle and try to set the squealing brakes by hand. Many a brakeman lost limb or life until, at the end of World War One, the government passed a law requiring all logging cars to be equipped with air brakes.

In 1917 — the year British Columbia surpassed all provinces in-cluding Ontario in lumber production — there were 62 logging railways in the province, 98 locomotives, 941 logging cars, 354 flat cars, and 400 miles of standard gauge railway. The growth of rail-way logging on the mountain slopes and shaky spur lines was due, as much as anything, to what in 1881 had been called "Shay's folly."

Around that time, the same year as Dolbeer started tinkering with a donkey engine, a Michigan logger named Ephraim Shay designed a light locomotive especially for logging camps. His moss-backed neighbours were understandably derisive since it was a queer-look-ing thing with lopsided gear transmission balanced on its right hip and a boiler on the left. Its top speed was little more than 15 miles an hour although, if it got away on a steep slope when pushed by a big load of logs, it might crash at 70. But Shay's locomotive could climb grades of nine per cent — nine feet of incline for every 100 feet of distance — and its universal joints helped it to take curves of 30 degrees. It could haul on mountains where a conventional rod locomotive would "lose its feet" and stall.

Between 1881 and 1945 the Lima Locomotive Works at Lima, Ohio, built 2761 Shays, including a special 90-ton model for the west coast. They were used in eastern Canada as well. In Ontario, the Abitibi Paper Company at Iroquois Falls had Shays hauling pulpwood on 70 miles of main and spur line over ungraded muskeg where they could be run only in winter when the ground was frozen.

"Those Shays would lean!" recalled Earle Wilson. "I've been in one of those things on one of the spurs in April when the frost was coming out and the engineer would say, 'You'd better slam that door in case she goes over.' They would just roll over. They just put them back on the tracks." There were other logging railways in eastern Canada — a couple on the Ontario shore of the Ottawa, a couple on the north shore of Lake Huron. A few Quebec camps had logging railways and there were nearly 50 miles of logging rail-way on Anticosti Island at the mouth of the St. Lawrence. But in the east there were always rivers to drive and rivers were cheaper

The Public Archives of Canada   C 19885

A No. 4 Shay locomotive hauling logs at Campbell River, B.C., in 1928. Since a Shay was driven by gears, instead of rods as on a conventional engine, it was ideal for the steep grades and hairpin turns of mountain logging.

Vancouver Public Library

Logging railways came to the British Columbia coastal forests around the turn of the century. Because of the great size of the timber and the lack of suitable streams to drive logs, such railways were more common on the west coast than in the east.

than rails, so it was on the west coast where rivers were scarce or too small for the big logs that the railways thrived. In 1924 there were 80 logging railways in British Columbia with 700 miles of track and 148 locomotives, mostly Shays and Climaxes. Climaxes, first built in Pennsylvania in the late 1880s, were handsome locomotives but their pistons, one mounted on each side, gave a rough and jerky ride. Conventional, direct-connection rod engines, or "hogs," were rarely used on woodland spur lines.

Waddy Weeks: The Hogger's Story

"The Shay was easy riding, rode beautifully, three cylinders on the side with a crankshaft split three ways. If you had the valves set right and tuned up, they ran like sewing machines. Shays were well-sprung whereas on a Climax you couldn't sit down when it got to jerkin'. I'd get mad and pull my shirt tight around my stomach and hold on tight. All the Climaxes just had damn curtains, greasy and blowin', and the cab would be half full of snow. The Shays, however, were fixed up with closed cabs and lovely seats. They figured a 90-ton Shay was adequate to handle anything they wanted to haul. Anything heavier required heavier bridges and rails. The steepest grade I ever worked was nine per cent and it took everything in your power to hold her. You had to watch like a hawk. If you hit that grade with a heavy load you just barely got over and if you ever went into a skid on the other side you were gone like a bullet. There's a point where friction ceases and if you broke over a grade too fast and went into a skid you'd just keep on skidding. The wheels would lock and you'd have to snap the throttle to make them start again — that's the trick to stop a locie skidding. In fog the rails got like slime, like slugs had been crawlin' on them, but after a damn good rain it was okay and snow was okay, like sand.

"A good hogger runs the locie by the seat of his pants. That's the whole trick. You watched your gauges. Those were your life lines. There were two air gauges with two hands on each one, a red hand and a black. The red hand was your main air reservoir pressure and the black hand was the brake pipe pressure on the cars. The other gauge was for the air pressure on the engine. Your air was the thing and you watched it like a hawk. The steam was okay, for if she got too high she would always blow herself off and if she got too low, well you just wouldn't go. But if your air got haywire you were in trouble. The air was the brains of the brake mechanism.

"A locomotive is like a violin. There are no keys. You can't run it by the book. You got to *feel* it and the guy who did that had no problem. The same with firing. Firing at night was tremendously hard for some people because you had to keep just a haze coming out of the stack. Too much smoke was no good. Blue smoke meant your fire was out and there was just gas coming up and you could wreck your boiler in a few minutes. I learned to fire by listening. You could tell by the sound if it's all right. One fellow who had been firing for 40 years had to go so far as to rig a light on the smoke-stack at night so he could see what was comin' out but I would only glance at the stack once in a while and if the smoke started to show dirty it meant the tubes were getting dirty and you'd put sand in to woosh it out. If I got a cold in my nose I used to have a helluva time because you used three or four different lubricants on different things and you learned to smell those if they were hot. So you would use your nose and your ears and the seat of your pants.

"I've been 'in the woods' — off the rails — many times and I remember I came down a canyon, around a curve, whistling, and spotted a rock on the track. There was about a foot of clearance, it seemed, and I thought, 'Maybe she'll clear.' But what actually happened is that the rock tipped the front trucks off the rails and dropped them 70 or 80 feet down into the creek. So I 'wiped the clock' — put on the brakes — and got her stopped awful damn fast. The locie had jumped the tracks and run 15 or 20 feet along the ground before I got her stopped. Sometimes we'd be rippin' up rails and wouldn't even know it. A truck might jump and rip up rails until the air line broke and put you on emergency — when every air brake will come on automatically. Boom. Just like that. And she'll go nowhere.

"One night at Elk River on Vancouver Island we dropped down the hill with 70 cars, a long load. I was sittin' on the sand box and happened to look up at the air gauge and saw the train line pressure suddenly go down and we started to come to a gentle stop. By the feel of it we had busted the train line — the air line to the brakes — for everything had stopped. So I grabbed a spare air hose out of the box and a 24-inch Stilson and started back up the track and when I come to the 10th car — there was no more cars! I shone my light up the track and there were no cars there! I walked up the track and came across a pile of logs 20 feet high with bits of broken cars showing underneath. Everything from the 10th to the 21st car lay in that broken pile. Eleven cars absolutely massacred. What a junk pile! It tore up 400 feet of track and we hadn't heard or felt a thing. One car had jumped and broke the air line and the others had piled up on top of it.

"But there's something that looks after a guy. I was brakin' one night, standing on the footboard where I usually stood, when I did something I rarely did and climbed up to get close to the boiler to get warm for it was colder'n hell and blowin'. We were chuggin' along and, God, I saw fire flyin' right in front of me, sparks and crashin' and bangin'. A boulder had slid down on the rails and was hitting the edges of the cars we were pushing ahead of us. That boulder hit the footboard where I usually stood and rolled it right up, tore hell out of that side of the engine. If I had been standing on the footboard where I usually stood it would have cut me right off at the waist. There's something that looks after a guy.

"Bear Creek trestle bridge was so rotten, at the end, you'd be looking more than 240 feet straight down, shaking and wobbling. There was one bridge where we'd just come down with the locomotive and stop before we got to it. Luckily it was on a down grade and one of us would walk across that bridge while the other climbed up in the cab, knocked the air off, let her go, and then jumped off. She'd roll across the bridge and we'd catch her as she came by.

"In the 1950s I pulled the last loads hauled by steam locie out of several camps before they pulled up the steel. The last 'tit' I pulled — the last throttle — was when I hauled the last load out of Bear Creek in 1957. Starting from 1936 I was 20 years in steam and I didn't like motor trucks as much as steam. You didn't enjoy the same prestige — because in steam everyone looked up to a locomotive engineer. All the kids idolized you."

The great age of steam spanned half a century although by the 1950s only 16 logging railways were left in British Columbia. By 1969 there were only two, and diesel locomotives had replaced the last of the steam locies. That year, at Ladysmith on Vancouver Island, the last haul of logs by steam locomotive in North America was made and men like Waddy Weeks took to driving the big "off highway" logging trucks which weighed 57 tons before you even put a log on. Weeks was in his 60s and the oldest man in camp when he finally quit. "I was gettin' too damn tired. You don't think you are under pressure but you are — under tension, a lot of tension. You are coming out 18 per cent grades with 120 tons on and awful switchbacks and canyons. You don't make mistakes. You can't let it get away from you." Logging had moved farther up the mountains and trucks could go places railway engines could not go.

There had been trucks — a few of them — on logging roads since 1920. The first were owned by contractors, gyppo outfits, and ran on solid rubber tires, had no cab, hardly any brakes, and ran on roads of planks or hewn timber called "fore-and-aft" roads because the planks lay lengthwise like rails rather than crosswise like a skid road. "Rip rap," old bits of cable, scrap metal, wood, anything they could find, was nailed in zig-zag patterns to the slippery planks for traction.

193

Vancouver Public Library

One of the first Duplex 4 hard-tired trucks used in British Columbia logging in the early 1920s. The trucks ran on "fore-and-aft roads" made of logs laid end to end and often more than 12 miles long. Sometimes the roads ran 16 or 20 feet high over gulleys that were as much as half a mile wide. "It was a ridiculous thing to do with a truck if you think about it," said Frank White. "But coming to it after years of skid roads and railroads, it must have looked like the only thing to do."

Cam's Photo Service

Bear Creek Bridge, on the west coast of Vancouver Island. More than 600 feet long, the trestle, at a height of more than 240 feet, was one of the highest wooden bridges in the country. It was built by a logging company in 1939.

Frank White: The Trucker's Story

"... The goddamn brakes on those things weren't meant to be taken seriously. You did have the emergency brakes. Great big squeeze-handle emergency brake on the side of the cab. That was the true measure of the truck, the emergency brake. The bigger the truck the bigger the handle. Some came right up to your chin ... Those old emergency brakes would work alright, but one good stop was all they had in 'em, and you damn well saved it for an emergency ... The steering wheels were great big wooden things about three feet across and flat. Had to be, because they had about as much reduction in linkage as a bicycle, you were hangin' on for all you were worth all day long. That was the main battle, to keep the front wheels going where you wanted to go and not where they wanted. You studied the road a long way ahead. Under normal conditions you had the edge in brute force, but a rock or a rut could tie you right in a knot. The spokes would blur just like an airplane propeller, jesus, if anything was in the way, you could write it off for about three months. . . . Come to any gully not real easy to fill and they built a timber trestle. Now let me tell you, coming down a plank road in one of them old hard-wheeled bastards, sittin' in the open on a board seat, a couple three-thousand-foot logs jiggling around up behind your head, no bulkhead for protection, just that steering wheel just like a bull's hind leg in your hands and mechanical brakes — you were earning your two dollars and eighty cents a day. Trestles rattling and jumping around, mud squeezing up between the planks. With mud or a touch of frost you could no more hold that thing on the track than you could hold a greasy pig with one hand. . . . You'd be looking through your floorboards going over a trestle and seeing straight down through 70 feet of clear open space. Boards broke and jillpoked all the time — God."[6]

Archie McCone of Vancouver was one of the pioneers of truck loading when he came to B.C. from a Manitoba farm in 1923. "Archie," his friends say, "was behind the door when fear was handed out." But even he shied clear of chaining logs to a truck bed because when a big west coast log over-balanced on a hairpin turn it could take the truck with it over a cliff "like a dog wrestling a bear."

"The first two years I was driving I just sat up there in the snow and rain in a pair of overalls that got soakin' wet. There was no cab and I dried out in the bunkhouse if I could. The first truck I drove, there was a little bit of frost on the fore-and-aft road and I stopped at the top of the hill and said, 'That road don't look very good to me. It looks too darn slippery.' The roadman assured me they had sanded it and it was okay. I took his word but they had only sanded a little piece and when I ran off the sand I started to slip and the truck was gathering momentum and there was a sharp turn in the road and I didn't want to go around that corner because there might be another truck on the road. I pulled off on a turn-out and came to a stop and the logs all shifted and slid forward right over my head. We didn't have any protection behind us except for a few railway ties bolted down with no strength in them at all. I wasn't hurt but when I got organized there I made a steel plate up the back so that when logs started to slide that steel bulkhead held them.

"Those roads were steep, up to 30 per cent, and when we had cabs the logs would slide right over the top. I had that happen two or three times and rolled over a few times but never was hurt — but I had a few friends killed on runaways. Generally, however, a driver would jump. We didn't have horns on the first trucks, or lights except for a coal-oil lamp as a tail light. Al Mann said, 'You should have a light for that truck,' so I rigged a little spotlight with a dry cell battery. Goldarn, the first morning I used it in the dark I ran right off the road so I never used it again. The old White trucks in those days would only do 12 miles an hour. I used to haul for 12 miles at Seymour Creek on those hard tires on a gravel road and, boy, it was sure rough. The seat of your pants would wear out about once a week. Pneumatic tires only came in about 1930.

"When I started hauling on my own as a contractor we had the pick of the drivers because the big company camps hadn't got into trucking on their own since contractors could haul logs cheaper. I selected contracts that most people would shy clear of. You could make more money hauling logs on steep and narrow roads than you could on fast, easy grades. This one logging show I was on, it was really a pretty haywire show, the guy there used to keep his old gas boat running with a piece of kelp when his gas line broke — he made a joint out of seaweed. He was a real haywire guy. His road there was steep and crooked. I started from the top on a 16 per cent grade and there was a left turn and a 28 per cent grade so abrupt the rear end of the truck hit the road and lifted the front wheels right off the ground. We came around there with the front wheels hanging over the bank, right off the ground, with only the rear wheels on the ground. As soon as I coaxed her around the corner on her rear wheels the front wheels came down again where they should be. Well, I hauled 70 loads and every load was the same, back wheels down and front wheels sticking out over the bank on that turn. I've known drivers who went into Horseshoe Bay and they just took one look and wanted to go back. 'I'm not goin' on that road,' they'd say. I never had any fear of any truck I was driving. You'd never take a load out until you made sure you were perfectly balanced."

By the 1950s diesel trucks had replaced the logging railways and diesel engines had replaced the steam logging skidders. "It was a sad, sad day when the steam went," said Waddy Weeks. "I don't know any steam engineer who didn't love steam. It had internal combustion beat a million ways. With steam, the power is right there. I remember standing watching the last steam skidder at work. It was a fine day and it was snapping up the loads with the tongs going, whistles blowing — sounded good. I heard somebody say, 'It *sounds* like a logging camp, doesn't it, Waddy?' I said, 'It sure does and it will be a damn shame when she goes.' 'That's the last settin', Waddy,' he said. 'From now on you'll see only those damn stinking diesels.' " The bulls, the horses, and finally the steam — all gone forever and the men who remember those times agree it was all proper, sensible, inevitable — and sad.

"After the Second World War," said Jack Bell, "there were new men, a different type of men. It was the power saw as much as anything else that revolutionized logging at that time. But there's been terrific change. Nowadays they don't have the same interest and I think I lived in the best era. It's different altogether now."

12 BEANS EVERLASTING: COOKS AND COOKEES

I pray dear Lord, for Jesus' sake,
Give us this day a T-bone steak;
Hallowed be Thy Name,
But don't forget to send the same.

LUMBERJACK'S PRAYER
A "WOBBLY" LOGGING SONG BROUGHT INTO
B.C. BEFORE WORLD WAR I

The first thing the men would ask when they were hiring on was, "Who's the foreman?" Then they would ask, "Who's the cook?" A cook could make or break a camp.

They thought about food, dreamed about food, talked about food. For months on end their lives were work, food, and sleep. They told time not by hours but by meals, especially on the river drives when they ate four times a day. "It was just before first lunch," the drivers would say, or "It was just after supper." They worked hard in the cold and wet, and burned tremendous amounts of energy. The logging legends of Paul Bunyan are spiced with gargantuan meals: "Hot Biscuit Slim's" Sunday dinners of roast pork, baked trout, cherry pie, and plum puddings; of how "Big Joe," Paul's cousin who came from "three weeks below Quebec," could make pancakes so fast because his griddle was "so big you couldn't see across it when the cookhouse steam was thick."

But in the early 1800s food was scant and monotonous: salt pork, hardtack, dried peas, pearl barley for soup, perhaps a hogshead of rum to ward off "camp fever," and a cask of molasses "to sweeten a decoction usually made of shrubs, or the tops of the hemlock tree, and taken as tea."[1] The cook in those days was a young swamper who remembered how his mother had parboiled salt pork back on the farm. The shantymen sometimes shot game on Sundays but fresh food was rare. Their delight when they got it is recorded in the old Ottawa Valley song, "The Chapeau Boys," which tells how Bob Humphrey, Ned Murphy, and their friends from Allumette Island dined at the Ruddy Farm on their way to log Black River.

> We had roast beef and mutton and good apple pie,
> Good bread and fresh butter which would make you surprise,
> We had cookies, rice pudding, our tea sweet and strong,
> And good early carrots, full six inches long,
> We had good cucumbers and cabbage, boiled and raw,
> And the leg of a beaver Bob stole from a squaw.

Camp meals improved as settlers pushed deeper into the wilderness to supply loggers with fresh food. The logging companies began to hire proper cooks who travelled from job to job with a "turkey," or home-made duffle bag, containing clothes, a bottle of yeast to start the bread and, occasionally, old-timers swear, a live rooster to serve as alarm clock since the cook was the first man up each morning. Until World War Two most cooks were men, except in the Finnish camps in northern Ontario or the small Quebec jobber camps where a *habitant* contracted to cut wood and his wife did the cooking.

Stoves were rare in the camps until the late 1800s and the cook scorched and sweated over an open log fire — the cambuse, the heart of the shanty.

Charles Macnamara, who worked in the Ottawa Valley camps in the second half of the 19th century, described the "camboose":

"It was a square of logs in the middle of the shanty, 12 feet each way, retaining a foot or so of earth and sand on which a fire for heating and cooking burned day and night. Four posts at the four corners rose to the low roof and to one of them was attached the cramier (French *crémaillère*), the ingenious adjustable crane that swung the pots over the fire. One end of the camboose was divided off by a log into a separate trough filled with sand. In this place, known as the bean hole, beans and bread were baked in cast iron kettles buried in hot sand. The 'cook shovel' used to bury the kettles was round-pointed with a short socket into which the cook fitted a long, straight handle. The 'cookery' consisted of about four camp kettles, large iron pots of 10 or 12 gallons with bails and tin covers, seven or eight bake kettles, cast iron 'ovens' 14 to 16 inches in diameter and 4 to 5 inches deep with cast iron covers and lugs, a five-gallon tin tea pail, and a large dishpan. Other appliances were several pairs of pot hooks of various sizes to handle the kettles and pots,

"The camboose cook's utensils and appliances were few. The large pot hanging over the fire was known as a camp kettle; a bake kettle is at the extreme right of the camboose and a tea pail is the second vessel to the left. The pot is hung on the cramier and the height of the pot adjusted by changing the far end of the horizontal bar into one or other of the holes in the vertical post, the bar held in position with a cotter pin. Hanging on the bottom of the cramier is a large, jointed pair of pothooks for handling the big camp kettles. The cook is holding a long-handled shovel used to bury the bake kettles in the hot sand in the trough partly seen along the near edge of the camboose. Paul Kittner was the cook and it was at McDonald shanty on Lake Travers, Black River, on the Ottawa, Nov. 1900."

CHARLES MACNAMARA

Charles Macnamara Collection, Ontario Archives, Courtesy of Mrs. Jean Cunningham, Arnprior, Ont.

what might be called tableware if there had been any table — but there wasn't — were tea dishes (pannikins), tin plates, and soup spoons. No knives or forks were provided. Each man bought a small butcher knife for himself for 25 cents. Between meals it stuck in the wall of the owner's bunk.

"Getting a tea dish, a tin plate, and a hunk of bread from the cook's shelves, the hungry man took whatever food he wanted from the pots and kettles around the fire; then sitting on the bench with his brimming tea dish beside him and his heaped plate on his knee, he proceeded to eat with the ready help of the butcher knife ... With his simple, open fire and his few pots and kettles, it was surprising what well-prepared food the camboose cook could set out."[2]

In the early shanties salt pork was the staple. Baked beans, so much a part of lumber camp life, did not appear until later, first in the Maritimes and then in central Canada in the latter half of the century. Some camps raised their own pigs and the cook stuck them and scalded them in maple sugar cauldrons over a bonfire in the yard and preserved them in saltpetre. Most of the pork was imported, however, first from Ireland and later from Ohio and Chicago. Suppliers called it "heavy mess pork," sides of 250- or 300-pound hogs with the ribs cut out, dry-salted, and shipped in 150-pound cases or pickled in brine in 350-pound barrels. Since the pork was mostly fat, suppliers advertised it, somewhat euphemistically, as "long, clear" pork. Shantymen called it "Chicago chicken," or "Yankee tiger," the latter being "sow belly with the tits of the sow still on it."

It took a good cook to handle those great "bricks" of salt pork. "We tried to cook it, boil it, fry it, but we couldn't eat it at all it was so salt. But those French cooks could cook it all right. I don't know what they did to it but they must have boiled it three days before it came to the table."[3] In Quebec they had learned to broil or fry salt pork into tasty grillades or, blasphemously, "les oreilles de Christ," slices of salt pork which during frying wrinkled up in an arc like an ear. Fried pork was so popular that the *Bytown Gazette* of May 7, 1857, reported "a good deal of excitement" in the camps when the bosses got together and decreed that frying used too much pork and henceforth all pork should be boiled. The shantymen were so incensed the bosses had to rescind their order.

"We'd get long, clear pork in rough boxes like those they used to put coffins in. The men liked that fat pork in winter because they had to have it to keep warm. But you can't boil it all the time. One cook we had, Bob Nesbitt, would cut it, not too thick, and parboil it to take the salt out. Then he'd put brown sugar on it and cut the pieces on a cookie sheet and put that in the oven and by the time it was cooked the grease was out of it and yet it wasn't. Did it ever taste good."[4]

When baked beans finally appeared in the camps the proper place for a fat slice of "long clear" was in a bushel of white beans in an iron pot. Although the Yankees from Boston had introduced baked beans in the Maritimes much earlier, Ulysse Duchine of Lac St. Jean recalled that as late as 1870 in Quebec he was still eating a crude, unappetizing ancestor of the noble baked bean. "The first beans were boiled in water with a white flour sauce. The men didn't like that. Then a cook came from the States, or perhaps he came from Trois-Rivières. His name was William Grant and for the first time he baked beans with pork. When we tasted that we said, 'Ah, that is right. That is correct.'"[5] The Québécois called them *bines* or *fèves au lard* and to the English they were "logging berries" or "echo plums." They were nourishing, delicious, portable, filling, and were served three times a day. "We had plenty of moose meat and fat pork but no potatoes, butter or sugar," H. T. Warne, a shantyman from Digby, Nova Scotia, wrote in the 1880s. "Even with beans 21 times a week we were all well-fed and happy."[6]

The last thing the cook did before he turned in for a few hours sleep was to bury his pot of beans to bake for breakfast. He scooped a 15-inch hole in the sand, lined it with live hardwood coals, put the eight-pound cast-iron pot in the hole, and covered it with a lid, coals, and hot sand. When he awoke before dawn the beans were brown. Shantymen swore that beans or bread or almost anything baked in a bean pot in the sand beat anything baked in an oven.

"The bean pot did its part to develop this country," said Robert J. Taylor of Arnprior, Ontario. "You can't beat an old cast-iron bean pot. I cooked tons of beans but for a special treat I'd take a partridge and put him in the bean pot, cover him with beans, and bake it all. The partridge would come out of there so tender you could just cut it with your fork."

A classic camp recipe of the time ran like this: "The cook sifts and washes 10 quarts of white beans for 40 men. He boils them over the fire. When they seem boiled enough take out a spoonful and blow on them and if the skins start opening up they are ready for the bean pot. Place layers of the cooked beans and large slices of fat, salt pork alternately in the bean pot, seal the lid against the air with a rim of dough and bury in the bean hole. Since the steam does not escape, the fat pork is dissolved by the heat and merges with the beans."

Bread baked in the pot was close grained yet light and of "a delectable, nutty flavour." It was raised with yeast cells mixed with flour and mashed potatoes, but old-time shantymen preferred bread made from fermented sourdough. They insisted the new-fangled yeast bread had no taste and spun yarns to the greenhorns about "Sourdough Sam" who made everything, even coffee, out of sourdough before, poor fellow, he lost an arm and a leg one day when his sourdough barrel blew up.

The ability to bake yeast bread came to be the common test of whether a man could claim to be a cook. "My wife's uncle, he was a good cook, he taught me to make bread. He said, 'I can show you in about three goes, because bread is really the easiest thing in the world to make.' It's the working of the bread that counts, you see, because all that goes into bread is salt, flour, water, yeast cake, fast yeast, although in them days it was always slow yeast, a little butter or fat. But it's the mixing of it, and let it raise, and the panning of it. That's what counts. It's the handling of the bread that counts. Nowadays they don't even bake bread in camp, they buy it."[7]

The iron bean pot was jack-of-all-pots not only for beans and bread but for frying pork, roasting beef, simmering stew and soup, and even for baking pies. "You never ate 'sea pie'? That's too bad. It's something really worthwhile. I used to love sea pie in the bush. You put a crust in the bottom of the pot and then a layer of meat and potatoes and another layer of crust and you put maybe four or five layers. Our cooks used to make it with rump steak every week-end."[8] It was a form of shepherd's pie.

"Raisin pie? When Paddy Kane was cook for us on the St. Maurice drive he says, 'I'll cook yuz a fine pie Sunday. Well, Sunday come and I wanted to see how Paddy made raisin pie in a bean kettle. So he made the fillin' just the same as they do for other raisin pies, then he took the bean pot and put a layer of pie paste in the bottom and another layer around the side and he dumped them raisins into there, put a layer of pie dough on that, and so on until he filled the pot. There were at least 30 men there and Sunday noon we took the pot out of the bean hole to cool and Paddy got out the big spoon. You brought your plate to him and he give you your share and you went off. I thought it was the best bloody raisin pie I ever tasted."[9]

Even when stoves came to the camps in the late 1800s there were cooks who continued to bake beans and bread in the sandy bean hole. Stoves had appeared in the towns before the middle of the century and earlier on the St. Maurice because of the old iron works at Trois-Rivières. There is record of a "three-foot double" stove in a Gatineau camp in 1860 and others scattered here and there. Adam Hall, Limited, of Peterborough, Ontario, made the first steel and iron range in 1878.

"In 1903," said Bob Taylor, "when I first went into the camps on the upper waters of the Madawaska off the Ottawa, they had a big Adam Hall stove and when the meal was ready the men lined up with tin tea dish, tin plate, knife and fork, and helped themselves. There were no tables and chairs so the men sat on their bunks or on

By 1903 a stove had replaced the cambuse fire in the Black River camp on the Quebec side of the Ottawa. "This man's name was Victor Lemaire and he came from Allumette Island. Shantymen looking at this photograph usually exclaim: 'My! What a stylish cook; wearing a necktie!' The fact is that when he saw that I was going to take his picture he went to his bunk and got out the necktie and put it on.

Charles Macnamara Collection, Ontario Archives, Courtesy of Mrs. Jean Cunningham, Arnprior, Ont.

"The stove-cook soon displaced the camboose cook and in a few years it was hard to find a man who knew how to cook in the sand. The bill-of-fare was enlarged with the better cooking facilities of the stove, and pies and cakes appeared on the table. Jam, figs, and cheese were added to the menu. In this shanty there was still no set table. The food was put on the wide shelf behind the cook, where loaves of bread are to be seen, and the large shutter (covered with newspaper) was pulled up, making connection with the main shanty. The men helped themselves, à la cafeteria."

CHARLES MACNAMARA

the grindstones with their plates on their knees just as they had done in the camboose shanty. Two years later they got tables and chairs and it all started getting better all the time."

The quality, quantity, and variety of food varied enormously throughout the years and from camp to camp. In the early years the shanty menus had been pretty well limited to salt pork, hardtack, dried peas, dried apples, and molasses. Later came bread, corned beef, white beans, China tea, sugar, prunes and raisins, fresh beef, vegetables, pies, butter, and jam. The introduction of stoves improved the bill of fare. At one time green tea was so expensive at $1 a pound, a shantyman would have to drink water or spruce tea unless he brought his own tea in from town. Coffee was unknown until Finnish and Scandinavian loggers began to demand it in the 1920s.

Potatoes were a problem because of the need to tote them 30 or 40 miles in freezing weather. Some teamsters defended the notion that so long as potatoes were covered with blankets and straw and the sleigh kept moving, potatoes would not freeze. Lumbermen who did not believe in miracles, however, baked the potatoes, packed them in rows in small barrels, and froze them before toting them to camps in winter.

The bigger camps could usually be counted on to provide good food but few could excel the Goulais River camp of the Algoma Commercial Company of Sault Ste. Marie whose grub list in October 1908 included the following: "Potatoes, carrots, beets, cabbage, sauerkraut, cucumber pickles, wheat flour, boiled oats, corn meal, fresh beef, codfish, pork, raisins, currants, evaporated apples, prunes, jam, figs, beans, barley, tapioca, rice, macaroni, dry split peas, custard, sugar, syrup, corn starch, mince meat and pumpkin pies, tea, and condensed milk and molasses." However, then and even 20 years later, a lumberjack was just as likely to land in a camp which served only beans, prunes, sow belly, good bread, molasses, pies, and tea. Some camps were so remote it was difficult to get provisions to them, and when the diet got too monotonous the men would go out of a Sunday to fish or hunt. "Beaver tasted good. We cooked it up just like beef and it tasted a little like deer."[10]

The worst camps were those run by the poorer sort of "packsack" jobber where food was sometimes such that a northern Ontario cook, George Wilson, tired of fighting with the jobber, laid out plates of hay and bowls of oats for the men one morning and then quit in disgust. "One jobber nearly starved us. He said he couldn't afford more food, he wasn't making enough money. He had a man shooting deer, and give him two cents a pound for the meat and boiled it, and those deer were shot in winter when they were eating only brush. That and bread and potatoes was all we got until we complained so he brought in some beef, but another jobber

205

we worked for was much better and even had hot beef brought out for the midday dinner in the bush."[11]

American outfits operating in Canada were known as good feeders and when a Minnesota firm moved into Blind River in 1928, anxious to hire 2700 men and 900 horses and get out the logs, "we had things we had never seen before, bacon and frozen salmon at 300 pounds to the wooden box, jam, and ham. Jack Smith, when he saw that real ham, said, 'That's the longest pig I ever ate. I've been eating through the fat for years and now I'm on the lean.' They even had lump sugar and the lumberjacks stuffed it in their pockets like candy."[12] When piece-work was introduced in the 1920s, the men had to pay for their meals and during the Depression men were known to work just for bed and board.

Camps that traditionally fed well were those run by Finnish jobbers. "The Finns liked *liha mojakka* and *kala mojakka*, meat stew and fish stew made with potatoes, onions, carrots, cabbage, and spices. Pork was a favourite. At Sunday dinner there was beef with carrot salad. Eggs were served several times a week and sweetened canned milk in 24-ounce tins, and fruit soup, *vellija*, made from blended raisins and prunes, or evaporated pears and apples. Sometimes there was custard and coffee bread coated with sugar syrup with cardamon seeds on it. They had real heavy Finnish pancakes for breakfast, thin, but rather tough, and made from white flour they never seemed to cook right through. They drank lots of coffee, the Finns never cared much for tea. From the Finnish bakers in Sault Ste. Marie they brought in *kovaa leipää* made from rye or wheat flour and half an inch thick and so hard it was a wonder they didn't break their teeth. There was *korppuja*, sugar toast, Finn toast, sweet bread made with white flour and sugar and cinnamon, and they bought that in barrels and they'd dunk it in their coffee. The Finnish lumberjacks also like *kaliaa* made of water, yeast and molasses. It was a mild, cloudy drink, fermented but non-alcoholic, that tasted of molasses diluted with water."[13]

Thousands of tons of food and fodder had to be toted, or "portaged," to the camps on trails that were, from April to December, a nightmare of mud, two-foot ruts, stumps, rocks, and broken wheels. To ease the shocks a teamster's seat was bolted on spring poles although a man was always in danger of being bounced like a jack-in-the-box unless he strapped himself down on his "dry-ass," or bag of hay, which was used as a cushion. "Each teamster had to be able to shoe horses. If we pulled a shoe off up in that rocky country a horse couldn't go a quarter of a mile before his feet were torn up. I lost a wheel once, a front wheel was smashed, so we took a hind wheel and put it on the front and fixed a pole to the hind wheel and used it as a drag. We had to go for miles that way and went in on three wheels, slid right along."[14] A good teamster, with one wheel in a rut and another in the air, could haul 1000 pounds.

On the Restigouche and Kedgwick rivers in New Brunswick they hauled supplies right up the shallow gravel river beds. Three horses, with one rider to guide them all, hauled 70-foot scows which carried five tons. When they struck deep water the tow line was let out to 200 feet and the horses did their pulling from paths on the banks. When bulldozers appeared in the 1940s to build good roads 200 scowmen lost their jobs.

At most camps, however, the rivers were not so accommodating and portaging had to be completed between December and April when the teams could take to the frozen lakes and rivers and when frost and snow had put a firm bottom on the trails.

"From the 15th of January to the 10th of March we hauled in supplies for a year: hay, oats, barrels of pork, flour, tea, anything that wouldn't spoil. We had 150 teams on the road. It was mostly the farmers did that. We had stabling for only 30 horses so the first 30 would start off Monday morning and they would send up 30 every day. It took good horses to stand it."[15]

In northern Ontario one teamster might drive three separate sleighs, walking beside them to keep warm, hoar-frost clinging to beard and brow until he looked like Santa Claus, and children would run out to watch them pass, bells jangling, steam standing up from the horses. In eastern Quebec, on the Saguenay, the Montmorency, or the North Shore, they hired teamsters from the south shore of the St. Lawrence, from L'Islet, St. Edouard de Frampton, and other farming communities. "It reminded me of those great migrations with people and animals in North Africa where they are strung out over miles of road. That's the way it looked when the little villages sent out their teamsters, perhaps 40 or 50 horses, single teams they were in Quebec."[16]

Portage men like Harry Garbison of Plaster Rock, New Brunswick, were famous. One winter's day he and Ernie McQuaid had to dismount to support one side of the sleigh to keep it from tipping. The team stepped ahead and a hogshead smashed, soaking McQuaid in 30-below weather. Harry, who was a small, wiry man with red hair and piercing eyes, loved to swear in colours and blaspheme in verse. He got down on his knees in the snow.

> Dear Lord of Hosts and Holy Ghosts
> And our Sweet Redeeming Jesus
> Come to our aid and save McQuaid
> Before the bastard freezes.

Since most of the eastern camps were empty all summer, food for the next season was stored in caches, or "keep-overs," which were

207

On the Restigouche River, in New Brunswick, horse-towed scows were used to tote supplies to camp. The 70-foot scows could carry five to seven tons. The three-horse teams, good swimmers with strong nerves, were trained when they were young and there were few drownings. When the scows came to deep water the horses would tow them from trails along the banks.

New Brunswick Provincial Archives

Toting, or "portaging," half a ton of supplies to camp near Iroquois Falls in northern Ontario. The two pulp cutters walking on the old corduroy road have tossed their duffle bags on the heavy wagon as well. A camp of 100 men and 20 horses consumed 1700 pounds of food and fodder every day and getting supplies over rough trails was a constant problem.

Abitibi Paper Co. Ltd.

208

log structures guarded by a watchman. Once a week he would up-end the bags and barrels to keep flour from "dying" and would shovel over the loose oats so they would not overheat and sprout or go musty. Brine barrels of pork, buried six feet deep, were dug up once each summer and if the brine had become strong enough to float a potato the liquid would be drained off and replaced. That was a big job in the camps of the McLachlin Brothers of Arnprior who brought 1000 barrels of pork to the Ottawa Valley in 10 carloads every December. Sometimes there were other problems. "The log drivers would bury a barrel of pork here and a barrel of pork there so they would have it for the drive in the spring. So the Indians there got wise and started to steal the pork, but Indians are very superstitious so the drive men decided to dig a grave and put a couple of barrels of pork in it and set up a little fence and a cross. The Indians were afraid to go near it and would pray for it instead of stealing it and the drivers would have their pork next year."[17] Most keep-over watchmen did not mind the solitude but there were cases when a foreman would return in the autumn to find his watchman "out of his head."

With such supply and storage difficulties the camp cooks were often called upon to improvise. "If you take raisins," said one, "you can make just as good apple sauce as you can with prunes." One cook's application for a job in northern Ontario rested on the boast that, "If we run out of pumpkins I can make pumpkin pie out of turnips and they won't know the difference."

Cooks came and went and varied tremendously. "We had more trouble with the cooks than with anyone else," said foreman Vic Hamilton who worked in camps around Chapleau. "It was a seven-day-a-week job, early and late. Ten men might sit down to eat supper and then an hour later 50 would get off the train and the cook would have to turn around and feed them, too."

Another foreman remembered they fired a cook every week for three weeks because the men kept getting diarrhoea. But lack of hygiene did not necessarily mean poor cooking, particularly on river drives where no one could keep clean anyway. "Old Paddy Kane, you never saw a blacksmith any blacker, and all he had on was a pair of calk boots, his mackinaw pants, and his woollen undershirt and an old felt hat with the band all gone so it looked like a hat you'd use to put in a funnel when you strained the gas. But Paddy could make the best pies you ever tasted. Charlie McKeer's cook on the same river, now he was something else. That fella, he had a white hat, white coat, white pants, but all he could feed his crew was biscuits and bean soup. He couldn't cook in the sand. He didn't know anything about it."[18]

No one seemed to mind too much if a cook was temperamental;

he was an artist who faced a critical audience at least twice a day. John Kelly, who was a teamster as well as a cook and served as a Chief Petty Officer in the galleys of the navy during World War Two, was merely "a bit nervous." "If a lumberjack didn't kick he wasn't healthy. There'd be something wrong with him, but they never kicked in front of the cook. That's why it made you nervous. You didn't know if they were kicking or no." Sometimes, in slyly criticizing a cook within his hearing, they might start telling Paul Bunyan stories of the cook who used so much grease he had to wear calked boots to keep from sliding right out the cookhouse door, or of the cook who had learned only to boil and did his cooking solely with a dipper. But if the cook was good he commanded respect.

— "Really the important man in the camp was the man who filled a fella's stomach. I know some cooks that was cross as hell but they were good and everybody put up with them. What's the use of having a nice fella if you get raw biscuits? When you were cooking in there you had to be the boss. There was no talk at the table. Absolute silence."[19]

— "Those cooks were strict. I remember at Lake Nipigon there was Joe Gordon from Fort Frances. He was a good cook but if anyone came in their undershirt or talked at the table he would go up to them and say, 'Out!' The first thing he'd do when he come out of the kitchen would be to grab that big butcher knife and walk down the aisle. I don't think he ever intended to use it but with him there was no talking."[20]

The origin of the monastic rule of silence at mealtime is obscured in the steamy past of the old cookhouses but Adélard Beaulne, who went to work in the camps at the age of 12 in 1918, had the simplest reason of all: "Quand on parle on mange pas."

— "After a while it got to be a matter of pride and you would not only be silent but you'd eat as quickly as possible. The foreman had to be the first through at any meal. Literally not one word was said except 'pass the bread' or something like that. But that all went out with the coming of the unions for to attract labour you had to make the place a little more home-like and in some cases talking was actually encouraged."[21]

— "Those fellas, they'd go in and they'd eat great big meals of meat, potatoes, pie, and stuff themselves. They had to do it in 10 or 15 minutes. Eat and get out. The cook didn't want the men to talk and loiter. We did a big business in Perry Davis Pain Killer and Enos Fruit Salts. At Iroquois Falls I said, 'These fellas have got to have at least 25 minutes or half an hour to eat,' so we finally got so they could talk and take their time. Our sales of Enos dropped off."[22]

The cook's assistants, called "cookees" in the east and "flunkies" on the west coast, were generally young men, new to the camp, the butt of practical jokes, the greenhorns sent to "fetch the bean hole." It was the cookee's job to blow the Gabriel horn, the three-foot tin trumpet that preceded the "gut iron," the big iron triangle that hung outside and summoned the men to meals. The "Gabreel" horn sounded like a moose — at least the moose thought so because sometimes there would be a moose on the other side of the lake answering it.

Then there was the "bull cook," an ironic title since he was no cook at all but a choreboy who cleaned the bunkhouse, carried wood and water, and was usually an aging lumberjack who could no longer work out in the bush. In Quebec choreboy was pronounced and spelled "showboy" from Gaspé to the Ottawa.

"At half past four in the morning," said Ralph Mills of Wawa, "the cookees set the tables, mixed a bunch of milk, half powdered skim milk and half canned, a couple of pailfuls. You rang the wake-up bell, dinga-dinga-dinga, with all your might at 5:30, half an hour before breakfast, and got out of the way of the thunderin' herd. That year at Magpie was the coldest I remember. We had a thermometer outside the cookhouse door and every day for a week it was 56 below zero. It was so cold I went out one morning, and my hands were wet, and I grabbed the iron bar. It was red hot. My hand blistered all up. After breakfast you cleaned the table off in a hurry to put out a bunch of junk for lunch: eggs left over from breakfast, cold, and nice and gooey, jam and cheese. In that camp they made their own sandwiches. They put their lunch in little canvas bags. Then you had to wash and dry the dishes, pots and pans, reset the table, butter and sugar, sets for every six guys. You'd peel spuds and turnips and cut up the meat. They'd take the frozen quarters into the cookhouse and saw it up when they had steak. They put it in a big roasting pan two feet long and stewed it. They were good meals but plain. Lots of rhubarb pie. The men used to take a chunk of that and pour corn syrup right to it. They ate their meal in 15 minutes and at 6:20 their supper was all over and you'd get into the dishes again and set the tables and at eight o'clock they were back for coffee with big barn door cookies made from lemon extract."

During the manpower shortage of the Second World War women were more frequently seen in the cookhouse, usually as cookees and sometimes as cooks, but even then women were only about two and a half per cent of the total work force in the woods. "The men never bothered women in the camps. They were more gentlemanly in the bush than they were in town."[23]

Noon meals were eaten out on the job. If the men were working far from camp they might tote a cotton bag with a cold lunch of salt pork, bread, molasses, and toast the bread on sticks over a fire

211

The Public Archives of Canada   PA 12609

Ottawa Valley camp cook and his two bowler-hatted "cookees" and the camp choreboys early in this century. It was the custom, almost a matter of honour, not to wear a coat around camp even in the coldest weather.

"At the dinnering out place," said W. H. Merleau of Maniwaki, up the Gatineau River in Quebec, "you'd have boiled pork and tea and a pail of molasses and toast your bread on a long stick in the fire and dip it in the molasses. You'd get some days 25 or 30 degrees below zero and you'd get a big fire started. In those days you were healthy and could take anything."

Ont. Ministry of Natural Resources

A pre-World War II cook camp, as the cookhouse was often called, ready for the supper rush with bread and bottles of maple syrup and graniteware dishes laid out and cooks and cookees standing by. In bush camps several days from the nearest town, with lumberjacks burning twice the calories of any city worker, the cooks could make or break logging operations.

The Public Archives of Canada
C 57057

and brew up strong and scalding tea. "Those fellows dinnering out would sit there with a rectangle of pork, about all fat, and a piece of bread, and with a jack-knife they'd cut off a cold cube of pork fat and a piece of bread and they'd chew them together."[24] If the work was a mile or two from camp there might be a lunch sleigh with a long box with a cover on it. The cook would prepare roast pork with gravy, all in special wooden containers with screw tops; also potatoes, and pies right out of the oven and still warm when they got to the men.

"There would be logs around for the men to sit on and a big fire but on a real cold day your plate would soon freeze. After they ate the men would leave their plates with meat and beans froze on them. The ravens and squirrels and meat birds and chickadees — the whiskey jacks or 'lumberjacks' or gorbeys — would gather around and come on your plate. The men had to hide their lunch bags so the ravens wouldn't eat their food."[25] There was a superstition that the grey, uncrested Canada Jay was really the ghost of dead lumberjacks. "I remember hearing about this man in New Brunswick, he worked as a teamster for Walter Clark. He caught this Canada Jay and pulled all its feathers out and then let it go, naked as a jay bird as the saying goes. It froze to death. Well, they say, when the teamster woke up next morning his head was as bald as that table."[26]

If the day was not too cold the "dinnering out" could be a pleasant break and was the sole place where the men could talk, and gripe, and even criticize the cook, while eating a meal.

"I liked cooking because the cook was really the most important man in camp." Having worked as jobber and camp clerk Len Shewfelt of Thessalon knew who was important. "At Camp 30 we had 200 men and we had to make every minute count. We'd have some things ready the night before and would get up an hour and a quarter before breakfast. There was a bedroom off the cookery for the cookhouse staff. Things were clean, you could almost eat off the cookhouse floor. As the cookees were serving breakfast I would get my pie filling ready and cooking. Then I'd turn to punching bread. After breakfast I'd start on my pies, 60 every morning, a pie a minute. A housewife making a pie might take 20 minutes but we made a pie a minute. You'd have only one handle on your rolling pin and keep your other hand right on the pin. On one end of the bread board you'd have flour and dip the pie dough in it and knock the flour off, it browns your pastry. I had an oven boy and all he did was watch the cookies and pies while they were baking. We had three big Adam Hall stoves and could make 24 at a time. I used to make 90 dozen cookies of various kinds. By the time I got my pies made I'd swing into the cookies and cup cakes and by then the bread would be ready to pan and you'd make big loaves, five in each long sheet-iron pan, 40 or 50 loaves at a time. It was all wood fires, maple and white birch and tamarack in the early morning to heat up the building although tamarack is too hot for baking. They would have pancakes every morning and we'd fry big pans of steak the night before and then simmer it so it had nice gravy. The men put the steaks on their pancakes. Every Sunday there'd be toast but you couldn't do that every morning because it would be too hard on your bread supply. We used to get our work done so there would not be too much to do on Sunday but there would be little extras, puddings and so on which you wouldn't have time to make on weekdays. To save the boys peeling too many potatoes, on Sunday we'd have baked potatoes and cold meats Sunday nights. There were always prunes on the table and sometimes we'd make prune pies or fig pies or pies from canned pumpkin and canned apples. After we started getting eggs in camp we made custard pies. 'Shoepack pie' was an imitation lemon pie made from cornstarch and a bit of vinegar. Stew and dumplings we had for supper. It was good, healthy food, maybe a whole lot better than we have today so far as nutrients go. The men I knew didn't do any kicking but then they didn't do any praising either."

Company-run camps fed the best and a Sunday menu in one of the better camps in 1935 read as follows:

Breakfast
oatmeal, stewed prunes
pork and beans — bologne — toast
raisin pie — ginger cake
bread — butter — sugar — molasses
tea — coffee — cheese

Dinner
pea soup — pot roast — mashed potatoes — mustard — pickled onions
steamed rice pudding, nutmeg sauce — blancmange — pie
bread — butter — sugar — syrup
tea — milk — sugar —cheese

Supper
pea soup
beef— cold salt pork — mustard
sugar pie — raisin pie — molasses cookies
bread — butter — molasses
tea — milk — sugar — cheese

At Arnprior in the Ottawa Valley, Bob Taylor, slim and spry at 90, sat amid his collection of antique bean pots, kettles, axes, harness, and muskets.

Pulp cutters' cook camp in northern Ontario. "They'd eat at long tables in those days, 20 or 30 men to a table. Everything was served right on the table and the men helped themselves. Later, in the 1940s, they got to the cafeteria system with the men lining up.

"I used to love the cookery," said Jack Matthews. "I used to go in there in the morning, steam over everything, and the table loaded down with food. At one camp they had big platters with a pyramid of T-bone steaks on them that high for breakfast."

Abitibi Paper Co. Ltd.

Everything, including the cookhouse, was on a grand scale in coastal British Columbia. This 1926 company camp on the mainland near Stillwater boasted not only the cook in his white hat, but a whole brace of flunkies, chore-boys, and a mascot in a stew pot. On the left is the "gut iron," a round piece of railway steel hammered to signal mealtime.

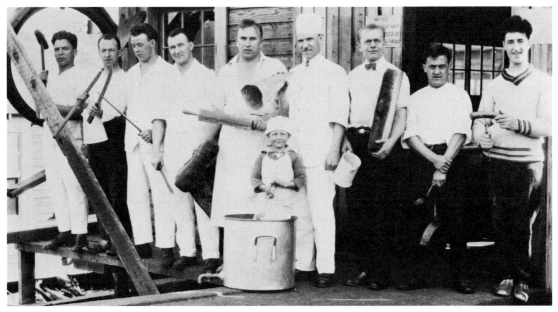

Provincial Archives, Victoria, B.C.

"I cooked in the camps for over 30 years. When I think of it now — it's hard work. I've been in camps where I had to get up at 1 A.M. On the river drives the cook was up at all hours. When I was cookee I never got time to peel potatoes in the daytime, there was so much work, so I had to peel three-quarters of a bag at night when supper was over. We had to give them meat three times a day. It was quite a job makin' pancakes for a bunch of men, a great smokin' griddle on top of the stove. To keep them fresh you had somebody to help. You'd have a stick with a rag tied to it for a swab and you'd grease it and dip the pancakes on and flop them over and fill up the plates, hundreds of pancakes.

"I used to make pea soup, rice soup, bean soup — anything soup. Raisin was their favourite pie. Roast beef was pretty near their favourite, or roast pork. We gave them meat three times a day. There were always some to complain about the cooking. Some would come in growling in the morning and others would come in all cheerful and smiling away.

"One spring I was cookin' on the river drive and some men came in to join the drive and wherever they'd come from they brought the measles. So we moved out into the tents in April — it was cold — there was snow on the ground. I always used to like to go out on the logs on a drive so I got a pike pole and got out on a log and would put the pike pole in the water and walk along the log and have a little 'sail.' But this time when I tried to pull up the pike pole it stuck on the bottom and I fell into the icy cold water. I could swim and I swum ashore and went into the tent and changed my clothes. I put on a fresh pair of winter underwear and a sweater and coat and got the men their supper and I made a big dish of hot ginger and wrapped myself in blankets and the next morning when I woke up I was red as a piece of flannel. As soon as the foreman saw me he said, 'You got the measles.' He said, 'You get into the blankets again and stay there.' I stayed there for three days and just lie there and told the choreboy and his helper what to do. That was in 1909 out of Whitney. Nowadays if anyone fell into ice cold waters and you had the measles people would think you would die.

"It used to be a seven-day week for the cooks, no such thing as an eight-hour day and no two-weeks holiday with pay. You'd not be through working until 9 o'clock at night and you'd roll up in the blankets until 4 A.M. Sundays were the same although I tried not to bake bread or cakes on Sunday. For years I spent every Christmas in camp, just the same as any other day. The men would not work Christmas day but of course the cooks did. The men just lay around like on a Sunday, smokin' or doing their washing or playing cards.

"I was 16 when I first went into the camps, in 1903. I had been living on the farm with my father. In those days there were no factories to work in as there are now so the young fellows went to the bush.

"Shanty life, they say it's hard but happy. I'd like to go back where there's any loggin' but it's so different now. . . they say. But in the old days men worked hard and I always tried to give them as good a meal as I could. It was hard work. Those 30 years along the Madawaska Valley at the turn of the century will never be repeated. Times change, logging has changed, the bush is ever-changing. The old-time loggers have long since been replaced by the new breed. However, the new ones in their return to the Valley to log the new growth must at times catch an unconscious glimpse of our days of logging, for it was only 75 years ago and the sapling is barely a full grown tree."

13 THE MIGRANTS

The long steel rails that have no end have taught me for to roam ...
They've taught me to leave my happy home.

TO THE PINES — TRADITIONAL

There were few trades more migratory than logging. If a man squared timber on the Ottawa there was a chance that he, or his son, would later be found hewing pine or cutting sawlogs around Lake Huron or even in Michigan and his grandson might be found bucking pulpwood amid the lonely lakes of northeast Ontario. Shantymen "followed the pine" and when pine ran thin they moved.

They moved from New Brunswick into Maine and on west, leaving a trail of stumps in New Hampshire, Vermont, and Tupper Lake in upper New York State. In the boom years after the American Civil War Canadian lumberjacks, riding the new railroads, arrived in Michigan in their thousands from the Maritimes, Quebec, and southern Ontario. By 1900 more than half the lumberjacks in Maine were "Provincemen" from the Maritimes or French Canadians from Quebec. "In New Brunswick you never counted for anything unless you had put in a winter in Maine. That made you a man. Some of the best lumberjacks in Maine were from the Maritimes. The Canadians made Maine."[1]

For generations, wood cutters from villages like St. Georges and St. Joseph in the farmlands south of the St. Lawrence had been crossing the American border in their tuques, red sashes, and homemade *bottes sauvages*, or knee-high moccasin boots. In the 1870s they were joined by *bûcherons* from the Lac St. Jean region. Cana-

"Every Wednesday night, Fraser's Special went up. That was the train you didn't have to pay — they'd give you a ticket and you could go as far as Plaster Rock from Newcastle, New Brunswick, on that train. It went right up the Miramichi River. You were 'going up for Frasers.' "

WILMOT MACDONALD, CHATHAM, N.B.

New Brunswick Provincial Archives

dian loggers paid little heed to borders or to the Yankee loggers who resented "Canucks" because they worked for lower wages than Americans would accept. American foremen, who knew good lumberjacks when they saw them, often came up themselves to hire men. Jigger Jones, who was probably the most colourful American foreman and liked to prove it by walking barefoot outdoors around his camp in the dead of winter, would make hiring trips to Sherbrooke, Quebec. "In Maine they were all French in the camps I was in. A foreman, he'd come to the church where we lived near Rivière-du-Loup and when the boys came out he'd announce what men were needed. When I first went to work in Maine I was 16 and we walked 40 miles through the bush to get to the camp."[2]

The logging legends of Saginaw or Bay City in upper Michigan, which was once the greatest pine producer in the world, are salted with the exploits of Joe Fournier from Quebec who was so tough everyone said he had a double row of teeth, or T. C. Cunnion, the "Peterborough Man-eater" from Ontario who wrestled bulldogs for fun and profit. The best-known Canadian in the Michigan woods was another Peterborough man, Silver Jack Driscoll, foreman, brawler, a giant with prematurely silver hair, who ran with a pal called "Pig Iron Jack." Driscoll, who boasted he could fell an ox with his fist and twist horseshoes with his bare hands, surprisingly died in his bed in 1895.

When lumber barons such as Isaac Stephenson from New Brunswick opened up the Wisconsin woods the Canadian lumberjacks followed. "There were thousands of them in the Menominee area, from the Miramichi and the Ottawa, the latter mostly Quebec French. At one community called Frenchtown there must have been six or seven thousand of them."[3] Many stayed, as the present-day telephone books in some of the Lake State lumbering towns will testify.

For almost a century men born on Canadian bush farms and apprenticed as boys to the camps had been the core of the logging industry. It was usual for boys to go to school until they were 12 or 13 and then go to work in the bush.

In an interview before he died in 1937 Joseph Tremblay said, "I went to the shanties in 1861 when I was 12 on Lac des Isles (now in Laurentide Park, Quebec). You had to walk seven miles from camp to the depot and portage provisions on foot, with 60 pounds on your back. The rest of the time you were cutting roads and felling trees. Many's the evening I spent on a stump crying. In those early years they employed lots of boys 12 to 15 years old and they were kept on when the camps closed to prepare for the drive and make black spruce pike poles to roll logs into the river."[4] By the 1920s the usual starting age was 16 or 17. "When I first started to work," said Geoff Randolph, "I bought a crooked-stem pipe so I would look like a man and went to Mr. Scott in Fredericton and said, 'Are you looking for men?' He said, 'Yes, where are they?' I said, 'I'm him.' It was 44 miles to camp on the Magaguadavic Lake and we carried our 'turkey,' or home-made packsack, and our blankets and looked like a walking caravan."

Shortly after the turn of the century, however, such traditional labour was getting scarce in the hiring halls, in Ottawa, at least. The May 1904 edition of the *Canada Lumberman* lamented that times were changing. "Until recent years the supply of men was equal if not greater than the demand . . . (but) the hardy, contented lumberjack of former years is surely passing from the land. High wages in other lines of industrial activity and the prospect of an all-year residence in town or city have lured men of the able-bodied fraternity from the (timber) limits." The *Canada Lumberman* lamented particularly that the French Canadians, at least for the time, had become less plentiful.

The *Canada Lumberman* need not have worried; under the Laurier government's open-door immigration policy of 1896 a new supply of bush workers was flowing into Canada from Europe. Some lacked experience and aptitude and brought instability to the camps — it was around that time the complaint of the foremen was born: "There was," they used to say, "one man coming, one going, and one working." The Scandinavians, however, and particularly the Finns and the Swedes, took to the work as if they had been born to it, as indeed many of them were. The Scandinavian forests were much like the lake-strewn Boreal Forests of Canada.

Although some Swedes logged in northern Ontario, a larger number went to the west coast, the biggest influx occurring between the early 1900s and about 1930. In May of 1903 the *Canada Lumberman* estimated that only 10 per cent of British Columbia loggers were Scandinavians, the rest being native Canadians, Americans, and Britons. By 1934 the proportions had changed to such an extent that a forester at Camp 6 on Cowichan Lake, Vancouver Island, estimated that more than half the loggers there were Finns and Swedes.

In northern Ontario, the Finns began to appear by the turn of the century, particularly around the Lakehead, Sault Ste. Marie, and Sudbury. Fred Niemi's father, William, was one of the first Finnish lumbermen to settle in the Algoma district around Sault Ste. Marie.

"Father had 50 or 60 men in his pulp camp around 1914, 99 per cent Finnish, a few Swedes. The French Canadians had not arrived up here yet. Later, Leonard Lafleur came up from Fassett, Quebec, on the Ottawa River, and brought a French crew. That was my first contact with the French and they were a good lot to get along with.

"Some of them were tremendous pulpwood cutters. The average was a cord and a half of four-foot bolts which meant a lot of cuts with the saw. It was nothing for Art Lampi to cut three cords a day, day in and day out, six days a week.

"A typical Finnish lumberjack, a *kämppä jätkä*, in the old days was a hard-drinking, hard-working man, maybe 75 per cent had no families here. Many would go up there and work to beat the band for six or eight months and then come down and sit in a hotel and drink it up and go back to the bush, shaky and broke, in a month or two, and then do it all over again. Quite a few had left wives and families in Finland, came over here, and worked all those years in this country, and sent monthly remittances to their people in Finland and never went back, never saw their families again. Worked here, died here, and their families never came over. Sometimes they'd sing songs in a homesick vein, sing and hum to themselves to release their feelings. There were Red Finns who favoured a Russian form of government and White Finns who didn't, but there were never any open fights in the camps over this. They were very hard working and apart from poker and listening to an accordion on Saturday nights they might have a dance and polka if there were three or four women in the cookery. We had Poles, Ukrainians, Czechs, Austrians, and a few Serbians at various times but there was no rivalry or bitterness."

The Finns particularly took to pulpwood cutting and by the 1920s their numbers had greatly increased. One of them, for a time, was Oscar Tokia who had been Prime Minister of Finland until, ousted by the Reds, he had fled to Canada with 38 countrymen. In the winter of 1921 he and his followers were working in the lumber industry at North Timiskaming, northern Ontario.

Frank Moran of Thunder Bay recalled he encountered his first Finns when he went to work in the woods, at the age of 17, in 1919. To get to the camp he had to walk 50 miles to the Black Sturgeon River. "I was green as could be, sitting there all by myself when the camp filled up with Finlanders. I'd never seen any before. Hardly anyone could say a word in English. I went up to a group of young Finns sitting around the table playing cards and I said, 'Would one of you fellows show me how to put my tools together?' One young fellow understood me and although he couldn't talk much English he said, 'Sure,' and by gosh he showed me how to sharpen my scoring axe and broad-axe and put my saw together and filed it and everything and, Gee, he looked after me like a brother and here I was a perfect stranger."

Fred Borrett recalled that those who spoke English would sleep

Finnish pulpwood cutters take a sauna bath at the Regan camp, east of Lake Superior, in 1950. The Finns brought the sauna to the camps. "In the early days," said Fred Niemi, "around 1911, it was just a big log cabin with an empty kerosene barrel for a stove and rocks piled around it. There was no stove-pipe and smoke would billow out of a seven-inch opening in the roof. Later they added a chimney. They took a sauna bath twice a week and would use cedar switches to work up a sweat and then jump out into the snow. In Finnish camps the sauna would be the first building to go up. It was very important."

Abitibi Paper Co. Ltd.

William Niemi's Finnish logging camp on Achigan Creek on the Algoma Central Railway, 38 miles north of Sault Ste. Marie, Ont., in 1912. The Finns had a reputation for neatness and hard work which was reflected in camps like these where women were the cooks.

Courtesy Fred Niemi, Sault Ste. Marie, Ont.

in one bunkhouse and the Ukrainians and Poles, who did not speak English, slept in another. "Lots didn't speak English, you'd see fellows out five years and couldn't speak English but we got along ok with them. There was an odd one prejudiced against foreigners but most got along well. Matt Brown, the barn boss, was as black as coal. He moved into the English bunk house and said, 'If it keeps on like this there'll be no place for us white fellows at all.' "[5]

In the early 1930s, the Depression brought new men to the woods looking for work, some wearing city shoes and carrying straw suitcases, with little or no experience at camp labour.

"During the Depression," said Hulme Stone, "10 or 12 fellas every other day might drop off the way freight at the camp. Those fellows were starving to death and trying to get work. They ranged in age from 18 to 40, some even had engineering degrees. This was below zero, in winter in northern Ontario, with no train again until the next day. But our camps were full, we couldn't hire them. So old Steve Gillis, a Nova Scotian from Antigonish, said to me, 'What can we do?' So I said, 'Well, Steve, supposing you gave them supper and a good breakfast, round up all the old newspapers you can get and inch-thick slices of bread and put a slab of beef in between and wrap it up in the newspaper and give it to them as they go by and see they get on the train. I never added up how much it cost. I was scared to. We were in receivership in those days. If we had openings we would hire them, but then World War Two came and it was different — we had trouble hiring men."

By 1940 there was a serious manpower shortage in the camps. Other industries were expanding rapidly and men were going into defence industries where the pay was better and they could work in town. To attract labour, camps were improved with better heating, lighting, and ventilation. Transportation and mail service improved and some recreation facilities were provided. Average bush camp wages, which had lagged behind the national industrial average by a considerable amount in 1939, were increased. But during the war the shortage was acute. Loggers by the thousands, perhaps 12 000, had gone into the armed forces, including 7000 who went overseas with the Canadian Forestry Corps. The shortage resulted in one of the most curious, and little known, episodes in camp history. For three years the pulpwood camps of northern Ontario were filled with German prisoners of war who cut wood to keep the mills running. There were almost 9000. The scheme was more ambitious than a similar one tried in the latter years of World War One when the workers used tended more often to be "foreign nationals," aliens from hostile European countries who had been interned for the duration of the war.

"We would have closed down in 1944 if it wasn't for the

P.O.W.s," said Al Buell who ran camps in northern Ontario. "We couldn't get labour. It was relatively easy to teach the Germans to fell trees but it was hard to teach them to handle horses. Most were mechanics, teachers, anything but lumberjacks. They had grey wool shirts with a big red patch on the back. There were 10 Canadian Veterans Guards (men who had served in the First World War and were too old to go overseas) for every 100 prisoners. The prisoners were sometimes divided into 'whites,' who were anti-Nazi, 'greys,' who were in the German army because they had no choice, and 'blacks,' who were real storm-trooper types. Ours were all storm-troopers, 530 of them."

The P.O.W.s, many of them veterans of Rommel's Afrika Korps, came to work in the woods under Order-in-Council PC 2326 in 1943 which authorized the Minister of Labour to use them on various projects across the country. The equivalent of a regular logger's pay for each man was sent to the Department of Labour but a prisoner himself got only 50 cents a day, and his bed and board.

"I was at Magpie Junction in northern Ontario," said Jack Mills, "when information reached us that 100 prisoners would arrive, and when this news got around the women living at Magpie went into seclusion, evidently under the impression that being ship wrecked on an uninhabited island with a sex-starved stoker would be a ball compared to what they could expect if the prisoners got out of hand. When the train arrived the ladies were surprised to see a snappy, clean-shaven, efficient group of 100 German Air Force men. They were dressed in German uniforms bearing the Nazi insignia and had a 'leader,' or 'speaker,' who was a senior non-commissioned officer. They were required to cut and pile three-quarters of a cord of four-foot wood per man per day but in many cases they produced their week's quota in two or three days and could take the rest of the week off to go fishing."

"There was no barbed wire or anything," said Wes McNutt of North Bay. "If they wanted to escape they'd just go down the road and there was a big sign there which said 'Boundary' and all they had to do was go past that sign and sit down and they had 'escaped' and were sent to Port Arthur for 28 days in detention. There was one fellow a bit older than the rest; I kinda got to like him, and I said, 'Franz, why do you fellas do this?' 'Well,' he said, 'I come from Cologne, I'm a city boy, and I get so lonesome out here in the bush — when they send me to Port Arthur I can look out the barracks window and see the street cars.' A lot of them were pretty good Joes, you know, just ordinary guys. But they got hard to manage toward the end of the war."

"There had been the Battle of the Bulge where the Germans damn near broke through in Europe and the P.O.W.s got pretty

Provincial Archives, Victoria, B.C.

By the 1920s logging camps in coastal British Columbia were running heavily to Swedes and Finns although they had made up only 10 per cent of the work force 20 years earlier. They were good fallers and buckers. Steam engineers on the donkey engines and locomotives, however, tended to be English, Irish, and Scottish. These bunkhouses at Lamb's lumber camp at Menzies Bay in 1926 were portable, housing eight men each and moving by rail from place to place.

Ontario Forest Industries Association

German prisoners of war, a tell-tale red diamond patch sewn on their grey jerseys, unloading eight-foot pulpwood at Long Lac, Ontario, during World War II. The thousands of P.O.W.s, many of them veterans of Rommel's Afrika Korps, kept the pulp mills running during the wartime labour shortage.

unruly," said Gordon Ball, who was Walking Boss in Magpie River camps near Wawa. "They knew what was going on from the radios and newspapers we let them have. They decided they could do their little bit by not working, especially once they got the idea the pulp they were cutting was being used for gun cotton in guns killing Germans in Europe. So they went on a sit-down strike and we told the government, 'We have to get this wood out before the end of March so you have to get these fellows to work or get them out and put in civilians who will do it.' It was in the dead of winter but the military got cracking and a colonel came up from North Bay with 40 soldiers. They went from camp to camp locking the P.O.W.s up on bread and water. They'd have bread and water for three days and then what was called a 'stirrup cup' which were pretty poor rations for three days and then back to bread and water. After 10 days of that they were ready to go back to work they were so hungry. We had to rest them for a couple of days, you can't imagine how effective bread and water is. Before that they were shouting, yelling, whistling, and when they came out they were different people."

When the German prisoners were sent home in 1946 and their departure left a shortage in the camps, their places were sometimes taken, with some irony, by Europeans "displaced" by the German Army during the war. Going to the camps was a quick way for displaced persons to get to Canada and at one time there were more than 3000 in the camps. They included clerks and professional men, and one foreman claimed he had encountered a former ballet dancer. They were unused to such work, had been badly nourished during the war years in Europe, and most left the woods after their year of indenture was over.

Despite such migratory ebb and flow the regional aspect of the camps remained clearly defined. New Brunswick camps were filled with men of Scots, English, and Irish descent and with French Acadians. In Quebec the lumberjacks were mostly French. In the Ottawa Valley the Yankee pioneers the Wrights were followed by Scots, Irish, English, Poles, and finally a preponderance of French. In northern Ontario there were Finns, French, Anglo-Saxons, Slavs, and Swedes.

In British Columbia the pioneer loggers, Americans and New Brunswickers, were joined by Swedes, Finns, Norwegians, and, in later years, some French from Quebec, and in the bush, as well as the mills, turbaned East Indian Sikh, Japanese, and Chinese loggers. In fact the Chinese might claim to be the first professional loggers working on the coast. In 1788 a Captain James Meares, an Englishman who sailed the China coast, brought 40 Chinese wood-cutters to Vancouver Island to cut trees to build a ship for the Chinese fur trade.

14 THE BUNKHOUSE BOYS

Some of the camps were pretty crowded. As one fella said,
"I've been putting socks on now for half an hour but none on my
own feet."

GEOFF RANDOLPH, MONTREAL, QUEBEC

When Bob Taylor first went to camp in 1903 the stove had just replaced the open-hearth cambuse in the shanties on the Madawaska south of the Ottawa. "The camp was a big, 40-foot building with two skylights but no windows and only one door. As you came in there was a water barrel and a big trough with half a dozen wash-basins. There were rows of bunks, two up, two down; two men slept in one bunk, 'muzzle loaders' we called them because you had to crawl in from one end. There was a bench went all around the rows of bunks, a log hewed on one side with wooden pins for legs. There was the cook's corner where he did all the cooking and everything was all under one roof. When a meal was ready the men lined up and took their tin plate, tea dish, knife and fork, and went to the table beside the stove and helped themselves. There was no such thing as tables or chairs. The men had to sit on the bunks or a block of wood with plate on their knees, but in 1905 they got tables in there and it started gettin' a little better all the time."

It took a dozen men two weeks to build a camp from spruce or pine logs with bark left on to hold a caulking of moss and lime. There were skylights but rarely windows in the early days. This kept the shanty warm and was regarded as no great hardship because the men rarely saw the bunkhouse in daylight except on Sundays. They worked from starlight to starlight, left the bunkhouse

A Miramichi, New Brunswick, lumber camp in 1898 — the type known as a "ragged cabin." It was built of chopped logs not evened at the corner, and roofed with "shakes" split from cedar blocks. The cook stands at the door of the "men's end." The man at right stands at the door of the "dingle," or storage room.

New Brunswick Provincial Archives

The Public Archives of Canada   PA 8394

The old-style bunkhouses could get pretty crowded, but not with furniture. About the only furnishings besides the bunks and stove in this one, at the turn of the century, were a bench or two and a grindstone.

"You were allowed three blankets. For a mattress you cut fir boughs and one blanket went over that, then two over you and there was always a little shelf for your doo-dads. Later on they cut out the double decker bunks since the man up top sweated to death and if you were below you were always getting his feet in your face. Then a government law came in and there had to be beds, two feet apart, and each man had to have a little box to keep his possessions in."

GEOFF RANDOLPH

before dawn and returned after sunset to dry their socks, eat supper, and sharpen axe and saw.

"You'd be lyin' around waitin' for lights out at nine o'clock and fellows would sing. Some couldn't carry a tune and would sound like a cat hollering but you never heard any dirty songs in camp."[1] Someone might play harmonica or fiddle or tell stories until the choreboy came in and called out, 'Ten to Nine!' and threw green hardwood into the stove. At nine o'clock he snuffed the coal-oil lamps. The lumberjacks were far too weary to hear the wolves howling on the hills or the snoring in the next bunk.

"At Magaguadavic Lake in New Brunswick," said Geoff Randolph, "the camp was a little grim. No mattresses, you made those yourself out of spruce and fir boughs but they were springy and nice and you put a blanket over them. Two men slept together and you'd get three blankets, two over and one under. Nobody undressed. There was a shelf by the bunk for your little doo-dads. The rough bench in front of the bunks they called the 'deacon seat,' named, I guess, for the seats deacons used to sit on in church.

"Smaller camps had field bunks where everybody slept in one long row. There were two decks to it and, oh, the arguments because those up top sweated to death and those down below froze. If somebody got steamed up and wanted to turn he would call 'spoon!' There was always one fellow who wouldn't turn at the same time as the others and threw the whole lot out of kilter. That was 'way back in the old days.

"The camp was roofed with a big square sheet of bark. It was waterproof and those tote roads were so rough you couldn't bring lumber in even if you wanted to. There was always two buildings, at least, there, the cook camp and the sleep camp and in between was a roofed-over section they called the 'dingle' and if there was a blacksmith he might work in there. The stable was called the 'hovel.'

"You had to wash your own clothes — outdoors — but a lot gave up and just put one layer on over the other. There's one fellow they tell of, he had to go to the hospital and they found seven shirt collars around his neck. The men wore 'rock maples,' Stanfield's underwear, which were drawers and a separate top which was always called a 'lender' for some queer reason. Their pants were 'Canadian Pride' homespun — like horse blankets, you couldn't wear them out. Out on the roads and the cleared places where the wind would come down like your mother-in-law's breath they wore mackinaw jackets. But right in the bush, the woods were called the poor man's overcoat because there was no wind there. On their feet they wore shoe-packs with moccasin bottoms, no heels. They were made from tanned beef hide. If the trails were slippery the men would put molasses on them and stick them in the oat bin and the oats would make kind of a rough surface on the bottoms. There always seemed to be someone in every camp whose dream in life was to be a barber and he would cut hair. The washing facilities were a hollowed out log and two granite basins in it and the looking-glass always seemed to be cracked.

"Sickness? You just laid in there and were sick, doctored yourself with Buckley's Mixture or the cook might mix up some concoction of ginger to take the poison out of you. They had Dr. Daniel's Colic Cure for the horses but that seemed to do a pretty good job on a man, too. The label actually said it was 'good for man or beast.' Some men suffered toothache pretty badly. Few seemed to brush their teeth anyway. I saw a man take an ulcerated tooth out with a horseshoe nail. Chewing tobacco was supposed to help that. The old-timers used to carry a file in their left boot to help prevent rheumatism and they used to have other superstitions. Never grind an axe on Sunday, you might cut yourself on Monday. Never sleep with your head downriver on a stream drive. It was bad luck and meant a man would drown. If they got hernia they used to say, 'I've forced my stomach.' If they didn't feel well they'd say, 'My food isn't going down well.' Then they'd buy a bottle of pain killer and down that and they'd be okay. That was in 1919 in New Brunswick."

Although no one wore a coat around camp, no matter how frosty it got, the common cold was rare unless someone who had a cold came in from town.

"Everybody in those days had his own remedies, the doctor being so far away. When we had colic we'd drink some gun powder in boiling water. That was in the days before you could die of belly ache, before there was such a thing as 'appendicitis.' If you cut yourself with an axe you put gum from the fir tree on the cut and you'd singe it three times with a flame, blowing on it each time, and it healed quickly."[2]

Aspen bark in boiling water, red spruce gum in brandy, and boiled beaver kidney were popular remedies and a common treatment for frostbite was a bath of lye from wood ashes mixed with a handful of salt. In 1901 a typhoid scare prompted the Ontario government to order camp operators to contract with doctors to inspect the camps and provide medical service for which the operator could deduct 50 cents from each man's monthly wage. There was a typhoid outbreak in 1918, the same year the influenza epidemic scourged the camps as it scourged the towns. When compulsory vaccination was introduced, foremen complained that the men did not hold with it and left a camp that tried to vaccinate them. Despite the sketchy hygiene in those days most of the men managed to stay healthy. They worked hard in the open air and usually ate robust meals. A man cutting trees had to be healthy to begin with or he would not be there.

Logging camps, before they became regulated by law and more or less standardized, and before the unions appeared, differed greatly from place to place. At one end of the scale you might find a company-run camp such as the one built 40 miles west of Sudbury in 1906 for 120 pine cutters. It boasted two airy bunkhouses, three stables, and a cookhouse as big as a village hall. On the other end of the scale, even into the 1920s, you might find a small packsack jobber's camp housing his family, a few cutters, and a horse under the same roof. "There was one I ran across up the Ottawa, a pole camp, not made of logs. There were 15 or 20 in the camp; the bunks were muzzle loaders, two men to each bunk. Their food was salt pork and beans and bread and treacle pies made of molasses and a few cookies. They had steaks as tough as leather, which they cooked in grease in a big iron pot. The bunks were at one end, the dining table in the centre, and the 'stable' at the other end, without a partition. If they tethered the horse with too long a halter he could dump right on the table. That," said Chuck Rowe, "would be in 1928 when I was going up the Ottawa on a cruise. Those little jobbers might spend a couple of years and then move on."

"Near Lac St. Jean in Quebec," said Buzz Lein, who came from Ontario, "they'd sit on the edges of their bunks and smoke that shag tobacco and I still remember the signs in the camp: 'Don't spit on the floor.' 'Don't swear.' There were pictures on the wall of Christ with a bleeding heart. Those guys would smoke and you couldn't see across the bunkhouse unless you peered. We didn't have windows. What the heck do you need windows for? We were never in camp in the daylight. We did have skylights but mostly for ventilation. Every night you'd hear 'chop, chop, chop,' for they'd bring their own tobacco from home and chop it up. They smoked pipes and I tried a packet of their shag one time and it nearly killed me; you get the same effect by running a file down your throat. They said their prayers every night and if you were outside the bunkhouse it sounded like a swarm of mosquitos droning. There was always a layman to lead them in prayers."

John Dunn of Sault Ste. Marie, whose 96-year-old father, Peter, had come from Gaspé at the age of 17 by way of Maine, the Lake States, and the Ottawa pine camps, recalled the varied make-up of the northern Ontario camps. "A lot of fellows came up from New Brunswick. Farmer boys came from the lower parts of Quebec and they had the old style of their ways. I used to get a kick out of them. They had big, long whiskers right to here. They slept not too far from me. They were tall, husky men. They'd get tobacco sent from home where they grew their own. This was in the 1920s. Their people sent it in a box. They'd say, 'Boy, does that ever smell nice, that leaf tobacco.' And they'd roll a cigar from the leaf, just like that, and they'd stand up and give it to you. 'Try some of our tobacco.' It tasted good. They had pig bladder pouches and would rub the tobacco soft like paper. Then there was one Polish fellow, Slim, who slept alongside of me and spoke seven languages. They used to read *True Story* magazine and cowboy magazines in those days and this Pole, who slept above me, kept all his money, $10 bills and $20s, among the pages of a *True Story* magazine."

One thing lumberjacks got used to and few forgot was the smell of the old bunkhouse: wool socks drying on the rafters, wood smoke, tobacco, coal oil, sweat, and the horse smell of the teamsters. "I could always tell a shantyman fresh from the woods by his smell," wrote Charles Macnamara of Arnprior on the Ottawa some 70 years ago. "In the days of the camboose he had a not unpleasant smoky smell like a new deerskin moccasin; after the stove shanty came in he had a disagreeable sour smell."

Working in northern Ontario camps a generation later Earle Nicholson, who later ran a general store near Bruce Mines, recalled: "You were healthy. You felt good, ate good, slept well, but I tell you there were nights, when all the socks were hung over the stove, boy, you could pretty near scrape it off your teeth. The bunkhouse got pretty ripe. It got hot and then it got cold. When the fire was on, the frost would come out of the logs on the inside and run down and freeze and when you awoke in the morning after the fire had died down you were lucky if your hair hadn't frozen to the wall."

Up to perhaps a generation ago all but the biggest and best company-run camps were apt to suffer from vermin. "The lice in those days — wuff!" said one veteran of Quebec and northern Ontario camps. "But we don't have lice any more."[3] "You could keep yourself free from being lousy," said another, "if you kept your clothes clean but sometimes a guy would come in lousy. Some camps I've been in, there wouldn't be anyone lousy, but again the lice would work from one bunk to the other in those old hay beds and before spring everybody would be lousy."[4] Some doused kerosene on the blankets and had a "boil up" on Sunday to steam out the lice. At Atikokan in northwest Ontario Bob Taylor recalled a camp with bed bugs which had appeared as the camp got old. "They thought they'd get rid of the bugs by steam. They had a big steam tractor so they put the pipe into the camp and steamed it for a couple of days. When they opened the camp up again, Mr. Bug, he was still there. Mr. Bed Bug." In another camp they succeeded only in warping all the tables and benches.

233

The Public Archives of Canada   C 56927

"We called our stove Jerry," said Wilmot Macdonald from Chatham, New Brunswick. "She took a three-foot stick and was made round like a barrel. No matter what camp you went in the stove was called Jerry." This 1916 camp was typical of the better camps of that time, including the cat befriended by the lumberjack at left. "Cats taken into camp would sometimes turn wild," said Geoff Randolph, "and we might have trouble with them. A mother cat would kill a rabbit and drag it back whole for her kittens and they would begin to run in packs. Old Tom Savage had a hell of a time with them when he was alone guarding a camp in the off season one summer. They used to follow him around in a pack with a hungry look in their eyes. Finally he boiled up a lot of rice and fed it to them."

The introduction of camp laundries did more than anything to get rid of the vermin. A more common amenity for any self-respecting camp was the five-holer with 20-foot double rails and splash board. "Eaton's mail order catalogue was used, and the last part of the catalogue to be used up was always the women's underwear section. The men would be in there for eight months and there were damn few women."[5] "One time we put a stove in the backhouse just to see what modern conveniences were like and believe you me the stove didn't stay there long."[6]

Oscar Styffe, a lumberman at Thunder Bay, recalled conditions before the First World War. "You washed your hands and face and that was it; you'd wonder the camp didn't get up and walk away by itself. No one took a bath except in the Finn camps where they had saunas. It is a peculiar thing but there are very few cases of severe sickness in the camps. There are minor colds and stomach troubles but no real sickness."[7] By 1934 Ontario, Quebec, and New Brunswick had drafted legislation to improve and standardize the camps. Ontario, generally considered in the forefront of improvements after B.C., insisted on windows and 400 cubic feet of space for each man and steel beds to replace wooden bunks. Separate washrooms were built and log shanties gave way to structures of lumber with tar paper roofs. "In Quebec the regulation for camp construction in the 1930s was laid down by the Department of Health. Inspectors used to come around. The walls had to be a minimum of eight feet high. There had to be so many square feet of window space per man, so many cubic feet of air. This limited the number of beds you could put in. The floor had to be boards — in the old days it was poles — so you needed a little sawmill in the camp. Doors had to open out, a door at each end. Two-storey camps were built on the St. Maurice. They required less heat. The only sickness I recall was related to bad water although we never had typhoid. But there were many camps deep in the woods that inspectors never saw. Before a union was established, regardless of what people may claim, the conditions . . . were primitive. But we thought it was normal. Times change, the standards of working and living changed."[8] Those days were a far cry from the camps of later years, with drying rooms for clothes, a recreation room, two men to a cubicle with steel beds, and a gleaming cookhouse.

Despite the crowding in the bunkhouse, and the ethnic mixtures, fights in camp were rare. "They were too tired. They got up too damn early to fight anything."[9]

"The idea was this: if you don't like the way I wear my hat don't look at it. If a man wanted to talk to you and get friendly, well, then he was part of your gang. You didn't sit on another man's bunk unless you were really friendly with him. Everybody in his place. You'd respect his place and he'd respect yours."[10]

The van. One of the camp clerk's jobs was to look after the camp shop, or 'van,' a name contracted from *wangan*, an Indian word for a container. The men could buy socks, pants, shirts, underwear, boots, Epsom salts, soap, tobacco, and odds and ends, the cost to be deducted from their earnings at the end of the season.
Abitibi Paper Co. Ltd.

Bob Duff sharpens an axe in a shanty on the Black River, up the Ottawa, in 1903, when stoves had replaced the open cambuse fire. What the windowless shanty gained in warmth from the change, it lost in fresh air. When a foreman went to the trouble of building a ventilator on the roof from an old pork barrel with the bottom knocked out, he found the men had stuffed it full of old clothes to keep out the draughts. They got enough fresh air, it seems, out in the winter woods.

Charles Macnamara Collection, Ontario Archives, Courtesy of Mrs. Jean Cunningham, Arnprior, Ont.

"They had a code against theft. The only time there would be any problem is when a man who really wasn't a lumberjack moved into camp and didn't belong there."[11] Problems of that nature generally arose in times of manpower shortage such as in the latter days of World War One when magistrates sometimes gave a convicted man a choice of serving in jail or working out his sentence in a lumber camp as a "Convict Volunteer."

The camp "van" was a sort of company store which sold boots, woollen socks, long underwear, pants and shirts, Epsom Salts, braces, gloves, liniment, carbolic ointment, cough syrup, and a variety of smoking and chewing tobacco — Stag, MacDonalds, Golden Rod, and Copenhagen snuff, or "snoose," as it was called on the west coast. Until the 1930s cigarettes were despised. "I remember one old guy smoking a cigarette and he said, 'Any man smokin' one of them pimp sticks is no good for nuthin'."[12] Purchases were deducted from a man's wages when camp broke up in the spring and the mark-up charged in such stores, particularly by some of the jobbers, was often a cause of grievance.

The "van," called the *wangan* on the east coast from an Indian word for "container of odds and ends," got its start as a simple iron-bound, padlocked wooden box in the shanties but over the years became a corner of the camp clerk's shack fitted with shelves. The supply and cook boat on a river drive was called a *wangan* boat.

Fancy goods were supplied to the camps by itinerant pedlars, known as "the Assyrian pedlar" in the early days no matter what their nationalities. The pedlar appeared in camp each winter with a pack full of cheap watches, playing cards, and mother-of-pearl brooches shaped like hearts, with "Sweetheart" or "Mother" spelled out in pliable gold wire. Another visitor, usually on Sunday, was the commercial photographer from town. In albums and attics across Canada there are thousands of yellowing photos of grandfather, arms folded across his chest, posed like a bearded Old Testament prophet with 20 or 30 workmates outside a log bunkhouse. Those photos are sometimes the only testimony of a vanished age.

15. TALES OF THE TIMBERBEASTS: LA CHASSE GALÈRE

On Saturday nights there would be fellows in the camps
up the Saguenay here who'd tell stories until two or three
in the morning. Real story machines. Everyone would listen
in silence as though they were in a theatre, while the
conteur des contes *told of beasts with seven heads who could speak.*
Those story-tellers had a whole repertoire in their heads.

GEORGES COTE, CHICOUTIMI, QUEBEC

A favourite of the Quebec *bûcheron*, who was often stuck in a distant camp on *le jour de l'an*, New Year's Day, was *La Chasse Galère*.

It told of how the Devil would come hunting souls on New Year's Eve in his big black boat. He would offer to transport the men to their homes hundreds of miles away in time to celebrate the holiday. In return they must forfeit their souls to the Prince of Darkness.

The homesick men were willing. They clambered into the boat and with the Devil leading were soon paddling hard, the boat climbing high above the tree-tops. They sped through the sky on a southeast course until, at dawn, the Devil deposited each man at his home on the St. Lawrence, at Trois-Pistoles, perhaps, or St. Siméon.

New Year's Day was theirs to visit families and girl-friends but at midnight the fun was over and the Devil picked them up and headed his boat back to camp. But, happily, the *bûcherons* always managed to outwit the Devil. As the boat flew over some lonely midnight town on the St. Maurice River or the Ottawa a lumberjack would suddenly lean out of the boat and touch the cross on the church steeple as they sped past. The instant he did so the evil spell was broken. The Devil and his boat disappeared in a flash of blue flame and the men tumbled into the soft snow drifts, freed from their hellish bargain.

There is a tradition that the story originated generations ago in France when a "Monsieur Galère" insisted on going hunting of a Sunday instead of going to church and was consigned to the Devil's black boat for eternity for his sins.

La Chasse Galère. With the Devil, in ghostly form beneath the bow of the canoe, Quebec *bûcherons* fly to their homes on New Year's Eve. A 1916 painting by Henri Julien, Montreal.

The Public Archives of Canada   C 17928

16 SATURDAY NIGHT AND SUNDAY

In the dark, tangled forest where lumberjacks sing,
And their saws and their axes, the music will ring
Oh the nights they are weary and the days they are long,
But my comrades they cheer me with music and song.

THE MAID FROM TIDEHEAD,

FROM THE BAY OF CHALEUR, NEW BRUNSWICK

Their music was fiddle, accordion, mouth organ, and jew's harp. Crusty old foremen were known to hire a good singer or fiddler even if he was not much of a logger.

"We had more entertainment in the pine camps than you'd have in town because we had every kind of man in the country there. Fiddle and dance, square dance, step dance, some of the greatest musicians you'd ever hear tell of."[1]

The men usually had Sunday off so when they came back to camp at nightfall on Saturday there was horseplay and laughter and perhaps something special for supper. In the pine camps they would light their pipes and sit around on bunks or benches in stocking feet or "stags" which were cut-down old boots they used for slippers. Some camps might even have a self-appointed "deacon," or master of ceremonies, for the songs, games, and recitations. The best fun was the stag dance, the "buck set" where they would "tamarack her down on the old pine floor." Since there were rarely any women in the early camps, half the men sported flour sacks around their waists or handkerchiefs around their arms to show they were dancing the lady's part. "They'd tie a dish towel around a fella's arm, and away you'd go."[2]

When they tired of that the men in Père Léandre Lang's camp might call for "a *gigue*, boss, a *gigue*" and while Onésime Filion

240

"Sunday in Camp" was "sketched from life" by Dan Beard. "The French were gay people, dancing, songs, teasing," said Geoff Randolph who worked in camps in New Brunswick and Quebec. "There was always a step dancer." This sketch is of one of the "stove camps" which replaced the open cambuse fire. Back under the windows are coffin-like "muzzle loading" bunks which had to be entered from one end.

Metropolitan Toronto Library Board

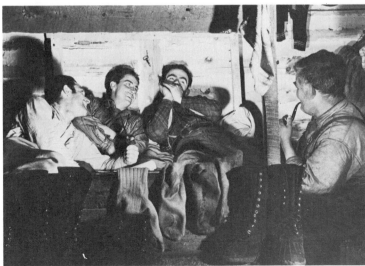

Mouth music in a pulpwood camp. After supper, when the men were sitting around smoking and talking, a man who could play a mouth organ was highly prized in the days before radios became common.

The Public Archives of Canada C 30813

241

tinkered with his accordion old Léandre would stand up and stretch. The "*gigue*," or step dance, was polished to a fine art in the Quebec camps, the body straight, head thrown back, arms folded, the upper body stiff — only the feet skittering to the beat of the tune. To signal a change of pace the dancer would thump the floor with one foot. The men usually brought in an old door or some planks for him to dance on so he would not break the pole floor.

Pierre Dupin described just such a dance. "Père Léandre cuts a pigeon wing, three inches off the floor, striking his heels together once, twice, before he comes down, then breaks in to a sudden, complicated cross-step. With a light leap he crosses his legs twice before coming down, all in the space of one square foot ... A strand of hair flops down and jigs on his forehead, the fringe of his sash flies out in its own dance.

"The dance lasts 10 minutes although it seems longer and then suddenly Onésime slackens the tempo, plays two or three chords, and accordion and dancer stop at the same time. While Père Léandre mops his brow the men applaud. 'In my youth,' says Père Léandre, 'I could have done better, but what can you expect when a man gets old?' "[3]

The dancing was already dying out by the 1920s when the first battery radios arrived and the Saturday "Hockey Night in Canada" broadcasts helped finish the tradition. There are men in their 70s, usually men of the pulp, rather than the pine, camps, who have never seen a stag dance, although they might remember step dancing, and some of the games.

Bunkhouse games were learned on the farm. "*Ça les hommes du chantier, ça m'fait penser à une gang d'enfants d'écôle,*" said Eugène Lavoie of St. Sixte, Quebec, and "*Sauter Le Cheval Blanc,*" played by the *bûcherons*, was a kid's game like leap frog. Indian wrestling and arm wrestling were popular in Quebec camps along with tug of war.

"Jack in the Dark" was a rough and rowdy blind-man's-bluff in New Brunswick camps with blind-folded men whaling away at each other with socks weighted with potatoes. In "Shuffle the Brogue" men in a circle shoved an old boot swiftly around behind their backs until one suddenly threw it at the victim in the middle who tried to guess who had thrown it. "Hot Ass" was a painful variation wherein the victim bent over, closed his eyes, and tried to guess who had swatted him. "Weighing the Sheep" initiated greenhorns: several men, including an innocent newcomer to the camp, draped blankets over their heads and a "buyer" lifted each blanketed man off the bench to guess his weight. When he lifted the greenhorn someone would slip a tub of icy water onto the dupe's seat before he was plumped down again. Another game was to leap over a broomstick held between their hands, frontward and back, higher and higher, or, standing in a three-foot-high barrel, risk a childless future by leaping into a second barrel nearby.

There was little to read in a pine camp and few who knew how in the old days and a good story-teller was almost as welcome as a good cook. "I remember one fellow with white hair, he must have been nearly 65. He started a story in November and it was after Christmas before he got to the end of it. He'd start about 7 o'clock every night and he'd talk for 15 minutes and then he'd leave off and say, 'Okay, tomorrow, boys, we'll go on with the story.' "[4] He was one of the famous *conteurs des contes*, the French-Canadian story-tellers who spun yarns of the *voyageurs*, of the *bûcheron's* hero, Joe Montferrand, and of the *loup-garou*, the werewolf who travelled hundreds of miles in one night through the great north woods. They told stories of the French-Canadian strongmen: Louis Cyr whose weight lifting record of 273¼ pounds was bettered by Victor DeLamarre from Lac St. Jean who lifted 309½ pounds in Montreal in 1914, although DeLamarre himself was only five feet six and weighed 154 pounds. DeLamarre had started his career as a *bûcheron*.

The liveliest story-teller of all was Joseph Lemieux, known as "Joe Violon," who shantied on the Ottawa, the Gatineau, and the St. Maurice. His stories of Ti Pit Vallerand of Trois-Rivières or Tan Fan Jeannot and Tom Caribou always began, "Cric, Crac, les enfants! Parli, Parlo, Parlons. To learn the short and the long pass the spittoon to Joe Violon! Sactabi sac-a-tabac!"

Stories were told not only in Quebec but in New Brunswick and Ontario as well. "Our foreman sat up with the crew and told us fairy stories and ghost stories. The crew were very superstitious and for that matter I am myself. That Christmas evening there was a fearful gale blowing and towards midnight when our foreman was in the middle of one of his blood-curdling and hair-lifting stories, the crew all gathered around him with their eyes fairly bulging out, crash, bang! down came right amongst us a big pine limb which the wind had broken from a huge pine that stood some distance from our shanty; the wind carried the limb and dropped it down our camboose chimney and it made a fearful crash when it struck our pots and kettles. A more frightened crew I never saw and I guess we all thought the devil had us."[5]

Before the First World War they sang *The Lumberjack's Alphabet* (A is for axe, that we keep strong and sharp . . .) or *Bung Yer Eye* or the Irish-Australian *Wild Colonial Boy*. They also had their own song-makers such as Larry Gorman, the red-haired six-footer from Prince Edward Island who was kicked out of many a New Brunswick camp for his satiric ditties about foreman or cook.

Saturday night in a shanty on the Severn River, in the Muskoka area by Georgian Bay. The foreman always made sure there was a fiddler in the gang. In Muskoka township lumbering began in 1871 when the eastern shore of Lake Huron was solid pine and hemlock.

The Public Archives of Canada   C 11738

Story time in a 19th century lumber shanty. "I worked with old Milmore and that's all he did, tell stories," said Steve Lewis. "He told one about this old fella, he had no relatives or friends that they knew of and he died in camp. But before he died he told a farmer he would give him money if he would bury him in consecrated ground. In those days they sometimes used to 'bury wild.' The farmer took the money but did not keep his promise. He buried the fella 'wild' on his farm. But the fella had been a good Roman Catholic and wasn't satisfied just being buried wild. So every night there'd be a light come out of his grave and go into the old fella's house and next night it would come out of the house and go back into the ground. The people living around there saw the bloody light and they went to the priest who told them, 'He's not satisfied, he wants to be buried in consecrated ground. You go there and dig him up and if that's the case he'll be just as fresh as the day he died.' Well, they went and dug him up and sure enough he was good and fresh. So they took him downriver by canoe to the graveyard and buried him again but by the time they got him there he was so rotten they could hardly stand the stink. That Milmore could keep on for days. He had more stories than any book you could have a mind to read."

Metropolitan Toronto Library Board

"Jack in the Dark." Both players were blind-folded. One knelt, clutching a peg driven into the floor and pivoted around this in a circle while the other player, with a sock in his hand weighted with a potato, would call, "Where are you Jack?" The one circling

The Harriet Irving Library, University of New Brunswick

the peg would call, "In the Dark!" The one with the sock would try to figure out his opponent's position and would say, "If you die before I do, take THAT!" Then he would strike out with the sock and try to hit the other player. He had three chances to swing at him and if he missed all three the players would change places.

Homesick ballads in the tall timber. Even the "Push," in the foreman's chair of honour, has a far-away look in his eyes. A favourite was *The Wild Colonial Boy*. "One song I used to hear about three times a winter," said Fred Kinnehan, "some old fella would sing *The Flying Cloud*, a ship that turned pirate. Before the First World War they used to sing all that kind of stuff but that all went out with the war."

Provincial Archives, Victoria, B.C.

245

Gorman could compose a 32-verse song and sing it on the spot, including one he wrote about himself.

> And when they see me coming
> Their eyes stick out like prongs,
> Saying, "Beware of Larry Gorman,
> He's the man who makes the songs."

In Quebec the songs had been passed down to the *bûcherons* from the *voyageurs* who had roamed the same rivers in the fur trade and, like the *voyageurs*, the early *bûcherons* wrapped coloured sashes around their waists, wore knee-high moccasins and coloured tuques, and sang the rollicking *En Roulant ma boule*, or in time of trouble, *Un Voyageur que si Détermine* (Virgin Mary, tender Mother, be his guide and his support). They sang of how poor Hyacinthe Brisbois lay dying in the forest without friends or sacrament, or they sang *chansons de réponse*, the "answer songs," and *chansons des blondes* of the girls they left behind. They sang homesick *chansons de départ* as they headed up the river in autumn and *chansons de retour* when they came home in spring. There were songs for almost everything in those singing camps until the gasoline age brought easy transportation and the radio arrived. By the 1940s *les bûcherons* were listening to Willy La Mothe sing cowboy songs.

"When the radios came in the first were only battery radios and maybe 20 per cent of them worked. There was a station on the south shore of the St. Lawrence, very powerful, and it was heavy on western music. It started, the damn thing, about 4:30 in the morning playing requests and a girl would be asking for a song for '*Jean Etienne Tremblay, présentement en camp sur la Rivière à Lac, de la part de son amie de Ste. Anne de Portière.*' "[6] "In northern Ontario one of our cooks built a crystal set but remember it was 9 P.M. before we could get reception — KDKA and WJR in the States. That was in 1924. We'd separate the earphones so two men could listen and each man had a turn."[7] By the 1940s there were Sunday movies in camp cookhouses, Tom Mix being the favourite character in the Quebec camps.

"Some fellows made gum books, little boxes with sliding tops with entwined hearts on them and filled them with fresh spruce gum and they'd go out in the spring and give them to their kids or a girl-friend. The French were not much to read. They went in more for whittling and hand work — fancy axe handles with painted deer heads carved on the end with a 'crooked knife,' the Indian knife that is drawn toward the whittler. They liked dancing, songs, talking, teasing — a gay people."[8]

"Those French fellas would come into camp with their woollen yarn, knitting needles, and sewing equipment and would knit socks, coloured mittens, even underwear, and if anyone tore a hole in his pants he would go to one of the French fellas and say, 'Would you fix this one for me?' and they'd make a wonderful job of it. Weekends were pretty heavy with poker. Some would lose a lot of money. There was always a few poker sharps around would get all the money and if there was no money they'd play for tobacco and later the winner would sell the tobacco back to the men when we were paid off at the end of the season."[9] By March there would be good poker players with half a case of tobacco, all getting dried out.

In the east, where wages were low, a big pot might be $100 but in British Columbia, where wages were always higher, there were wild games after World War Two. "It would be nothing to see $10 000 or $15 000 change hands on a weekend."[10]

At cards, like almost everything else, they poked fun at themselves, often in songs, like *McKinley's Brook*.

> Their nights are oft in gambling passed
> and some will win tobacco fast
> and then like Satan they will cheat
> and swear at cards, they can't be beat.
> Out in the dark they dare not stray,
> for fear old Nick takes them away.

Apart from the French and some of the Irish they were not regarded as religious men. A writer in 1867 feared that lumberjacks were "like sailors, very loose in their habits and careless with their own souls . . . It is hard to make any provision to reach their moral and spiritual wants."[11] An old logger from New Brunswick recalled that only once in his long life had he seen a lumberjack reading a bible in camp. In 1927 a writer in Chicoutimi, Quebec, while conceding that "blasphemy and drinking are two plagues that are growing less," feared that "Sunday is less observed than ever in the camps . . . All say it is a pity they are so long without priest, mass, confession, the eucharist, resulting in a loss of faith, particularly among the youth . . . "[12]

Missionary priests from the Oblate order or curés from some nearby parish visited camps each winter. "The priests would make two visits a year, one in the fall when they would spend a night in each camp, and if you had 10 or 15 camps you would have the priest around two or three weeks to hear confessions and hold mass the next morning. The second visit might be Christmas midnight mass. The priest would come in the day before, hear confessions, preach

Lumberjacks were great whittlers and in New Brunswick they spent many nights and Sundays carving ornate "gum books," which they filled with spruce gum from the trees and carried back as presents to their loved ones in the spring.

Northeast Archives of Folklore and Oral History

Poker in a pulp camp, northern Ontario, 1955. These men — the one on the far right seems to be winning — were playing for money but if they were short of cash they played for packets of tobacco. "But in our camp near Lac St. Jean," said Benoit Girard of Chicoutimi, "we were not supposed to play cards and there were notices everywhere saying, 'It is strictly forbidden to play cards for money.' David Durand wrote under those notices, 'It is necessary to play cards! — in the woods!' "

Abitibi Paper Co. Ltd.

a little sermon during the evening, and hold midnight mass followed by a banquet with chicken or turkey."[13]

Arriving after a long, cold journey by horse and cutter the priest would curtain off a corner of the cookhouse with a blanket or two. After supper his portable altar would be set up with the crucifix in the centre and candles burning on each side. Short vespers were said and the priest would hear confessions far into the night. Next morning mass was celebrated and after final benediction the men resumed work in the forest. "Apart from the annual mass we always kept a religious aspect to our camps in Quebec and every night we said the rosary on our knees."[14]

Protestant churches made determined efforts to reach the lumberjacks. In the 1860s the Anglican Diocese of Montreal established a mission to the "Lumber Districts" along the north shore of the Ottawa from Buckingham to the Coulonge River and in the Laurentian hill country. Bishop Oxenden, on his first confirmation up the Ottawa in October 1869, wrote, "The life of the shantymen who fell the timber is a very peculiar one ... They meet with many privations, but they live well, having plenty of good beef and pork. They are restricted, however, from the use of spirits, and indulge in no stronger drink than tea ... "[15] The Presbyterian Church established The Lumberman's Mission on the Ottawa and although services were rare the Reverend Joshua Fraser was pleased that "on the first Sunday after my arrival at Monahan's shanty more than 100 turned out to sing The Old Hundred" and hear Fraser preach on the hoary age attained by the patriarchs of the Old Testament. "There is not the least levity," he reported. "A more repectful, attentive and apparently devoted audience I never preached to."[16] The "Go Preachers" of New Brunswick were less sedate and like the Salvation Army, which also visited the camps, preached a more muscular faith. "They would come in with violin and bible and go to it! They'd walk from camp to camp and everybody was very polite to them but nobody reformed. We used to like the music. That was the main thing."[17]

"Vital religion," declared the Reverend Alfred Fitzpatrick, a lean, bespectacled Presbyterian minister from Pictou County, Nova Scotia, "is impossible on a foundation of ignorance." And in the 1890s, when less than half the country population could read and write, Fitzpatrick took to carrying books in his packsack so that those who could read would not have to "treasure the wrappings from a patent medicine bottle because it gives them something to read." Since bunkhouses were cramped, noisy, and poorly lit he talked J. R. Booth and other Ontario camp operators into building "reading cabins" and founding the Reading Camp Association. A similar project was started later in Quebec by La Bibliothèque des Chantiers at Chicoutimi under the guidance of the Catholic Church "to

The Public Archives of Canada   C 56826

The young Norman Bethune, long before he achieved fame as a crusading doctor in Spain and China, stands with hands on hips in Martin's camp west of Sudbury, Ontario, where he taught his workmates at night after labouring all day with them in the woods. Third from right, wearing a fedora, is Alfred Fitzpatrick, founder of Frontier College which brought basic education to the woodsmen.

The Public Archives of Canada   C 82910

Mass in a lumber shanty, *Picturesque Canada*, 1882. Once or twice each year a priest would travel 20 or 30 miles over forest trails to visit a Quebec camp.

preserve the *bûcheron* from bad conversations and unwholesome pastimes."

Fitzpatrick found that unsupervised reading camps were not enough. Lumberjacks who could read often preferred the pink *Police Gazette*, *True Story*, or *Argosy* magazine. Teachers were needed to go into the camps, work beside the loggers by day, and teach by night. Only that way, said Fitzpatrick, would the teachers be accepted in the camps. Thus Frontier College was founded, financed by modest donations totalling $49.50 in 1900. Thirteen years later Frontier College boasted 71 worker-teachers. "The man would work and earn his keep and do his teaching at night. Very dedicated young people. I think the men respected the fact the teacher was one of the gang, so to speak. The teachers were not politically inclined. They taught English and arithmetic mostly, with lectures in citizenship to the immigrants."[18] During the 1920s Frontier College reported that perhaps half the men in the logging and railway camps would attend regular classes. One problem was to find young men who could handle the physical labour in the camps.

In the winter of 1911–12, Norman Bethune, who was to die as a surgeon on the battlefields of China in 1939, represented Frontier College at Martin's Camp near Whitefish, west of Sudbury. He wrote that he enjoyed the work, despite "lack of time and sore hands," as he cut trails by day and taught English to his Croatian workmates by night.

In 1908 William Henderson, a Presbyterian Scot, founded the Shantymen's Christian Association. Carrying a mail-bag full of bibles, he tramped the bush trails with evangelical zeal spreading fundamentalism and attacking the communism he feared was spreading through immigrant camps in northern Ontario. He died of tuberculosis at the age of 52 in 1925 but spread his gospel across the country. "I knew them well," said Bob Taylor. "Fine fellows. They'd come in once or twice a winter. They used to walk all the way into the camps and I've often given them dry socks and a good supper. They'd go to the bunkhouse and sing songs or something. They never took up collection. If you gave it to them they'd take it but they never asked for it. They didn't wear collars, it was non-denominational." The shantymen preachers usually worked in pairs and claimed that in a good year they might reach as many as 55 000 men. Their journal, *The Shantyman*, claimed "the most surprising result" of their work was to turn men against drink. They liked to call their brand of faith "the lumberjack's religion."

By the 1920s another sort of proselytizer was tramping the bush trail with packsack full of tracts and the west coast "Lumberjack's Prayer": "Oh hear me Lord, I'm praying still, but if you don't our Union will . . . "

251

17 WORKERS OF THE WOODS: LOGGING UNIONS

*The trouble was that it was seasonal work in eastern Canada.
The camps were occupied only from September until March and
then the men would be laid off and the bulk of them wouldn't
go back to work until next fall. They couldn't hold the
organization together. Every fall there'd be a new attempt
to start a union.*

GORDON BALL, CAMP SUPERINTENDENT,
NORTHERN ONTARIO

As early as the 1880s the Noble and Holy Order of the Knights of
Labour, a Protestant organization with roots in Philadelphia, was
trying to organize woods workers but with little effect. Until well
into the 1900s most labour organizing in the logging industry in the
east was done in the mills where the strikes occurred.

On the west coast, where year-round work in the woods may
have made labour organizing somewhat easier than in the east, the
skid road loggers of Vancouver got their first real whiff of American
fire-and-brimstone unionism in 1907 when "Wobbly" agitators followed steam logging up the coast from Seattle. With their Little
Red Songbook of revolutionary songs and their call for control of
industry by the workers, the International Workers of the World,
despite internal dissension and lack of cash, managed to implant a
lasting belief that unions should be organized by industry rather
than by craft. Founded in Chicago in 1905 it sought to organize the
unorganized and influenced logging unionism for many years both
in British Columbia and in northern Ontario, particularly around
the Lakehead. In one of the IWW's internal disputes, a union official
once suggested it be called "the industrial workers of the woods,
and not of the world." No one is certain how the IWW came to be
called "The Wobblies," although old organizers like to tell how a
Chinese restaurant owner in Kamloops, B.C., had trouble with his

w's and took to calling IWW men the "I-Wobbly-Wobbly." The IWW left a firm imprint on young immigrants like Tom Hill from Finland who joined the IWW in Chicago and carried its teaching to his new home at Fort Frances and Thunder Bay in 1917. "We established the Lumber Workers Union, a local group with no affiliation at that time. They were mostly Finns but there were others too." Hill eventually became a member of the Communist Party of Canada when it was established in 1922. In the tangled skein of union organization both in northern Ontario and on the west coast, the red thread of communism ran until well after World War Two.

During the long fight for recognition which finally saw the International Woodworkers of America emerge as top union on the coast and the Lumber and Sawmill Workers Union triumph at Thunder Bay, more than half a dozen bush unions came and went amid breakaways and jurisdictional disputes. The first effective union was the Lumber Workers Industrial Union (LWIU) which brought the eight-hour day to the west coast just after World War One and organized branches in northern Ontario. By the late 1920s, and the Depression, it had tumbled into obscurity and the early gains seem to have been more shadow than substance. It was during those years that a few dedicated men, such as Hjalmar Bergren, a Scandinavian immigrant logger on Vancouver Island, kept the union idea alive.

"When I started work in the camps in 1925 I never heard of union organizing — oh, there was the odd organizer. I remember I attended a meeting in Vancouver in 1928 but it was only a start. There was no membership; the trade union movement was very weak then. Nothing much was done except talk because there were too few working and those who were working were too scared. If the bosses thought you were in any way connected with the union, out you went. I became a job steward in 1931 and a full-time organizer in 1935. We didn't get paid very much. It was difficult getting unions started, nobody knew what they were all about. Conditions when I started in the camps weren't too bad, there was all kinds of food. The main problems were safety, wages, and individual rights.

"If the men elected a committee the boss said, 'We don't deal with committees. If you have any grievance you can come on in here and see us.' Of course if you came in there and saw them they gave you your walking ticket. If you got someone to sell the *B.C. Lumberworker* — the mimeographed union bulletin started in 1932 — they got fired. If anyone from outside, such as myself, came to camp they got chased out. I used to walk from Cowichan Lake to Camp 10, 12 miles on the railway ties, and then walk home at night. At other places on the west coast of Vancouver Island it was a whole day's march. We kept goin'. You had to keep the dialogue goin'. If they had guards we found ways of getting in. When the police came and told you to go we'd go but we'd be back next day. I used to say, 'What the hell are you running here, a concentration camp?' I'd say, 'These people are paying for their bed and board and they should have some rights.' One time at Elk River we went into camp to distribute the *Lumberworker* and the superintendent followed us and took all the papers out of the men's hands. He collected them as fast as we gave them out and as we reached the end he handed them back to us. We thanked him kindly and moved on.

"The work we did — unionizing — started to get noticeable in 1939 after we had a convention in Vancouver and laid down very definite strategy. Before that it was haphazard, each man had his own scheme and his own idea. After 1939 we were pretty sure of ourselves. Of course we had to keep on propagandizing. If you forgot the propaganda the boys forgot to pay their dues. You had to keep the dialogue going. Of course we'd had the 1934 and 1936 strikes and those provided the experience."

The 1934 strike on Vancouver Island, the first major walk-out in Canadian camps, brought out 3500 men for more than three months. It was organized by a revived version of the old Lumber Workers Industrial Union which was called the Lumber Workers Industrial Union of Canada (LWIUC). It had appeared on the west coast and at the Lakehead as part of the Worker's Unity League, the union arm of the Communist Party. The B.C. loggers demanded higher wages and protection against work speed-up and accidents. Police were brought in, there were many arrests, but in the end the union claimed a partial victory and 11 000 new members.

At Thunder Bay progress had been even more uncertain. Autumn after autumn, as the camps filled up for the cutting season, there were scattered strikes. In the autumn of 1929 these annual confrontations were dramatized by tragedy. When a camp at Shebaqua went on strike two Finnish organizers of the new LWIUC went to Onion Lake to try to spread the strike to other camps. They never got there and in the spring the bodies of Viljo Rosval and John Voutilainen were found in a shallow creek. Since they were experienced bushmen the union rejected the official finding that the men had died accidentally. Their funeral in Port Arthur brought out 4000 mourners.

In 1931 eight of the Communist Party leaders who had organized a "work and wages" campaign were arrested under the since-repealed Section 98 of the Criminal Code. This was a First World War measure which had been used against subversives and broadened in scope during the Winnipeg General Strike in 1919. One of those imprisoned was Tom Hill, pioneer organizer in the Lakehead logging camps.

Myrtle Bergren, Nanaimo, B.C.

After several years of preparation the Lumber Workers Industrial Union succeeded in organizing logging camps in Vancouver Island's Campbell River area and the men came out in a general strike. The three-month strike brought an improvement in wages and camp conditions.

Myrtle Bergren, Nanaimo, B.C.

Loggers at Campbell River, Vancouver Island, set up a picket camp in the first major lumber camp strike. "The 1934 strike," said Harold Pritchett, a British Columbian who became president of the International Woodworkers of America, "firmly established unionism in the logging industry."

The annual strikes continued and it was during such a strike at Port Arthur in 1933 that Bruce Magnusson first appeared. Magnusson, an immigrant from Sweden, was to join A. T. "Tom" Hill in the work of organizing bush workers.

"I got involved in the strike at Port Arthur," he said, "by acting as recording secretary at the strikers' meetings. 'Pigeon' Johnson tried to take his horses out to the bush and we had about 400 people at his barn and they stopped them from taking the horses out and next morning we must have had 1000 people there, mostly bush workers. It was a big strike and I was blacklisted after it was over. I started to read books on socialism and the communist manifesto and to think about political activity and the working-class struggle. I was 24. We used to get along on practically nothing; I walked around for three days once with nothing to eat. In 1935 I was elected secretary of the Port Arthur local of the Lumber Workers Industrial Union of Canada, affiliated with the Workers Unity League. We had our meetings in the small Finnish Hall; the big Finnish Hall was run by the Wobblies, the IWW." Magnusson played a key role in the first formal agreement between companies and bush workers in northern Ontario — a general wage schedule in 1935.

About this time came a change which was to split the woods unions in B.C. and northern Ontario and set them on the separate paths they follow to this day. The communist Workers Unity League had persuaded its LWIUC affiliates to merge with a new union, the Lumber and Sawmill Workers Union which had appeared in the American northwest as the industrial wing of the Carpenters and Joiners of America. The marriage lasted in northern Ontario but in British Columbia led to divorce and formation in 1937 of the International Woodworkers of America which remains the bush union in B.C.

During the Second World War both unions entrenched and immediately after the war both tested their new strength by calling the biggest logging strikes ever seen to back wage demands and to gain union recognition. With the industry booming, as many as 160 000 loggers might be employed across the country during fall and winter.

The B.C. strike set the pace and when it was over the IWA, which had boasted only 3000 members before the war, claimed 27 000 members and had become one of the biggest unions in Canada.

In northern Ontario the 1946 strike was credited with establishing the Lumber and Sawmill Workers Union on a broad basis. "The result," said a company official, "was recognition of the Lumber and Sawmill Workers Union as bargaining authority for woods employees and the signing of collective agreements, all similar, by the companies in whose camps the strikes had occurred. The first years of negotiated labour agreements with the Lumber and Sawmill

Abitibi Paper Co. Ltd.

Pulpwood cutters on White Lake near Regan, Ontario, read the *Sault Daily Star* headline, "12,000 Bush Workers Strike." The month-long strike for recognition of the Lumber and Sawmill Workers Union started on October 12, 1946, and hit the Lakehead and Hearst areas hardest, although it was also felt in northeastern Ontario.

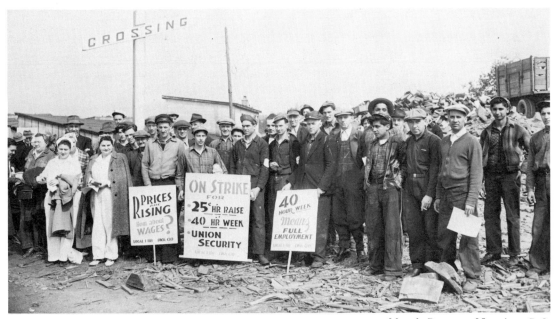

Myrtle Bergren, Nanaimo, B.C.

British Columbia loggers trek to the provincial capital, Victoria, with demands for the 40-hour week and higher pay in the strike of 1946. When the strike ended, the union emerged with a membership of 27 000 in the woods and the mills.

Workers Union was a trying one due, in some degree, to the inexperience of camp stewards as well as that of the employer's representatives in the camps, although, in the main, the agreements were lived up to by both parties in a commendable way."

Within a few years both the IWA and the "Lumber and Saw" faced threats from within. For years the rank and file had not been averse to communist leadership but after the war anti-communist pressures built up at international union headquarters in the United States, and in Canada members were concerned that their leaders were neglecting bread-and-butter issues in favour of international communist dogma with little Canadian relevance. The first union to be split by the temper of the times was the IWA in B.C. in 1948. To meet the challenge the communist leadership made secret plans to disaffiliate and set up a breakaway union. The IWA loyalists fought back. "A surge of loyalty for the IWA soon became evident. Our first problem was dealing with the breakaway union, the Woodworkers Industrial Union of Canada. They were attempting everywhere to woo the IWA members to their breakaway union and to take over our certification. Gradually we signed up those who had gone over and the WIUC was completely defeated and went into oblivion."[1] Those involved in the "October revolution" were banned and the IWA, badly mauled, was rebuilt.

In northern Ontario the power struggle came in 1951 — efforts to form a breakaway union failed, and the Lumber and Sawmill Workers Union shed its slate of communist officers.

East of Ontario, bush unions prospered only in fairly recent years. In Quebec the Church had long opposed international unions on the grounds they were secular and materialistic. The Church built its own confessional labour organizations under the guidance of priests. "Around 1945," said Théophile Savard, who was 82 and who started working on the Saguenay at the age of 13, "many things started to change. We began getting paid for overtime. Around 1950 the Union Catholique des Cultivateurs was voted in. We needed a union and it was the only one around. It brought changes — standard working hours, improvements in camps." According to his son, William, "When Maurice Duplessis became prime minister of Quebec many things changed: he standardized the working hours to 10 a day, six days a week, with overtime paid. Camps became separated into three buildings: kitchen, bunkhouse, and stable instead of having it all in one building as in the old days. They got rid of the old pole beds, the *bêtes-à-boeufs*, and had them replaced with proper beds with space between them." So things were changing in the east as well, but in Newfoundland, as late as 1959, an IWA effort to organize was defeated amid violence, repression, and jurisdictional disputes.

With standardization, mechanization, and unionization, west-east discrepancies evened out, but for half a century west coast camps led the way in pay and conditions, followed by Ontario, and then by the east. "I used to visit camps from the Queen Charlotte Islands to Newfoundland," said the late Alexander Koroleff, manager of the Woodlands Section of the Canadian Pulp and Paper Association. "There were tremendous differences."

Joe Morris, before he became president of the Canadian Labour Congress, had started in the B.C. woods as a chokerman and then as an organizer for the IWA. "Up to World War Two I doubt there were any more than 3,000 members in the union. It got impetus during the war. There were only a few full-time organizers but we had a lot of people carrying cards as 'walking delegates.' I was one of those. Those were the guys who went into the camps, sounded out the people, and signed people up into the union. The whole thing was underground at that time and lots of times the professional organizer had to walk miles into camp and if they were discovered they'd get the run put to them. There was evidence of some of them being physically manhandled. There were many things militating against union organization. Hell, camps were scattered all over creation. The food was generally good and in the bigger camps the living conditions were not that bad; the camps on the coast were made from lumber and for that time were fairly good accommodation but I've seen camps in the interior of B.C. where conditions were very primitive. There were lots of things I didn't like. I didn't like the fact you could be told to pack your bag and go at any time. There was a great deal of favouritism. The boss's 'boys' got all the best jobs. So we started to organize. It was tough. We really didn't start to solidify the union until we started to organize the sawmills as well. British Columbia was the most progressive. They were organizing more or less at the same time as they were organizing in the States. I think the union was progressive because it was always a pretty rank-and-file-controlled union. When we had the 1948 split the communist group tried to personalize it on the basis they were the ones who had built the union. Conversely, those who opposed the split said it was the union that was important. It was on that basis that the fight was won."

"I was a union man," said Waddy Weeks on Vancouver Island, "all my life. I fought for it and got fired for it time after time . . . When young fellows today say, 'What the heck do I want to go to a union meeting for — what the hell do they ever do for me?' that's when I blow my top. I say, 'You're in a nice, clean room, two men to a room, you have your own wash-stand, clothes closet, easy chair, light, and there's a bathroom between each two rooms. You think we didn't do anything for you? I could show you where I used to go when I went to the bathroom: over a peeled sapling stretched 20 feet long.' "

18 "BLOWIN' 'ER IN": THE LOGGER GOES TO TOWN

They tell the story of the old lumberjack sitting on the side of his bunk on a Friday night and somebody said, "What's the trouble, Joe, you're looking down in the mouth." "Well," he said, "I go out tomorrow for my annual drink and how I'm dreading it."

Few adventures in "blowin' 'er in," spending a winter's pay in a few riotous days in town, have been preserved in more detail than that of Baptiste Fortin during 72 merry hours in Ottawa in 1890.

When Baptiste finally arrived home in L'Ange-Gardien, Quebec, that spring, his wife, Exina, horrified to find he had only $54.13 to show for six months' work in lumber shanties up the Ottawa, wrote to his employers to ask why. The company discovered, through some detective work worthy of Sherlock Holmes, that Baptiste had spent $96 of his $150.13 winter wage in the following manner:[1]

One bottle of whiskey	$ 1.25
One briar pipe	$ 1.25
Ear rings	$ 1.75
A breakfast plate of oysters	$ 1.50
Hair cut and shampoo	$ 1.50
Hair dyed, black	$ 2.00
Hair dyed, brown, when black did not suit	$ 2.00
Drinks and tobacco with friends	$30.00

One photo, 25 copies	$ 5.00
Sightseeing, with horse and buggy	$ 7.00
One suit (real value $7)	$17.00
Red-topped boots (value $1.75)	$ 5.00
Watch and ring, later exchanged for 2 plugs of tobacco	$ 3.25
Advance to boarding house for room and meals, only one of which he ate	$ 5.00
Tip to Marie Christine for sewing button	$ 2.00
To organ grinder for damage in knocking over organ	$ 2.00
For stitches in face after fight with Xavier Lacasse	$ 1.00
For losing bet he could wrestle Narcisse Plamondon to the ground in the gateway of his hotel	$ 2.00
Hire of cab to railway station	$ 1.50
Railway ticket to L'Ange-Gardien	$ 4.00

What Exina said to Baptiste is, alas, unrecorded.

There were many places to welcome the well-heeled, or "stakey," logger, from Mother McGinty's tavern in Bytown and the fly-by-night Ottawa River grog shops with their barrels of raw white whiskey to the dives of rue Champlain in Quebec's Lower Town, Helltown in East Bathurst, New Brunswick; "Place des Dames" in Chapleau, Ontario; and the skid roads around Carrell and Cordova streets in Vancouver.

"The preachers who came to the camps used to tell us boys that when we came down in the spring instead of going to a saloon why not go to a nice library or drink coffee or things like that. One fellow told them, 'Well, Reverend, when I go to town after six or eight months fighting the elements I don't want libraries and I certainly don't want coffee. What I want comes in bottles and step-ins.'"[2]

Mary Chekman, a cook in northern Ontario camps who used to hear the men talk when they returned to camp, figured a lot of their adventures in town were just hot air.

"When they went to town all they did was sit around and drink and talk and boast, like 'If it wasn't for me that tote road wouldn't have got built yet.' Most of them wouldn't even get to *see* a woman in town but when they got back to camp you should hear them talkin'. They'd say, 'There wasn't one decent woman in town' and most of them hadn't even seen a woman. So all winter in camp they'd be talking about women and all summer in town they'd be talking about cutting wood."

If there was little fighting in the camps where bunkhouse etiquette sensibly forebade it, once the timberbeasts got to town the rules changed and a good booze-up and brawl were often part of the fun.

"There used to be great brawls in the old days in town between loggers from different camps. Nanaimo in the early days had Vancouver Island's biggest red-light district. Sunday morning we'd get a call saying all or part of our crew was in jail. The police would give us the sum total of bail, fines, and damages. We'd put a check in the mail and the crew would be back in time for work Monday morning."[3] For those who could not get to Nanaimo or Vancouver there were always a few scattered places like the Red Lantern House at "Pecker Point" on the lonely coast near Ocean Falls, where the 300-pound Bertha acted as bouncer when things got rough.

All over the west coast there were rough-and-ready bars wherever a trading post and a shanty of a "hotel" could be found. One at Knight Inlet was described thus in 1908: "The bar was roaring day and night. Billy had a band of bully boys tending bar for him; about 16 strong they were, and there was always some of them sober enough to work the cash register — right around the clock. Gee, them was great times. If a man liked he could keep drunk right along and never cost him a cent. I seed some of the finest kinds of fights, too, in this very barroom, four or five a night. There was always a card game going on, $10 or $20 the bet. I've seen a fellow go up to $900 on a single jackpot. In the morning you would see the boys lying scattered all over the rocks and down on the beach — just like a lot of dead flies when you've emptied out a jug of stale milk." That was in the boom years on the coast when logs were selling for $10 per 1000 board feet.

The lumber-town bars in the east could be just as active. "I was in Blind River one spring when the camps had broken up. This Sunday morning another fellow and I walked uptown to see what was going on. We came to this hotel and although the bar was closed we could see a pile of men in there on the floor all fighting and drunk as owls. In one corner was a fellow sittin' with two black eyes, crying away. I'll never forget that, such a mess of human beings. Some of them had their calk boots on. They would walk in with their calk boots if the hotel keeper would let them but it would tear your floors to pieces."[4]

There was usually someone like "Peg Leg Billy" LaFlamme of Blind River, big and tough despite his wooden leg, to bounce a trouble-maker but sometimes things got out of hand and the unthinkable would happen. In 1906 at Blind River a young logger who had been bested in a fight with the blacksmith Edward Morin pulled a gun and shot the blacksmith dead.

During the First World War the prohibition act stopped the sale of legal liquor, except for beer and wine in Quebec, and there were no more bar fights because there were no more bars. But there was lots of bootleg liquor and battles in the back alleys.

"They used to raise hell on Saturday nights and they'd fight, in good spirit, bet a week's chewing tobacco on a fight. Real serious fighting with bare knuckles. After the fight was over, that was it."[5]

"Things had changed a lot in the bush when I got back from the First World War. Before prohibition the lumberjack might work six months in the bush and he'd be broke three or four days after he got to town. Got drunk and somebody might roll him. Fellows would come down with their old lumberjack clothes and never get a new suit. They'd get drunk and the first thing you knew they'd be broke with the same old clothes on."[6]

But law, of course, did not stop drinking. "Prohibition just turned the lumberjacks to rot-gut. Sometimes the moonshiners put lye in it, sometimes chewing tobacco — to make it taste interestin'."[7]

The bolder bootleggers even managed to get into the camps where liquor had been more or less banned since the mid-1800s. The ban had been imposed during the great national temperance movement of the 1850s on the grounds that a crowded bunkhouse or a rumbling load of logs was no place for drunks.

"I remember a guy coming with a load of potatoes for a camp five miles from our depot. The next day the depot foreman went out to that camp and when he landed back at the depot that night he said, 'You know what I ran into? The horses were there standing around in the snow and there was a big stag dance in the bunkhouse and everybody drunk. There had been booze under that load of potatoes. Paddy Elliott was calling off and I don't know what all.' I said, 'What was the foreman there doing?' He said, 'The foreman was the biggest toad in the puddle.' I said, 'What did you do?' He said, 'I asked them if the work would be going all right tomorrow. I'll go again in the morning. They'll be working again in the morning.' "[8]

Camp cooks were always well placed to produce a surreptitious brew. "There was a Swedish cook at Minnipuka in northern Ontario who, every chance he got, put on a good brew of prunes and rice, beans or raisins. The trouble was we'd never let the darn stuff cool off. We'd sit around and try it every once in a while. They used the cans flour came in, with a top like a funnel. They'd put water and the ingredients in a pot and fire up. They tipped the can upside down over the pot and fashioned a dish under the apex of the inverted can and the steam would hit the can and drain down into the dish . . . pure moonshine. No copper pipe in those days. It was hot but by God it was good."[9]

In Quebec, although they preferred gin when they could get it, they made *chien* from almost anything lying around: oats, potato peelings, raisins, prunes, molasses, and they matured it for eight days in an old salt pork barrel behind the stove. Diluted with cheap wine it became *caribou*. There were some weird and wonderful concoctions. "We were making a brew out of Australian currants once and it turned black as ink. We'd make it in a 50-pound lard can to get a gallon plus a gin bottle full. It would burn like gasoline, blue. The two of us there didn't happen to drink so we made it for fun."[10]

But the last liquor most of the bushmen saw was on the long journey back to camp. "During most of their journey," warned the *Traveller's Guide* to the Upper Ottawa, written for genteel tourists in 1873, "they are probably singing ... Some of them know they will not see or taste John Barleycorn until they return to the city and have been bidding a too affectionate adieu to that potent monarch, for there is no grosser violation of regulations than the introduction of intoxicating liquors to the shanty or raft."

FIRE 19

In order that you may understand what these burnt woods
are I will tell you that the Heavens, being one day all on fire, full
of tempest and thunder which rumbled and made itself heard
in all parts, a thunderbolt fell at a time when the dryness was
extraordinary, and not merely set in flames all the woods and forests
which lay between Mirimachis and Nepisiquit, but also burnt
and consumed more than 250 leagues of country in such manner that
nothing was to be seen except very tall and quite blackened trunks
of trees, which showed in their frightful barrenness the evidence
of a conflagration wide-spread and altogether astonishing . . .

FATHER C. LE CLERCQ, 1677[1]

Since the 17th century, summer after summer, explorers, fur traders, and missionaries described forest fires across the land. Some were so great they darkened the noon skies and, carried high by the westerlies, fell as black rain on ships at sea. Less than 150 years after Father Le Clercq, a Recollect from Quebec ministering to the Indians, had described a lightning fire "between Mirimachis and Nepisiquit," another holocaust struck the same pine forests of New Brunswick.

In late September 1825, the people of the twin Miramichi towns of Newcastle and Chatham were prospering from the white pine trade. In Newcastle, a town of 1000, the talk was about a woman who awaited sentence in jail for murdering her baby and about the dry heat which had lain, week after week, across the province. It shrivelled crops and dried out streams until the Miramichi River itself sank low in its banks. October came but instead of mists and autumnal chill the sun shone hot through a sepia haze and there was smoke in the still air. Settlers and loggers, in town to buy winter supplies, spoke of the unusual number of fires in the bush. On the sixth day of October the heat was suffocating and away to the north-

265

west there were rumbles of thunder and flashes, like lightning, in the night.

The next day, Friday, October 7th, started like the others, the air still, the sun a small, hazy disk. By early afternoon a purple cloud appeared but was blown away by the light northerly breeze. Twilight came early, followed by a night so dark that people could hardly find their way home along the roads. Some thought the slash of red they had seen in the west had been the setting sun. The fresh breeze, at first welcome, had become a gale. William Wright, a lumberjack who had arrived from the north and knew the danger, somehow got hold of a drum and ran drumming through the streets but few heard him above the wind. Just before nine o'clock there was sudden silence and then a crash like thunder on a mountain.

"Suddenly a bright light pierced the darkness and a moment later a sheet of flame flashed from the woods at the top of the hill. Near this place was the new Presbyterian church . . . It was the first building to take fire and it vanished almost in an instant. The wind had increased to a hurricane, and the burning brands were carried over the town, spreading destruction in their path. There was no longer darkness, and in the awful light the terrified people were seen hurrying for their lives and knowing not where to look for safety . . . many of them believed the Day of Judgment was at hand."[2]

Men, women, whole families fled into the river or to the swamp west of town. Some climbed on floating logs and tried to paddle across the river to the safety of Chatham and were drowned in the waves whipped up by the gale. Cries from the jail caused men to pause long enough to break down the door but the prisoners, including the woman who had murdered her baby, perished in the smoke.

On the back lots behind town only one girl survived among the 13 families. Ann Jackson, 41, a farmer's wife at home with six children, sought safety in a brook. All the others died and their memorial stone in St. Paul's churchyard bears the words:

> Forests were set on fire, and hour by hour,
> They fell and faded, and the crackling trunks
> Extinguished with a crash,
> All earth was but one thought,
> And that was Death.

The fire was halted by the broad Miramichi and within 10 hours had burned itself out of fuel. At daybreak on Saturday only 12 of Newcastle's 260 buildings remained standing and in Douglastown, a few miles downriver, only six out of 64 homes. More than 160 bodies were counted and many of the injured died later. Hundreds of square miles of forest around Newcastle were destroyed and at the same time fires were burning over one-fifth of New Brunswick, from Chaleur Bay to Maine, and homes were burned in Fredericton. Although ships were burned to the waterline in the Miramichi River, Chatham was spared.

The firestorm known as The Great Miramichi Fire was born of several bush fires which united, creating hurricane winds with their heat, and whirled through the dry woods on a 15-mile front, throwing fire balls and flaming branches miles ahead. Whether it reached the "mile a minute" claimed by survivors, its speed was tremendous because it was "crowning," leaping through the tops of the dry pine. Such a crown fire has been described by the geographer, Dr. Robert Bell.

"When the fire has got under way the pitchy trees burn with almost explosive rapidity. The flames rush through their branches and high above their tops with terrifying sound. The ascending heat soon develops a strong breeze, if a wind does not happen to be blowing already. Before this gale the fire sweeps on with a roaring noise as fast as a horse can gallop. The irresistible front of flames devours the forest before it as rapidly as a prairie fire licks up the dry grass. The line of the gigantic conflagration has a height of 100 feet or more above the tree tops, or 200 feet from the ground. Great sheets of flame disconnect themselves from the fiery avalanche and leap upwards as towering tongues of fire, or dart forward bridging over wide spaces, such as lakes and rivers, starting the fire afresh in advance of the main column ... The immense shooting flames are probably due to the large quantities of high inflammable gas evolved by the heat from the pitchy tree tops just in advance of actual combustion, and they help to account for the incredible speed ... "[3]

In the Ottawa Valley the first great recorded fire swept the "Big Pine Country" on the Bonnechère River in 1851 and was started by burning wadding paper from a river driver's musket. In 1855 an Indian burning off a blueberry patch near Lady Evelyn Lake, west of the Lake Timiskaming stretch of the Upper Ottawa, set off a tremendous fire which burned, first eastward, and then turned northwest up the Montreal River and west 200 miles to Lake Superior near Michipocoten. Two thousand square miles of spruce and pine were burned but since the country was unsettled there were no deaths. In later years, however, a great triangle of country north of Lady Evelyn Lake was to be the scene of repeated fires and human tragedy.

Until the arrival of European settlers forest fires were caused by lightning. For the most part the Indians appear to have been careful

"Great sheets of flame disconnect themselves from the fiery avalanche and leap upwards as towering tongues of flame..." A crowning fire turns the tree-tops into torches at Youbou on Vancouver Island.

British Columbia Forest Service

burning off their vegetable patches, but to the settlers forests were for burning. The forest was the enemy, hiding dangerous beasts and hostile natives and preventing cultivation. Although a forest fire prevention law was passed in Nova Scotia as early as 1761 it had no teeth. It was 1921, in fact, before the first settler was convicted in Canada for causing a forest fire and he was sentenced to one month in jail at Sudbury for starting a fire which destroyed thousands of acres of pine.

Although, by the turn of the century, there had been no tragedy to equal that on the Miramichi in 1825, there were serious fires year after year. In 1870 a gang clearing brush near St. Félicien, west of Lac St. Jean in Quebec, neglected a dinner fire which got out of control and within three hours had burned an area 100 miles long and 15 miles wide. Many communities were burned, 500 were rendered homeless, and Chicoutimi was threatened, but miraculously only five persons were killed. Many escaped the blaze by seeking shelter in caves.

The advancing railways had become a major source of fires until the Board of Railway Commissioners ordered the companies to cut the brush back from the tracks, prohibited use of poor quality coal, and ordered spark arrestors on locomotive smokestacks. Slash from logging and the clearing of mine sites was also a serious hazard. As more settlers, miners, and loggers moved into the north, man replaced lightning as the major cause of fire.

On June 13, 1886, bush fires around Vancouver rushed through the growing lumber town, killing 20 people. In the logging country of southeast British Columbia 80 lost their lives and 3000 lost their homes in 1908. The town of Fernie was destroyed and survivors claimed the heat was so intense that dry buildings caught fire even before flames reached them.

In the east, on the Canadian Shield in Quebec and Ontario, weather conditions which breed forest fires are all too common — weeks of drought, southwest winds, high temperatures, and low relative humidity of 30 per cent or less which sucks billions of gallons of moisture out of the trees. In July 1911, all three conditions prevailed in northeastern Ontario. The settlements of South Porcupine, Timmins, and Cochrane were so full of prospectors in for the gold rush that tents were pitched along the transcontinental railway line. For weeks smoke had been seen southwest of the tracks as far as Elk Lake, which had developed into a busy centre in the silver mining rush. As on the Miramichi in New Brunswick 86 years earlier, everyone was much too busy to pay heed to the fire danger, and besides, they argued, it was about time for rain anyway.

Black Tuesday, July 11, brought not rain but wind. Bush fires were swept up by the southwest wind into a firestorm and by mid-afternoon the country from Porcupine to Cochrane, some 50 miles, was ablaze. Hundreds fled into the lakes. Tent camps, farms, the settlements of South Porcupine, Porquis Junction, Cochrane, Matheson, and a part of Timmins were destroyed. Ed Caswell was trying to rescue a trunk of family keepsakes when a teamster drove through Cochrane shouting, "Jump on, the whole world is on fire!" Down at the Cochrane railway station a locomotive, its whistles blowing, was shunting people to safety in boxcars. All but three houses were razed in Cochrane but amazingly there were no deaths directly attributed to the fire in Cochrane itself. In settlements farther south at least 73 perished before the fire swept northeastward and burned itself out around Lake Abitibi. The second day after the fire, rain came down in torrents on half a million acres of black, smoking desolation.

In 1914 the Ontario government began to keep records of forest fires and of the 2300 reported that year nearly 70 per cent were blamed on railway operations along the 2000 miles of track passing through Ontario forests. By 1915 there were 900 fire rangers in the woods. As well as fighting fires, a ranger was expected to patrol long beats, usually in pairs on foot or by canoe, build cabins and look-out towers, clean up dangerous areas of slash, post warning notices, issue or withhold permits for settlers wishing to burn off their land, and investigate the cause of fires.

By 1916 Cochrane and Matheson had been rebuilt in the wake of the 1911 Porcupine fire and care had been taken to cut back the bush far from town limits. With 10 000 people living in the clay belt triangle bounded by Timmins in the west, Matheson in the east, and Cochrane to the north, the worst fire in Canadian history occurred.

There had been a month of drought and heat, settlers were burning brush, and there were fires in the woods to the southwest where a breeze began to stir on July 25th. A fire front near the Mattagami River began moving northeastward, making its own gale, until it stretched, irregularly, for 100 miles in a J with its western hook near Timmins, its lower curve near Matheson, and its cross-bar centred on Cochrane. On Saturday morning, July 29, the curtain of smoke parted a quarter of a mile from Cochrane and settlers reported "one seething cauldron of flame." It was 1911 all over again. The southern tentacle of fire struck Matheson, a town of 800, early Saturday afternoon.

"It was not so much a matter of fire as of wind," Mrs. C. R. Keeling told newspaper reporters from Toronto after the fire was over. "You must think of this in terms of a tornado and a cyclone, not so much as fire. The very air was burning. The rate of speed was anything between 50 and 90 miles an hour. It seemed to leap from the forest to the buildings and in about three minutes the whole town was ablaze."[4]

At Nushka, a French-Canadian settlement of 20 frame houses a few miles up the Timiskaming and Northern Ontario Railway, Father Wilfrid Gagne, a 27-year-old priest, led 35 parishioners out of the burning town and left them in the comparative safety of a railway cutting to return to Nushka to try to rescue 28 others. Both groups suffocated to death except for one man who managed to breathe by scooping a hole in the moist clay of the cutting and thrusting his face into the hole to filter the smoke. When Nushka was rebuilt it was named Val Gagne.

Farther south searchers found 21 bodies in a root cellar with no burns on them, while near Cochrane nine bodies were found, one with face thrust in the scorched and powdery muskeg. Part of Cochrane was saved when a rain storm dampened the flames on Saturday evening but 3000 were left homeless. The fire raced on to burn Kelso, part of Monteith, and Iroquois Falls, a town of more than 1000 where many took refuge in the concrete pulp-and-paper mill. Part of Timmins was burned. By Sunday night heavy rain drenched the north and the tragedy played itself out.

Since most of the deaths were in the clay belt farming area around Matheson, it was known as the Matheson fire. Officials wondered how it was that the death toll, 60 or more, had been so high in the town since a wide tract of open land had been cleared around the town when it was rebuilt after the 1911 fire. An Englehart undertaker, L. Soper, sent to bury the dead, had an answer.

"To my mind 90 per cent of the deaths were caused directly by burnt oxygen in the air. The flames leaped ahead of the fire, ignited the oxygen, and the people fell to the ground from lack of air. All the bodies recovered have been burnt but that was quite natural after the fire passed over them. Most of them were suffocated before the fire reached them."[5]

The fire burned over 1329 square miles, killed more than 220 people, and was the worst, if not the last, in northeast Ontario. Because it had suffered the worst forest fires, Ontario began to lead the way in fire fighting legislation. In 1917 a new Fire Prevention Act was passed. Fire towers, first wooden and then steel, were erected since proper early warning would have saved lives in both the 1916 and 1911 fires. Portable back pumps came into use. Settlers were forbidden to set fires for land clearance between April 15 and September 30 unless they had a permit. The regulations did not forestall still another tragedy in northeast Ontario, however, in an area 50 to 80 miles south of Matheson.

Despite hot, dry weather in 1922, municipalities around Haileybury decided that fire protection service was too costly to continue

Cochrane, Ontario, before and after the fire of 1911 which razed all but a few buildings. Three thousand people were left homeless.

Ont. Ministry of Natural Resources

Ont. Ministry of Natural Resources

Photograph by MALAK, *Ottawa*

A fire ranger behind his map table was reporting by bush telephone from a look-out tower in the Gatineau forest, north of Maniwaki, Quebec, in 1950. Once he spotted a fire from his tower, a ranger was expected to relay the location and distance in words such as these: "I have spotted a fire with azimuth compass bearing, from my station, of 24 degrees, 30 minutes. Distance approximately 19 miles." In the days before phone lines were rigged through the woods, he used heliographs or semaphore signalling and the standard code for the fire warning above would have been simply "OG DS."

past September 15. In an isolated region to the west bush fires were gaining strength around Montreal River and Elk River. The humidity dropped, the days were hot and cloudless, and by October 2nd the fires had joined and travelled 20 miles on a southwest wind through unsettled forest to within striking distance of Tarzwell, Charlton, and Englehart. By October 3rd the fire front was creating its own 75-mile-an-hour hurricane as its tremendous heat rose and cooler air rushed in below. The fire struck Tarzwell and by the next morning was speeding southeastward, with a change of wind, toward the town of Haileybury, 45 miles away. Charleton was destroyed and part of Englehart, along with farms and hamlets on the railway line. The fire reached Haileybury by mid-afternoon and clothes drying on the line caught fire and swept down Main Street. The roof of the Catholic church caught fire and people praying inside ran to the river. Within 30 minutes 100 buildings were afire; the town's volunteer firemen were forced back, block by block, from the north end of town, and by nightfall most of Haileybury was destroyed.

At Cobalt the miners fought back with dynamite, blasting wide ribbons of forest, clay, and rock as a fire-break. They worked all night and saved the town and the next day snow fell and the fire guttered out. All told, 43 people died and 6000 homes were destroyed. It was the last of the fires with high death tolls apart from one in 1938 which killed 20 in Dance Township in the Fort Frances area.

There were three types of forest fires: the common brush fire, a surface fire which runs through dry leaves, duff, and bush; the ground fire, which burns deep into dry muskeg and humus gases; the crown fire, which leaps through the tree-tops and, short of a firestorm, is the worst of all. In the days before the bulldozer which carves out fire lines, before the airplane and water bombing, they fought with water from portable back tanks or water pumped through hoses from the lakes and rivers; they fought with axes, grub-hoes, and the Pulaski tool — a combination of shovels, axe, and hoe — named in 1910 for Edward C. Pulaski, a hero of the Coeur d'Alene fire in Idaho. Sometimes they fought fire with fire: the area ahead of the main fire would be burned off with a "backfire" to deprive the main blaze of fuel.

"With a backfire you were counting on it setting up a counterdraft of its own. If the main fire is moving one way you want to set up a backfire that will draw in the opposite way so the two fires will come together and burn out. You don't just go into the bush and set it. You have to make a fire line you can hold, dig trenches, and clear away the bush and wet it down and have men and pumps handy."[6]

"With a backfire," said William Sleeman, Director of the Forest

The early fire towers were rickety-looking affairs built of poles. This tower, on Deadman's Mountain between the towns of William's Lake and Soda Creek, to the east of the Fraser River in the British Columbia interior, was built of jack pine in the 1920s and was 40 feet high. By the 1930s steel towers were the rule, some 80 or even 150 feet high. Since most of them swayed in the wind, a tower man needed a good head for heights.

British Columbia Forest Service

Woodsmen cutting out underbrush and digging a "fire line" in an effort to stop an advancing forest fire near Sudbury, Ontario, in October 1947, by depriving it of fuel. Many fires, blown by the wind, leaped such lines and swept on.

Ont. Ministry of Natural Resources

Fire Control Branch of the Ontario Ministry of Natural Resources, "you attempt to develop natural fire-breaks first of all, such as lakes or big muskegs. You run a fire line from one lake to another, then you pick your weather to set a backfire. If you have a 40-mile-an-hour wind there's nothing you can do. Once the wind is up and the relative humidity is down and the wind is in the wrong direction there is nothing you can do. But even if the wind is only blowing the fire about 10 miles an hour it will create its own draft: that is to say, if you get a mile in front of the fire the wind will be blowing in the same direction as the wind behind the fire. But if you get within an eighth of a mile in front of the fire the wind will be blowing back toward the fire. The fire will be creating its own wind and will pull air against the prevailing wind. That is when you can backfire.

"There is a fantastic amount of energy being created and hot air has to rise and the only place cool air can come in is at the bottom, so you get wind coming in against the prevailing wind at the bottom of the fire. But it gets pretty critical in there and getting in front of a fire like that to make a backfire can be pretty hazardous. If you get relative humidity down around 15 per cent and 40-mile-an-hour winds behind the fire it will jump one-half or three-quarters of a mile ahead.

"The basic reason a fire crowns is relative humidity. When you get humidity at 70 per cent you couldn't get a crown fire going. When you get around 30 per cent and a week without rain and 30- or 40-mile-an-hour winds the fire will go through anything, even poplar, hardwoods, or anything else."

"They are pretty tricky," said Buzz Lein, who fought dozens of forest fires, "but when the whole countryside is on fire what difference does another fire make? The only thing you'd better make sure is that if you are setting a backfire you don't get caught in it. About half of those fires worked. Fighting fires is probably the worst job in the world. It requires a special type of fella with a special type of knowledge. You read about these huge forest fires with 600 men on the fire. Well, I'll tell you something. If you've got a fire and you have 600 men, at no time is there ever more than 100 working. The rest are just goofing off.

"I remember one fire, around May 24th, and that thing really burned. It must have been started by lightning. It swept across a river and I guess it caught a river drive crew. One of the guys died of heart attack and when the fire was out and I went back to pick him up we had to haul him out like a deer. I still remember the hole above his breast where his gold watch had melted."

In the Depression years men were setting fires in order to get jobs fighting them and in 1937 more than 270 incendiary fires were reported in Ontario.

Jack Matthew's Story

"I became Chief Ranger at Chapleau in 1936. The Chief Ranger is the guy who gets the noisy end of the fire-fighting job. You'd go down to headquarters about 8 o'clock on a bright, hot, sunny day and there'd be 15 or 20 fellows sitting there with little haversacks and their bush boots on and I'd say, 'Okay, where is it?' Some of the local people said, 'They only do this around the 24th of May or the 1st of July to get money to buy some wine.' One guy set 52 fires along a road three miles behind town. All in one afternoon. He walked along the road with a box of matches and lit the birch bark and threw the matches in the bush – 52 starts. The fire was less than 50 acres but it was so close to town we just jumped on it. If you passed the word around town you soon got a fire-fighting crew because those were Depression days. At one fire, a place called Dalton, fire burned 25 million feet of lumber and it was suspected the fire was set. I simply sent up to White River and said send me 150 men on the next train and I called the local men together and said, 'Okay boys, you are all laid off. Somebody started this fire and some of you are going to suffer but all of you are going to go.' We didn't have any more incendiary fires. Another time I needed men I just took 127 off the next train that came through town and all of them were happy as clams to get $2 a day and their board.

"There was one fire which burned 10 square miles where a bunch of bachelors had settled in little shacks. One had a hobby of cutting birch firewood which he split up nice and fine and he had piles running all through the woods, roofed with big sheets of birch bark. His shack took fire and spread to the wood piles and those big sheets of birch bark took off like quoits in the southwest wind and flew into the bush. It was an old burned area, dry as tinder, and fire started all over the place. By midnight you could read a newspaper with all this dry wood burning. We nailed it next morning at 3 o'clock. You'd do your fire fighting in the early morning or at night when the humidity is high and the fire drops down.

"One time in Chapleau on a Sunday afternoon the sky suddenly got a greenish colour and you should have seen people scuttle out of the bush. It made me nervous because I was responsible and I didn't know of any fires and it turned out to be one 100 miles away on the other side of White River. A cloud of ash came over, light grey ash. Oh, you can smell fires and tell what's burning. You can tell a muskeg fire from a bush fire. A muskeg fire has acrid smoke. But if you have a lot of fires around you wouldn't know where it is coming from. They had steel fire towers by that time, 80 feet high with little octagonal houses on top and from them, normally, you would figure on seeing smoke for a 15-mile radius. There is not much use going up on a fire tower before 10 A.M. The humidity is

276

still too high and there's not much going on in a fire. The humidity drops and the sun comes out and the breeze comes up and the fire will fan up so that's why you do your fire fighting at night and in the early morning. The worst time for a fire is 2 or 3 P.M. when humidity is low and the wind gets up. It depends on the size and nature of the fire whether you can work at it in the afternoon. People used to say it was like fighting a war. Tactics. We were on the job seven days a week and no shifts. You just stayed."

Two of the worst fire months were May and June after the spring sun had dried out the woods and before the new growth was well established. The forests most at risk were softwood stands which had suffered from some earlier fire, where trees stood like scorched kindling, or forests which had been killed by the spruce budworm. The budworm destroys hundreds of thousands of acres of fir and spruce each year, feeding in its caterpillar stage on the trees until they are dead, resinous Roman Candles awaiting a match. It takes three years for budworms to kill a tree and they come and go in cycles.

It was under such conditions that the 1948 Chapleau-Mississagi fire, one of the biggest in the world, began. There were actually two fires, which started at the same time but far apart; they finally joined, and burned the beautiful Mississagi Forest Reserve which runs east of Sault Ste. Marie from the north shore of Lake Huron up to Chapleau. The Mississagi River and its tributaries had long been logging country. There had been an unusually dry spring which had parched the sub-soil, and the budworm had killed off tracts of forest in the last great pinery in northern Ontario. On the day the fires started, May 25, winds were from the southwest at 20 miles an hour, the temperature was 66°F. but was to go up to 90°F. later, and humidity was 27 per cent.

The southern, or Mississagi, section of the fire burned an area 50 miles by 40 miles and was unusually well documented from the hour it started. As it happened, the forester Holly Parsons was flying over the area near the Thessalon-Chapleau road doing aerial mapping and he spotted white smoke 20 miles away at 12:50 P.M. Within 10 minutes he was over the fire and reported 15 to 25 acres alight. The fire had started near a small lake on the headwaters of the Sharpsand River in trackless, hilly country strewn with dead jack pine and balsam fir which had been killed by budworm. Lightning had been reported in the area a night or two before. Ranger Lake Tower 102 sighted the smoke at 1:10 P.M. and at 3:30 Jimmie O'Meara at the Peshu Lake Ranger Station reported 50 acres afire. By 4 P.M. this had spread to 100 acres under a strong wind and was crowning rapidly. Logging had finished for the year and there were few men in the camps so O'Meara sent for 25 men at the Mississagi Indian Reserve to the south, the home of some of the best fire-fighters around. The fire was two miles southeast of Trolling Lake but there was little to be done that night. There were various accounts of how the fire started; some blamed campers from Michigan and others blamed trappers. Within a few days lightning started at least a dozen new fires.

Anatomy of a Fire

May 26 (Wednesday) — The 25 fire-fighters were on the fire by 6 A.M. At 10 A.M. aerial reconnaissance plotted the fire over 2000 acres although it was barely 21 hours old. It was spreading rapidly northeastward through dead slash left from logging operations which extended 10 miles from Trolling Lake to Peshu Lake. By 1 P.M. another 44 men had arrived by truck over the Thessalon-Chapleau road from the hydro project 40 miles to the south. After the fire had forced them to abandon the fire lines southeast of Trolling Lake, the fire-fighters concentrated along the Mississagi River from Trolling Lake to the southwest arm of Rocky Island Lake.

May 27 (Thursday) — Blown by southwest winds of 40 miles an hour, the fire jumped the Mississagi River at three points during the afternoon and spread along the south shore of Rocky Island Lake. The fighting force numbered 137 men and 11 pumps and the fire covered 7000 acres 48 hours after it had started.

May 28 (Friday) — Half an hour of light showers during the early morning failed to stop the fire from crowning and it burned around Rocky Lake as far as Rouelle Lake to the northeast and it spread to the west of Rocky Lake and through the slash north to Rimrock Lake three miles southeast of Peshu Lake. The men made a stand at Rouelle and Rimrock lakes using bulldozers to build fire lines, but were forced to abandon the lines next day. Flames swept within 25 yards of a lumber camp west of Rocky Island Lake and two men barely escaped entrapment. Four were burned but the camp was saved. The fire had spread over 29 000 acres and the fighters numbered 250.

May 29–31 (Saturday–Monday) — The wind had fanned the fire over 65 000 acres and south toward Finn Lake. Four hundred and fifty men had been trucked in but the heat was so intense they were unable to make a frontal attack and had to work from well back. By Monday, with no hope of rain, they were on 24-hour duty

The start of the great Mississagi fire in northern Ontario in 1948. Holly Parsons, who happened to be flying over the area at the time, took this picture shortly after smoke began to drift from the head of Sharpsand River.

Ont. Ministry of Natural Resources

By June 5 the fire was burning around Peshu Lake, threatening the ranger station which was the command post for the fire fighters. The fire was "crowning" and leap-frogging in the wind.

Ont. Ministry of Natural Resources

279

and lumber camps between Trolling Lake and Peshu Lake were evacuated.

June 1 (Tuesday) – When the wind suddenly shifted from west to northwest a group of men trying to check a prong of fire near Gravel River were forced to flee, throwing their equipment into the river. There was speculation that a muskrat trapper had started the fire, which was now being fought by 800 men.

June 2 (Wednesday) – Only six miles now separated the Mississagi fire from the Chapleau fire to the north but smoke made aerial spotting so difficult there was uncertainty as to where the fires were actually burning. Tower men could see no farther than four miles and smoke was reported as far away as Peterborough, 250 miles to the southeast. The Mississagi fire was still crowning in the wind and extended 20 miles from Peshu Lake in the north to Finn Lake in the south and had jumped eastward to Kindiogami Lake.

June 3 (Thursday) – The wind swung into the northeast, forcing the fire toward the south where there were few big natural barriers, lakes and rivers. More than 100 000 acres were afire in the Mississagi sector and more than 35 000 in the Chapleau sector. Heavy smoke was blown 2000 miles into southwestern United States and, in Texas, street lights had to be turned on in daylight. Pilots flying across America reported poor visibility in smoke at 4000 to 8000 feet.

June 4 (Friday) – Only four miles of white pine, cut-over slash from logging, and acres of dead balsam fir killed by budworm now separated the Mississagi and Chapleau fires.

June 5 (Saturday) – In an effort to keep the two fires from joining, relays of Norseman and Stinson aircraft carried canoes, tools, pumps, and hose to Rocky Island Lake and Seven Mile Lake. Three hundred men were ferried to the east side of Peshu Lake and walked eastward three miles to the height of land where one force headed north to attack the Chapleau fire and the other went south to fight the Mississagi fire.

Jump fires had appeared to the north, south, and west of Peshu Lake Ranger station, practically encircling it in smoke so thick the float planes could no longer land. By 4:30 fire had almost reached the small huddle of cabins where Tom Woodside, a ranger from Sault Ste. Marie, had organized the defence.

"Eight pumps were placed at the dam and the main wooden part and log sides were kept well wetted down. Barrels of aircraft gas

Ont. Ministry of Natural Resources

After a month of fighting the Mississagi fire, tired woodsmen lean on their shovels in the black and smoking ruins. When the worst was over they made patrols to make sure there was no flare-up.

Ont. Ministry of Natural Resources

Peshu Lake ranger station after the fire had passed over. The rangers saved the buildings by building a backfire and soaking the wooden huts.

were placed in the lake to avoid any possible explosion. The fire approached on a 15 to 20 mile front. All buildings were kept sprayed with water and small buildings covered with wet blankets. The fire reached Peshu in the afternoon. It was so hot, there was little smoke. It struck like a gigantic red hot furnace and in a short time it was gone . . . Peshu Lake buildings were saved. In spite of the pumps at the dam the woodwork was badly scorched. If the dam had gone out the water in Peshu Lake would have gone with it.

"I was keeping Mr. Art Leman, District Forester, Sault Ste. Marie, fully informed by phone. Over the span of years I can still remember saying, 'Art, here she comes, the telephone will soon be gone.' Then all was quiet except for the roar of the flames."

Just before the fire had struck, the half dozen men at the camp had built a backfire which, while it destroyed the camp's only transport, a truck, it did save the buildings. After the fire had swept past, the cook, despite intense heat in the cookery, managed to prepare a supper of steak and gravy, mashed potatoes, chopped lettuce and tomatoes, and pie.

To the south, that same afternoon, a crown fire overran the Black Creek fire tower forcing the tower man to race into the lake and from his canoe he watched the tower collapse. To the west of Rouelle Lake, towerman Slim McCaskiff and 22 men were forced to leap into the lake up to their necks, dragging 3600 feet of hose, two pumps, and six gasoline tanks with them. The road between Thessalon and Chapleau was cut by the fire.

June 11 (Friday) — District Forester Leman, in a Norseman, seeded clouds with dry ice but the cloud formation was inadequate for real rainfall. The wind had boxed the compass and was now back in the southwest where it had started 18 days before. No rain had fallen for two weeks.

June 12 (Saturday) — The Mississagi and Chapleau fires finally met near Seabrook Lake, northeast of Peshu Lake. The Chapleau fire began to burn in areas which had been scorched a few days earlier by the Mississagi fire. In the teeth of a 45-mile-an-hour wind from the southwest, the battle was concentrated north of Mount Lake, Distant Lake, Kirkpatrick Lake and, in the west, around Aubrey Falls and Peshu Lake where the Chapleau fire was pushing in through the earlier burn.

June 14 (Monday) — Showers (.26 inches) were too light to affect the fire. Half the construction workers on the $14 million dollar power development to the south on the Mississagi River were thrown into the fight and the Hydro Commission flew in an amphibian at 13 000 to 16 000 feet to drop dry ice into the clouds with no success.

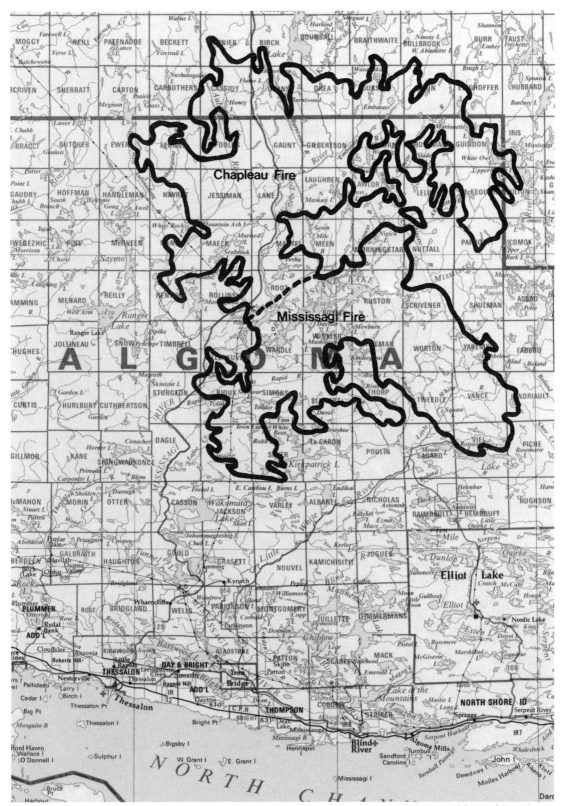

Chapleau Fire

Mississagi Fire

An Otter aircraft making a water drop over a forest
fire in the Sioux Lookout area of Ontario. The dropping of water from aircraft floats equipped with
special valves began in 1945.

Ont. Ministry of Natural Resources

June 22 (Tuesday) — On this day, four weeks after the fire had started, substantial rain began to fall for the first time and continued for eight days permitting the men to hold their fire lines. The holocaust was reduced to "smudges," scattered grey mushrooms of smoke.

July 23 (Friday) — At 2 p.m., two months after it started, the fire was officially declared under control.

July 31 (Saturday) — All fighting crews were withdrawn by 6 p.m. although air patrols continued for another month.

The Chapleau-Mississagi fire was now history. More than 1500 men, with 43 portable fire pumps and 107 000 feet of hose, had fought the fire. A total of 645 340 acres were burned but no one was killed. Thirty planes were used in the battle but water bombing, then in its infancy, was considered still too ineffective.

The primitive system of dropping water from planes, adopted in 1945, consisted of scooping up and releasing water through valves on a Norseman, which could lift a load of 1800 pounds. Sometimes the plane scooped up too much water and risked crashing on take-off. There was danger, too, over the fire when the pilot cut from his 130-mile-an-hour cruising speed to a near stall to permit a gravity flow to dump the water through the valves. A faster bombing method was developed in 1950 when salvoes of paper bags, each containing three gallons of water, were dropped. Just before he reached a fire the pilot would cut his speed to 55 miles an hour, barely above stall level, and while the "stall horn" blared its unnerving warning a helper scrambled to toss the bags down on the fire where they burst in an explosion of steam. Occasionally the bags broke prematurely or fell on the heads of the fire-fighters.

The Chapleau-Mississagi fire left 300 million board feet of salvageable timber and late that year the provincial government moved 2000 loggers into the blackened woods to bring it out in "Operation Scorch." It was hard, dirty work and they would come back to camp at night as black as coal miners but they saved millions of dollars' worth of lumber and pulpwood.

Although the days of great loss of human life have passed, forest fires have continued and there is little to indicate they will ever disappear as long as there are great tracts of trees diseased by spruce budworm, as long as there is lightning and high winds, and as long as people are in the woods in the dangerous dry seasons. But at least, said one official, fire losses could be reduced to a minimum if "every individual developed a state of mind that would cause him to avoid any single act that could possibly start a forest fire."

20
GHOST CAMP

*Those old camps seem like ghosts out of the past. But I still
remember the men who used to work in them and the things
we used to do. I guess someone coming along now would see the
remains of our camps and wonder what sort of men worked
there and who we were.*

GORDON FLETCHER AT PUKASKWA

Along the lonely northeast shore of Lake Superior there is no place
more inaccessible than Pukaskwa. It is a federal wilderness park now,
700 square miles of unpeopled forest, but barely half a century ago
its hills and swamps were alive with lumberjacks. Their trails have
disappeared, their cabins are in ruins, and the trees have grown again,
but for 13 years, from 1917 to 1930, the logging camps of Pukaskwa
cut 30 000 cords of spruce each winter for the pulp mill at Sault Ste.
Marie, 150 miles down the lake.

Most of the lumberjacks were single men, Québécois from Buckingham on the Ottawa River 500 miles to the east. Each autumn
they would take the train to the Soo and the tug boats which hauled
logs down to the mill carried them, along with horses, pigs, and
supplies, up to Pukaskwa, a journey of a day or two. From the
freeze-up in December until the April thaw their only link with the
world was the two dog teams which carried mail twice a month
over the 70 pathless miles from the railway town of White River.
There were, at times, 375 loggers and, perhaps, 20 women and children at Pukaskwa.

There is little left to mark their passing — the remains of a small
graveyard lost amid wild roses, honeysuckle, and raspberry bushes;
one building stands amid the bushy mounds which were the cookery,
bunkhouses, warehouses, and stables of the base camp on Imogene

PUKASKWA

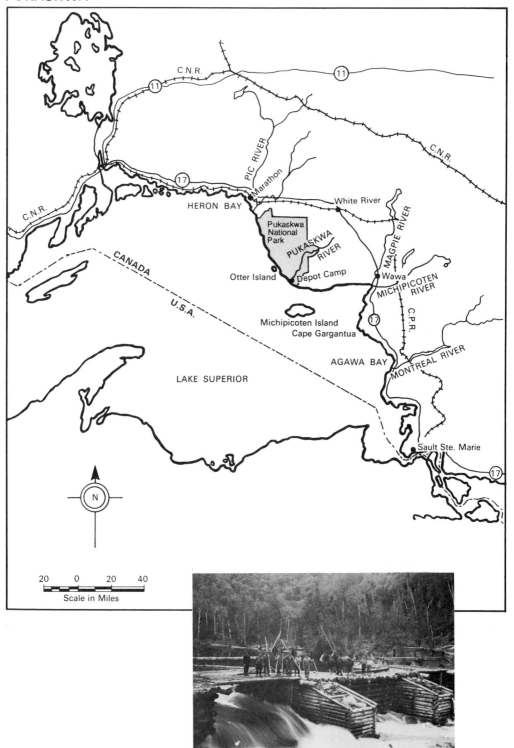

Courtesy of Gordon and Lee Fletcher

287

Creek, a mile west of the Pukaskwa River. You have to search for other signs: the mouldering logs of a dam, a rusted steam boiler that winched sleigh loads of logs up hills too steep for Amab Raby's horses. The Indian grave of Old Lady Pukaskwa is just a tumble of bunch berry and rotten logs. They say that Sarah Pukaskwa died by Imogene Creek early in the century after her husband and sons were drowned on a canoe trip to tap maple sugar on Michipocoten Island 10 miles off shore.

Logging started at Pukaskwa — called "Pukasaw" by those who worked there — about 1905 when Frank Perry from Sault Ste. Marie, Michigan, cut timber on the flats a mile up the Pukaskwa River. Perry rafted logs to Michigan until his holding boom broke on the lake and he lost thousands of dollars' worth of wood. Cutting resumed only in 1917 to supply spruce to the mill which had opened in Sault Ste. Marie, Ontario, in 1895. The new men built their camps as far as 20 miles up the north branch of the Pukaskwa River and 16 miles up the wilder East Branch, and logged on the Tagouche and Imogene creeks and on the rivers Pipe, Julia, and Ghost, or Floating Heart. Cutting began each October and ended in January when the 12- and 16-foot logs were hauled by horses to the river banks. In April and May the wood was driven to the mouth of the Pukaskwa and stored for the tugs in a giant boom.

Gordon Fletcher lived there as a boy with his mother, his brother, Lee, and his stepfather, Jack Mills, the camp clerk. Their cabin by Imogene Creek, the only building still standing, has been immortalized by A. Y. Jackson in a painting called "Bear Cabin."

"Oh, it was isolated in the winter. The odd man used to take off, couldn't stand it any longer, and go 70 miles up the White River trail. But there weren't too many. You needed snowshoes and there were no snowshoes. Once in a while the Scandinavians used to make their own skis and take off but if you didn't have skis or snowshoes there was no way you were going to get out. Pukasaw is still one of the most isolated places in Ontario. In those days the same men kept coming back — year after year you'd see the same faces. It was a good place to make a stake for there was no way of spending it. I went in with my parents in 1921 when I was 10 and I was 14 when I got my first job there, at Schist Falls. I had to watch out for log jams and when a jam started I had to wave a flag which they could see a quarter of a mile upriver and they'd swing the boom across the river with a horse to keep more logs from coming down. They just logged along the sides of the river, a mile or two on each side. I started as a clerk in one of the camps when I was 15, a camp of about 30 men. They still had muzzle loader bunks. Some of those small-time jobbers, they didn't have any more buildings than they had to, cookery and bunkhouse combined in one building. In the

288

Courtesy of Gordon Fletcher

Pukaskwa depot in the 1920s. The Walking Boss's cabin in foreground is flanked on the right by the Mills-Fletcher cabin and on the left by the depot office. The big buildings behind them, across Imogene Creek, are the bunkhouse at left and cookery at right, with hardwood for the stoves piled almost to the eaves. The depot staff consisted of the Walking Boss, doctor, clerk, scaler, harness maker, barn boss, blacksmith, cook, and choreboy. Between 1917 and 1930 there were more than a dozen buildings at the little community on the shores of Lake Superior. The people in the logging camps, which stretched miles back in the woods, made only occasional visits to the depot.

Courtesy of John Kelly

The men of Pukaskwa. Leon Raby's camp on the Pukaskwa River in the winter of '23. The men came back from Quebec every year to spend six months in the wilderness. It was a great place to build up a "stake" — there was nowhere to spend it.

289

camp I was in and most of the French camps there were no bathing facilities, you washed your hands and face and that was it, but in the Finn camps down around Ghost River they had saunas.

"I was there, while they were logging, from 1921 to 1930. It was hard country to log and hard country to drive wood, too."

John Kelly
Born 1902 — teamster and cook

"The first time I went into Pukasaw on that tug I said to myself, 'Boy, if I have to live here forever I don't know what I'm going to do.' All I could see were those big, dark hills and all that bush. It was my first job and that night was the first I ever spent in a bunkhouse with all the guys, 30 of them. I was only 14 but after I started working I liked it.

"I had driven horses on my grandparents' farm at Buckingham so Dad took me to Pukasaw as a teamster along with 60 men from Buckingham. Pukasaw had opened up the year before and times were good. There were a lot of young fellows in camp because the First World War was still on and men were hard to get. Age was no barrier in those days but now if you are under 17 you can't get into a camp because of compensation regulations. But in them days they'd take anybody so long as you could handle an axe.

"We had some Indians working there. Bob Saulier was part Indian and his wife trapped there and she made more money than he did. She was in her 50s and kind of adopted me, knitted me socks and mitts and made moccasins for me because I was the youngest in the camp. The other fellows used to kid me, but I'd say, 'I don't care, my feet are warm.' I'd go out on snowshoes with her and she'd teach me to snare and set traps. In the winter it used to get down to 40 below zero.

"We used to go up there year after year in July and never come back to Buckingham until the following June. We'd always say there were five seasons — summer, fall, winter, spring cut, and spring drive. We'd make that extra cut in the spring if we had not filled our quota during the winter. Ten months was a long time to stay in the bush. The best part would always be the sleigh haul because then you'd look forward to the river drive and after the river drive you could go home.

"The other day I was writing down the names of the men who were in Pukasaw from 1918 to 1930, the 12 years I was there. One hundred and fifty of them had died, many in the past few years. There are not many left. Up there when somebody died they'd send up a lead coffin in the spring and ship the body to the Soo, but sometimes they'd bury him at the depot. The first man ever

Courtesy of John Kelly

Kelly's lumber camp on the Pukaskwa River, 1923. Bill Kelly, John Kelly's father, came from Buckingham, Quebec, and his crew were mostly French-speaking loggers from that region.

291

buried there was Hiram Shelson, a one-armed man who had once been a cutter and who died of Spanish flu.

"But it was a healthy place to work and you were well treated. You had to learn to live together. I don't think I enjoyed working any place as much as I enjoyed working at Pukasaw, but the first time I saw Pukasaw I was 14 and it was awful lonesome lookin'."

Joe Lefebvre
Born 1900 – lumberjack

Small and lean and sharp as a squirrel, Joe Lefebvre had come to Blind River from Lachute, Quebec, to work in the pine camps at the age of 13 when he was still too short to harness the team he drove. He was a cutter, and tried his hand at jobbing with his own crew. He was also a cook in a camp of 125 men. *"We worked in our lives, you know,"* he said.

"I went to Pukasaw when I was 22 with my wife, Ida, and our two kids, and cut logs, skidded, and drove sleighs in the haul for Mr. Kelly, Johnny's father. In the spring we used to drive horses through the shallows to haul logs over the sand bars on the river. The cutters used the crosscut saw, there was no bucksaw in the woods in 1922. An old Finn, who later drowned in the Julia River, brought the first bucksaw in.

"I began jobbing on my own with a crew of 35 half a mile this side of McDougal Lake. I contracted to bring out 2000 cords which was a big contract at that time. That was pretty rough country, black spruce swamp. I had to haul wood by dog team one spring, the dogs hauling 200 loads of wood a quarter of a mile. You see it was in a swamp and the water would never freeze over properly. You couldn't take a horse in there, you could hardly walk there yourself. I made a sleigh eight feet long and four feet wide with a rope to hold it back so it wouldn't run over the dogs on the steep hills. Me and my brother-in-law, Joe, we'd go early in the morning and we'd put half a cord of eight-foot-long wood on that sleigh and off the dogs would zizz! In one week we had cleared all that wood out. If you had put a horse in that swamp he would have gone right through.

"It was in Léon Lafleur's camp in 1925, three and a half miles back, that I had my accident. My brother and I had rigged a block and cable to take sleigh loads down a son of a gun of a steep hill. My brother, Jean, was watching the cable. I was going down with a big load. It was steep, a hill about a quarter of a mile long. We were using one log as a brake and suddenly that log swung and hit me on the side of the head. It broke my jaw and threw me out in front of the horses. I managed to grab the sleigh pole between the

Eric Skead prepares to set up the White River trail for the 70-mile dash to hospital with the injured Joe Lefebvre. They made the trip, which usually took a week, in less than a day and a half.

Courtesy of Gordon and Lee Fletcher

horses and they stopped. I got out of there but everything was blurred and the blood coming from my eyes and ears. I grabbed the reins but the horses couldn't hold that load back and the sleigh hit me and hurt my chest. I started to holler and my brother ran up and said, 'Jesus!' I tied my jaw shut with string and he helped me walk the three miles and a half to camp where I lay down in Mr. Lafleur's cookery. I didn't pass out but two hours later I could see nothing. I could eat nothing because of my jaw. I was 18 days in that camp before they took me out. Angus Baker, the Walking Boss, the Superintendent, had a special sled made with two handles on it and Eric Skead, one of the jobbers and a very good dog sled man, drove me out 70 miles to White River in 30 hours. The usual trip took a week. My wife had to stay in camp because she had three children, the youngest born six days before the accident.

"When they brought me to the hospital Dr. Castleman thought I'd be there for months but I was off work only a month and a half. Before the accident I weighed 145 pounds. Afterwards I weighed 98 pounds. Even now I can't open my mouth the way I did before that accident. Maybe that's a good thing! When I left the hospital and took the trail back on snowshoes I was still weak. On the way I met a young fellow, about 22, who was going into camp for the spring drive and he was wearing just a pair of ordinary shoes that were too small for him. About two-thirds of the way into camp he said, 'Jeeze, I can't walk any more.' I had a pair of good lumberman's rubbers, they fit like a glove, so I said to him, 'Give me your shoes and take my boots.' He said, 'No, you don't want to do that.' But we did it and I walked through to the camp with his shoes on and it was 25 miles from where we traded shoes. Jeeze, my toes hurt. If you tried to make people do today what they did then they'd die."

Ida Lefebvre
Born 1904 — Joe's wife

A slim, white-haired grandmother, her stone house on the out-skirts of Sault Ste. Marie neat and blue-carpeted, she did not look like a woman who had lived her life in the bush.

"I didn't know he was coming and when I saw him walk through the door I thought, 'Oh, no! I'm seeing things!' He was like a skele-ton. His toe-nails, they had all come out, wearing those shoes. He took off his packsack and said, 'You take care of this, honey, and be careful.' I thought, 'Be careful of what? in this country?' And do you know what he had? Some Easter eggs for the babes. When we first went to Pukasaw our son was 19 months and our first daughter three months. I had never been in the bush before. I had been in a convent near Ville Marie in Quebec and was supposed to have be-come a Sister. Look where I ended up!

"Sometimes I look back and think, 'It's a dream.' When I think of it now, when you're young what you do! There were times I even skidded logs for Joe. Yes I did, with a horse, a big white horse as gentle as could be but when I got mad at him, boy would he get it. I was not as heavy then as I am now. I'd go out at daylight, ride the horse out and ride him back at night, and I was good enough, when I think of it. I would chain those logs good and get six or seven logs chained together and skid them 500 feet to the river. Sometimes I'd jump on a log and ride it. Mrs. Ainsley, the jobber's wife at the next camp, used to laugh at me. I'd skid most of the day and I'd be so tired I'd just about drop. I must have good legs. No wonder my doctor says I have good legs.

"I remember the time at Lafleur's camp in the winter of 1923 when Fred Lafleur's two children, a little girl and a little boy, were burned to death. The mother had just run over to her mother-in-law in the next cabin to get milk for the baby. Her cabin just went up in flames, that quick. Nobody could get in. The men ran with shovels and snow but it was no use. They tried. A friend was passing along and said, 'Oh my God, Ida, you should see it!' It was that bad. They had coal-oil lamps and the cabin had been built of spruce logs and chinked with moss and the moss after it was dry, you know how it is. They buried those children in the little cemetery and the blacksmith made a wrought iron cross painted white with their names on the cross-piece in black. The graveyard was not far from the cookery and there were six or seven buried there. Every spring old Angus Baker would go and fix the rosary on the grave of Old Lady Pukasaw if it had been broken in the winter weather. And now, do you know something? I hate the bush. I just detest it. I won't even go fishing."

Mrs. Tim Devon
Born 1897 – jobber's widow

"The first time I went to Pukasaw on the tug *Reliance* in 1922 she was a-rollin'. I was so seasick. We were four days making the 150-mile journey and arrived at the depot in time for supper and had macaroni. Tim had been a brakeman on the railway but times were hard and he went to Pukasaw with 29 men to cut wood because there was nothing else. I can't say we made much money jobbing but I felt happy going in there. I was with my husband and children and knew at least we were not getting into debt. I was born in Eganville in the Ottawa Valley and always loved roaming the woods. I had three children when I went to Pukasaw and three children were born there. I had three boys and nine girls altogether.

"Our camp was on Tagouche Creek eight miles from the depot. We had a big cabin ourselves with office in front and sleeping quarters in back. We had four horses in the stable across the swale and there was a cookery and a bunkhouse for the men. Being the only woman at that camp and having small children you kept pretty much to yourself and kept your children away. When it got dark the kids had to be in and I didn't allow them out when the men were coming back and forth. Sometimes when the men were coming back and Tim was with them the kids ran out to meet them and they'd put the kids on the horses' backs. But I watched them. You take men cooped up from September to May — there were little problems here and there. You watched your children. We never had trouble with moonshine but they had at some other camps.

"We put in a garden but the rabbits got in and we gave up. Tim caught a rabbit once but it looked so much like a cat when it was skinned that I cut it in two so it would look more like a partridge. The men would get a craving for eggs and on Sunday, when we kept hens, we'd send some over so they could at least have one each. When they came into camp in the fall they'd crave pie so much they'd even want it for breakfast. I could never get over that.

"At night we could hear wolves over around Otter Head. There was a big hill they sat on. One dusk Tim was away and the kids were in bed and I looked out and saw a she-bear down by the coal-oil barrel, with her cubs up on the hill behind. There was only cheesecloth screening the window between that bear and me. Oh, me! I went to the wall and got the .303 and fired through cheese-cloth and all. The bear got out of there in a hurry, and so did the cubs. Just at that moment I heard a team out on the tote road. I thought it must be Tim, but then I didn't hear it any more. When Tim finally came in he said he heard me shooting but didn't want to come in and risk getting hit. As long as their food was good the bears didn't bother you. Old Charlie Fairfield, the trapper over at Otter Cove, said he was picking on a berry bush once with a black bear eating on the other side.

"I was happy in there and I used to think, 'This is what I call pioneering.' The thing about Pukasaw, there were quite a few women there. In the French camps jobbers brought their wives in and with all the men around the idea was you knew your place and they knew theirs. It was rough, hilly country but lovely, the birch and spruce, and to look out on a sunny day in the fall it would be beautiful. Lots of nights, now I'm older and can't sleep, I let my mind go back to dwell on some of the most beautiful scenes. Our camps there have long since fallen in. The snow in winter would be quite a weight on the roof."

Dr. Bertram Henry Harper
Born 1896 — camp doctor, 1922–23

"I was supplied with medicines which consisted mostly of cough syrup, aspirin, laxative tablets which were called No. 9's and were left over from the First World War, and some ether and chloroform, but a very limited amount of morphine. You had to make do with what you had, good training for a young doctor just out of medical school. There was a man who used to make salve out of pine gum, clarified and melted down, and I used some of his methods myself. Once I wanted to put heat on a broken leg to get down the swelling and I had the foreman knock the end out of the oven of the old wood stove. I lit a small fire in the wood box and had the injured man stick his leg through the oven and out the back.

"There were quite a few accidents. One man's axe slipped and I had to amputate his toe and, although he had been one of the best men on the log drive, because of losing his toe he could not balance well on the logs. The more than 300 men under my care were quite healthy but once in a while they'd have a head cold or bronchitis.

"I had two cases of suicide, one of them hard to understand. The man was Ukrainian, very well-educated, and had been editor of the Ukrainian newspaper in Toronto. For what reason he came to the lumber camp I never did ascertain. We noticed that he started refusing to get up in the morning and go out to work although he had been a good worker from the fall well into the winter. It was around Christmas that he started to act rather odd. He'd sit for hours during the day in the cookhouse where it was warm and write constantly in his own language, ream after ream of paper, even borrowing wrapping paper that had been saved by the cook. He said he was writing to tell his people never to come to a lumber camp.

"Finally, one morning, I think it was on the 18th of February, 1923, he had his breakfast, a good meal, and turned to the cook and said, 'I'm going to finish myself off this time.' The ice was a foot and a half thick on the lake but he went to a hole that had been cut to bring out buckets of water for the cookery. He pulled his cap down over his face, crawled down into the hole which was about the size of his body, and got himself under the ice. And of course he didn't come out. Everyone who saw him doing this ran down but they couldn't do anything. We didn't know which way he went. The foreman had his men start to cut the ice away from the hole out towards the middle of the lake. They cut out 16 or 20 feet and piled the ice on each side but couldn't find his body. It was two days before they found his body and everybody felt very badly because the man was quite well liked.

"The other case was a Finlander who selected a horrible way of doing it by drinking pure carbolic acid. His throat had been burned to a horrible degree I don't like to dwell on even now.

"When the men were cutting they were too tired for any enter-tainment at night but there were occasional celebrations. The French had a celebration at New Year's with cakes and the odd bottle of brandy saved from the fall. Poles and Ukrainians cele-brated at Christmas. Once in a while they had an evening of singing hymns or songs of their own countries. The men were happy, I think. Working among the evergreen trees in the fresh air may have had its effect in keeping them in good health."

Charlie Lampi
Born 1902 — Finnish cutter and jobber

In the mid-1920s Finns came to Pukaskwa to work as "shackers" who cut stands of timber too small and scattered for a large camp to handle. Most Finns were excellent pulpwood cutters and they tell of "The Thousand Dollar Finn" who came in every fall and went out in the spring with $1000 earned from the wood he sold to the company. In the 1930s Lampi became a typically successful small Finnish jobber cutting 1000 cords a year with a crew of a dozen men whom he supervised while also doing his own scaling, blacksmithing, and occasionally driving one of his three teams.

"I came to Canada from Kilvkka in central Finland in 1923. Times were bad in Finland. I went to Pukasaw for one year in 1926 with a five-man crew on the East Branch 12 miles from the depot. There were a few Finnish camps there then, five-man, three-man, two-man camps. We were the shackers. We made our own bucksaw frames and sometimes our own blades from gramophone springs.

"We worked. From dark to dark we worked. We even worked on Sundays. I cut 210 cords myself that season. Four-foot wood, piece-work. Our crew cut 1000 cords and we got $5 a cord. It was good, big wood, 10 cords to the acre. You had to each cut two cords a day if you wanted to make money.

"The Finns didn't like the white pine log camps. They just liked the pulp camps. I worked in the pulp woods 31 years. Only once did I work in a pine log camp. Gee, those pine log camps were dirty and the food was not good. That was a shacker camp, too. A Finn would not stay in a dirty camp, they had to have good food and clean camps. You see, they worked hard, really hard.

The Finns don't go in for bush work like they used to. It's not like it used to be."

During the Depression, in 1930, the Pukaskwa operation was closed down, never to reopen. Lee Fletcher, who became a profes-sional forester in the years after he left Pukaskwa, said, "The expense would be such these days there would not be enough wood at Pukasaw to justify it. You couldn't run an operation now the way they did then, just landing a bunch of men to stay in there until

The author, left, and his father-in-law, Gordon Fletcher, in 1976, at the door of the cabin where Fletcher lived as a boy when Pukaskwa depot served a scattered logging community of more than 300 men.

Bill Wyett, Marathon, Ont.

Pukaskwa depot, 30 years later. The only building still standing on Imogene Creek is the Mills-Fletcher cabin. In the background across the creek are remains of the bunkhouse. By the summer of 1976 the cabin had dwindled to little more than two rooms, one part roofed in, and the bunkhouse was a tumble of rotting logs.

Courtesy of Gordon Fletcher

spring. A lot of the men came from Quebec where I suppose they were used to working in isolated camps. They got their fare paid if they stayed all season, 'stayed the run,' as we used to say. I suppose it was a place to save money, there was no way to spend it. But despite the fact they were so isolated many look back on those as the happiest days of their lives."

Before he died, Jack Mills recalled those days at Pukaskwa. "There was an awful lot of hard work for we had no power equipment in those days but we had a lot more fun than they have now. At least I think we did because now it's strictly business and it's completely unionized. You are working like a machine, not like an individual. When we started at Pukasaw it was a ball, we had lots of fun there."

They took their fun where they found it, but part of the fun must have been the individualists who came and went in the restless "glory days" of logging. Al Buell, who has retired after years of bossing big camps in northwest Ontario, believes there is just no room now for such men as Joe Montferrand, "Gentleman Charlie" Sproul of New Brunswick, or "Roughhouse Pete" and "Eight-Day" Wilson of B.C. "I really believe there are not the characters in the bush now there were then because you can't put up with characters. The costs would be too high. The equipment is too expensive and has to be kept operating. We mechanized because of the cost and scarcity of labour. No, you can't afford those characters, but they sure made life interesting."

Viewed through the mellow light of time and distance, like a faded sepia photograph, those old camps have something of the same nostalgic romance of old sailing ships and times at once more simple and more vivid. Certainly it was hard, and many men who went to the woods quit as soon as they could get better jobs in less remote surroundings, but even more men, such as Théophile Savard of Chicoutimi, Quebec, kept going back, year after year.

"Nowadays," said Théophile Savard, who first went to the camps at Lac Bouchette at the age of 13 in 1908, "it's not so hard working in the woods but in our day we worked very hard, to say the least. But still we were happy and if I had to do it all over again I would. I had a big family, 15 children, but had a little piece of land, didn't have to pay any rent, and the whole family always ate three meals a day; my wife worked hard and made all our clothing and we were all properly dressed and the children were happy."

"While the camps may not have seemed so pleasant at the time, I look back now and it is something I like to think about," said Harold Green of Sault Ste. Marie, who started in the bush at the age of 16 in 1910. "Those camps were rough-and-ready but there were great men in those days. You worked with great men, great workers; they could lay their hands to practically anything. I never saw anything like those men anywhere else. There never will be."

NOTES

Major sources are listed here according to the appropriate chapter when not previously mentioned in the narrative.

Those interviewed by the author are identified by their names and the location where the interview was taped.

CHAPTER 1. THE LOGGING FRONTIER 13-34

[1]Philemon Wright's Account of the First Settlement of the Township of Hull, before a committee of the House of Assembly of Lower Canada, 1823. Andrew Picken, Appendix *The Canadas* (London: Wilson, 1836).

[2]Joseph Tassé, *Philemon Wright, ou Colonisation et Commerce de Bois* (Montreal, 1871).

[3]Sir James M. Le Moine, *Annals of the Port of Quebec* (Quebec, 1901).

[4]Deeds of 1662, Suffolk, Massachusetts: "sayled in said ship being freighted in Boston, New England with Beames for houses, Boards, pipestaves, tarr and other lumber." In New England, lumber came to mean boards, although in England lumber meant simply odds and ends stored in a "lumber room," derived from "lombard room" where Lombard bankers stored unredeemed pledges.

[5]John McGregor, *British America* (Edinburgh: W. Blackwell, 1832).

[6]McGregor.

[7]Ralph Connor, *The Man from Glengarry* (Toronto: Revel, 1901).

[8]John Langton, *Early Days in Upper Canada* (Toronto: Macmillan, 1926).

[9]Thomas Carr, letter in *Cobourg Star*, 10 May 1831.

[10]Samuel Strickland, *Twenty-five Years in Canada West* (London: R. Bently, 1852).

[11]George S. Thompson, *Up to Date, or the Life of a Lumberman* (Peterborough, Ontario, 1895).

[12]J. J. Bigsby, *The Shoe and the Canoe* (London, 1850).

[13]J. W. Thomson, *Lumbering on the Rivière du Lièvre* (Ottawa, 1973).

[14]Unpublished journal of Charles Macnamara, Arnprior, Ontario; courtesy of Mrs. Jean Cunningham.

[15]George S. Thompson.

[16]Steve Lewis, Devil's Lake, Ontario.

[17]John MacTaggart, *Three Years in Canada, 1826-7-8* (London: Colborn, 1829).

CHAPTER 2. TALES OF THE TIMBERBEASTS: JOE MONTFERRAND 35-39

One of the first published Paul Bunyan stories was in the *Detroit News* in 1910; however, P. S. Lovejoy of Ann Arbor, Michigan, an expert on the Bunyan stories, traced them back to the Tupper Lake camps in the Adirondacks, perhaps as early as the 1850s, and reports that these stories reached their peak between 1880 and 1900 along with the pine lumber trade.

CHAPTER 3. THE RAFTSMEN 40-54

[1]MacTaggart, *Three Years in Canada, 1826-7-8* (London: Colborn, 1829).

[2]Thomas Coltrin Keefer, paper delivered to Montreal Mechanics Institute, January 1854.

[3]John McGregor, *British America* (Edinburgh: W. Blackwell, 1832).

[4]George S. Thompson, *Up to Date* (Peterborough, Ontario, 1895).

[5]Thomas Carr, letter in *Cobourg Star*, 10 May 1831.

[6]Captain Fred Harrison, Sault Ste. Marie, Ontario.

CHAPTER 4.   GREEN GOLD: THE TIMBER CRUISERS   55-72

[1]J. B. Benson, *Canada Lumberman*, May 1905.

[2]Edwin Kerry DeBeck, Victoria, B.C.; interviewed in Aural History Program, British Columbia Archives, Victoria.

[3]John McGregor, *British America* (Edinburgh: W. Blackwell, 1832).

[4]Wes McNutt, North Bay, Ontario.

[5]Ellwood Wilson, *American Forestry*, May 1912.

[6]Hulme Stone, Midland, Ontario.

[7]Fleetwood Pride, interview in *Northeast Folklore*, Vol. 9 (University of Maine, Orono), 1968.

[8]Geoff Randolph, Montreal, Quebec.

[9]Pete Charlebois, Sault Ste. Marie, Ontario.

[10]J. B. Benson, *Canada Lumberman*, May 1905.

[11]Stuart Moir, interviewed for *Journal of Forest History*, Santa Cruz, California.

[12]*Canadian Forestry Journal*, Vol. 4, 1908.

CHAPTER 5.   THE SEASONS: FALL — CHOPPERS AND SAWYERS   73-88

[1]Pierre Desbiens, interview in *Saguenayensia* (Chicoutimi, Quebec), Nov.-Dec. 1962.

[2]Dan Hill, Bruce Mines, Ontario.

[3]John S. Springer, *Forest Life and Forest Trees, Lumbering on the various rivers of Maine and New Brunswick* (New York: Harper and Bros., 1851).

[4]Robert Harrison, *Peterborough Daily Evening Review*, 27 Oct. 1902.

[5]Harrison.

[6]J. E. MacDonald, *Shantymen and Sodbusters* (Thessalon, Ontario, 1966).

[7]H. W. Withrow, *Our Country, Scenic and Descriptive* (Toronto, 1899).

[8]Henry Hansen, Delta, B.C.; interviewed in Aural History Program, British Columbia Archives, Victoria.

[9]Frank Moran, Thunder Bay, Ontario.

[10]Gordon Withenshaw, Thunder Bay, Ontario.

[11]Charlie Lampi, Sault Ste. Marie, Ontario.

[12]Buzz Lein, Midland, Ontario.

[13]Joe Sarazin, Blind River, Ontario.

[14]Ralph Mills, Wawa, Ontario.

[15]Moran.

[16]Lein.

[17]J. W. Challenger, *Canada Lumberman*, 1 May 1946.

[18]Murray Bean, Bruce Mines, Ontario.

[19]L. D. Gaffney, Ottawa, Ontario.

CHAPTER 6.   THE SEASONS: FALL — THE SKIDDERS   89-98

[1]J. E. MacDonald, *Shantymen and Sodbusters* (Thessalon, Ontario, 1966).

[2]Geoff Randolph, Montreal, Quebec.

[3]Paul Assam, Poplar Dale, Ontario.

[4]Randolph.

[5]Dan Hill, Bruce Mines, Ontario.

[6]Hill.

[7]Randolph.

[8]Randolph.

CHAPTER 7.   THE SEASONS: WINTER — THE TEAMSTERS   99-119

[1]R. J. Taylor, Arnprior, Ontario.

[2]Geoff Randolph, Montreal, Quebec.

[3]Randolph.

[4]Harold Green, Sault Ste. Marie, Ontario.

[5]L. D. Gaffney, Ottawa, Ontario.

[6]Bill McNeil, Braeside, Ontario.

[7]Joe Sarazin, Blind River, Ontario.

[8]J. E. MacDonald, *Shantymen and Sodbusters* (Thessalon, Ontario, 1966).

[9]Unpublished journal of Charles Macnamara, Arnprior, Ontario; courtesy of Mrs. Jean Cunningham.

[10]Wilmot MacDonald, Chatham, New Brunswick.

[11]Frank Moran, Thunder Bay, Ontario.

[12]R. J. Smith, Renfrew, Ontario.

[13]Dan Hill, Bruce Mines, Ontario.

[14]Shannon Assam, Poplar Dale, Ontario.

[15]Len Shewfelt, Thessalon, Ontario.

[16]Randolph.

[17]Jack Hughes, Chicoutimi, Quebec.

[18]Mike Scorback, Thunder Bay; interviewed in Aural History Program, Confederation College, Thunder Bay, Ontario.

[19]Roy Murphy, Iron Bridge, Ontario.

[20]Hill.

[21]Lorne Nicholson, Sault Ste. Marie, Ontario.

[22]Lee Fletcher, Sault Ste. Marie, Ontario.

[23]Randolph.

CHAPTER 8.   THE SEASONS: SPRING — RIVER DRIVERS   120-143

[1]Geoff Randolph, Montreal, Quebec.

[2]Randolph.

[3]Tom Pond, Fredericton, New Brunswick.

[4]Steve Lewis, Devil's Lake, Ontario.

[5]Charlotte Whitton, *A Hundred Years A-Fellin', The Story of the Gillies on the Ottawa* (Ottawa: Runge, 1943). In this book David Gillies said calk boots appeared on the Ottawa River only late in the 1860s.

[6]Wes McNutt, North Bay, Ontario.

[7]Harold Green, Sault Ste. Marie, Ontario.

[8]McNutt.

[9]R. O. Sweezey, "Life in a Lumber Camp," *Canada Lumberman*.

[10]Murray Bean, Bruce Mines, Ontario.

[11]Gordon Withenshaw, Thunder Bay, Ontario.

[12]C. C. Pickering, *Northern Monthly* (Portland, Maine), 1860.

[13]Harding Smith, Boiestown, New Brunswick; interviewed by Carol Spray of Fredericton and reproduced here with her permission.

[14]Fred Kinnehan, Sault Ste. Marie, Ontario.

[15]Mrs. John Dunn, Sault Ste. Marie, Ontario.

[16]L. D. Gaffney, Ottawa, Ontario.

[17]Kinnehan.

[18]Fleetwood Pride, interview in *Northeast Folklore*, Vol. 9 (University of Maine, Orono), 1968.

[19]George Gilbert, K.C., *Account of Early Logging*, Bathurst, New Brunswick.

[20]Walter Gaunce, Ottawa, Ontario.

[21]McNutt.

[22]Fleetwood Pride.

CHAPTER 10.   THE BULL OF THE WOODS   147-157

[1]Steve Lewis, Devil's Lake, Ontario.

[2]Geoff Randolph, Montreal, Quebec.

[3]Fred Kinnehan, Sault Ste. Marie, Ontario.

[4]Walter Gaunce, Ottawa, Ontario.

[5]Wes McNutt, North Bay, Ontario.

CHAPTER 11.   LOGGERS OF THE RAINCOAST   158-197

[1]Henry Hansen, Delta, B.C.; interviewed in Aural History Program, British Columbia Archives, Victoria.

[2]Ira Becker, *The Daily Colonist* (Victoria, B.C.), 10 Dec. 1961.

[3]Albert Drinkwater, interviewed in Aural History Program, British Columbia Archives, Victoria.

[4]Ralph D. Paine, "The Builders, The Heart of the Big Timber Country," *Outing Magazine*, Sept. 1906.

[5]Peter Trower, "Like A War," *Between the Sky and the Splinters* (B.C.: Harbour Publishing, 1974).

[6]Frank and Howard White, "How it is with Trucks," *Raincoast Chronicles* (B.C. Coast Historical Society, Madeira Park), No. 3.

CHAPTER 12. BEANS EVERLASTING: COOKS AND COOKEES 198-217

[1]John McGregor, *British America* (Edinburgh: W. Blackwell, 1832).

[2]Unpublished journal of Charles Macnamara, Arnprior, Ontario; courtesy of Mrs. Jean Cunningham.

[3]Frank Moran, Thunder Bay, Ontario.

[4]Mrs. Tim Devon, Sault Ste. Marie, Ontario.

[5]Ulysse Duchine, interviewed in 1934 when he was 87; *Saguenayensia* (Chicoutimi, Quebec), July-Aug. 1960.

[6]H. T. Warne, *Canada Lumberman*, 1 Aug. 1930.

[7]John Kelly, Sault Ste. Marie, Ontario.

[8]W. H. Merleau, Maniwaki, Quebec.

[9]Steve Lewis, Devil's Lake, Ontario.

[10]R. J. Taylor, Arnprior, Ontario.

[11]Dan Hill, Bruce Mines, Ontario.

[12]Thomas Nash, Blind River, Ontario.

[13]Fred Niemi, Sault Ste. Marie, Ontario.

[14]Hill.

[15]Bill McNeill, Braeside, Ontario.

[16]Wes McNutt, North Bay, Ontario.

[17]L. D. Gaffney, Ottawa, Ontario.

[18]Lewis.

[19]John Joseph Gillis, North River, Nova Scotia; interview in *Cape Breton's Magazine* (Wreck Cove, Nova Scotia), No. 7.

[20]Gordon Withenshaw, Thunder Bay, Ontario.

[21]Jack Matthews, Toronto, Ontario.

[22]Hulme Stone, Midland, Ontario.

[23]Mary Chekman, Sault Ste. Marie, Ontario.

[24]McNutt.

[25]Taylor.

[26]Geoff Randolph, Montreal, Quebec.

CHAPTER 13. THE MIGRANTS 218-227

[1]Geoff Randolph, Montreal, Quebec.

[2]Henri Rioux, Iroquois Falls, Ontario.

[3]Wilbur S. Sherrard, Newcastle, New Brunswick; interview in *Halifax Chronicle-Herald*, 31 December 1960.

[4]Joseph Tremblay, interview in *Saguenayensia* (Chicoutimi, Quebec), Jan.-Feb. 1963.

[5]Fred Borrett, interviewed in Aural History Program, Confederation College, Thunder Bay, Ontario.

CHAPTER 14. THE BUNKHOUSE BOYS 228-237

[1]Spurgeon Allaby, Passekeag, New Brunswick; interview in *Northeast Folklore* (University of Maine, Orono), 1954.

[2]Pierre Desbiens, interview in *Saguenayensia* (Chicoutimi, Quebec), Nov.-Dec. 1962.

[3]Albert Bordeleau, Iroquois Falls, Ontario.

[4]Fred Kinnehan, Sault Ste. Marie, Ontario.

[5]Lee Fletcher, Sault Ste. Marie, Ontario.

[6]Buzz Lein, Midland, Ontario.
[7]Oscar Styffe, interview in *Canada Lumberman*, 15 Jan. 1938.
[8]J. A. McNally, Montreal, Quebec.
[9]Dan Hill, Bruce Mines, Ontario.
[10]Joe Sarazin, Blind River, Ontario.
[11]Wes McNutt, North Bay, Ontario.
[12]Geoff Randolph, Montreal, Quebec.

CHAPTER 16.   SATURDAY NIGHT AND SUNDAY   240-251

[1]Dan Hill, Bruce Mines, Ontario.
[2]L. D. Gaffney, Ottawa, Ontario.
[3]Pierre Dupin, *Les Anciens Chantiers du St. Maurice* (Trois-Rivières: Bien Public, 1953).
[4]W. H. Merleau, Maniwaki, Quebec.
[5]George S. Thompson, *Up to Date* (Peterborough, Ontario, 1895).
[6]Lucien Bergeron, Quebec City, Quebec.
[7]Mrs. Tim Devon, Sault Ste. Marie, Ontario.
[8]Geoff Randolph, Montreal, Quebec.
[9]Harold Green, Sault Ste. Marie, Ontario.
[10]Jack Bell, Qualicum Beach, British Columbia.
[11]W. Fraser, *The Emigrant's Guide*, or *Sketches of Canada* (1867).
[12]Eugène L'Heureux, *Progrès du Saguenay* (Chicoutimi, Quebec).
[13]Bergeron.
[14]Benoit Girard, Chicoutimi, Quebec.
[15]John Irwin Cooper, *The Blessed Communion: Origins and History of the Diocese of Montreal, 1760-1960* (Archives Committee, 1960).
[16]Joshua Fraser, *Shanty, Forest and River Life in the Backwoods of Canada* (Montreal: J. Lovell and Son, 1883).
[17]Geoff Randolph, Montreal, Quebec.
[18]Wes McNutt, North Bay, Ontario.

CHAPTER 17.   WORKERS OF THE WOODS: LOGGING UNIONS   252-259

[1]Edwin Linder, *Centennial Edition* (Duncan, B.C.: Local 1-80, IWA), 1971.

CHAPTER 18.   BLOWIN' 'ER IN: THE LOGGER GOES TO TOWN   260-264

[1]*Arnprior Chronicle*, 18 April 1890.
[2]Geoff Randolph, Montreal, Quebec.
[3]Jack Bell, Qualicum Beach, British Columbia.
[4]Len Shewfelt, Thessalon, Ontario.
[5]Harold Burk, Espanola, Ontario.
[6]Fred Kinnehan, Sault Ste. Marie, Ontario.
[7]Harold Green, Sault Ste. Marie, Ontario.
[8]Bill McNeill, Braeside, Ontario.
[9]Green.
[10]Shewfelt.

CHAPTER 19.   FIRE   265-285

[1]*Nouvelles Relations de la Gaspésie* (Paris, 1691).
[2]Robert Cooney, *A Comprehensive History of the Northern Part of the Province of New Brunswick* (Halifax, 1832).
[3]Dr. Robert Bell, *Geographical Distribution of Forest Trees in Canada* (Toronto, 1897).
[4]*Toronto Globe*, 2 Aug. 1916.
[5]*Toronto Daily Star*, 4 Aug. 1916.
[6]Jack Matthews, Toronto, Ontario.
[7]Based on unpublished manuscript, "The Mississagi Fire — 1948" by Don Gord Campbell, by permission of William Sleeman, Director, Forest Fire Control Branch, Toronto.

GLOSSARY

Alligator Flat-bottomed, amphibious barge invented by John West of Simcoe, Ontario.

Bark mark Symbol chopped into the side of a log to prove ownership.

Beaver Unskilled lumberjack who cleared roads with double-bitted axe and grub-hoe. Swamper.

Bitch chain Short, heavy chain with hook and ring for loading logs.

Board feet Unit of measurement for lumber and sawlogs; 12 inches wide, 1 inch thick, 12 inches long.

Bolt A short log, a four-foot length of pulpwood. (Quebec: *pitoune*.)

Boom A floating corral of logs chained together to impound timber (holding boom) or to haul it across a lake in the form of a loose raft (bag boom).

Bridle Chain wrapped around rear runners of a sleigh as a brake on steep, icy roads.

Broad-axe Short axe with 12-inch blade bevelled on one side like a chisel, for hewing masts, square timber, railway ties.

Brow Logs piled on a river bank to await the spring river drive.

Bûcheron French-Canadian lumberjack. *Forestier*.

Buck To saw fallen logs into lengths. When buckers had to saw through a log from below, rather than from the top, they often used a small gadget called a "hootnanny" to hold their crosscut saw steady.

Bucking board Record of a cutter's daily ouput.

Bucksaw Thin-bladed, one-man saw for felling and bucking pulpwood. Pulp saw, Swede saw, Finn saw, bow saw.

Buck beaver Assistant to the foreman, in charge of clearing and building roads.

Bull bucker Boss of a gang falling trees in B.C.

Bull cook Choreboy, usually an old logger, who cleaned the bunkhouse and hauled water and firewood. In the early days he also fed the oxen or bulls.

Bull of the Woods A camp foreman; a Walking Boss or Superintendent who had charge of several camps. (Quebec: *Contremaître*.)

Bull rope Attached at each end of a log with a "pigsfoot" hook to draw logs up onto the skidway pile.

Bull whacker Driver of an ox team. Bull puncher.

Bunk Lumber camp bed; also heavy timber crossbars forming the bed of a logging sleigh.

Cache Wooden shelter for supplies. Keep-over.

Calk boots High-cut boots with quarter-inch nails in soles and heels to hold a man on slippery logs.

Cambuse (Camboose) Fire for cooking and heating built on sand in the centre of a 19th century shanty.

Camp foreman Boss of a camp and all its logging operations. The Push. (Quebec: *Contremaître*.)

Cant To turn logs with pole, cant-hook, or peavey.

Cant-hook Wooden stock, three or four feet long, fitted with a swinging hook and shoed with an iron ferrule with a jutting toe. Used in loading logs; an early cousin of the peavey.

Chaland Barge for hauling men, horses, and supplies in Quebec.

306

Chantier In Quebec, shanty or bunkhouse.

Chaser In B.C., logger who unhooked logs hauled into the pile in the donkey engine skidder system.

Chickadee He cleaned winter roads of debris and, like the bird of the same name, of horse manure. Road monkey.

Chicot Dead, dry, standing tree trunk. Rampike.

Chokerman The man on a B.C. yarding crew who fastened the choker, a loop of cable, around a log to haul it over the ground.

Chopper Axeman who cut the trees down; "feller" in the east but "faller" on the west coast.

Choreboy Pronounced and spelled "show boy" in Quebec. Bull cook.

Chute Long trough of logs or lumber to shoot timber down off hills or over ravines by gravity or water power.

Contremaître Quebec camp foreman.

Cookee Cook's assistant, usually a young man, but after World War Two women were also employed.

Cord Stack of pulpwood four feet high, four feet wide, eight feet long, although somewhat larger in Quebec camps.

Corner bind Four short chains to secure the two outside logs of the bottom layer of a load to the bunk of a sleigh.

Cow's mouth A notch axed into a tree to fell it.

Crazy Wheel Patent Barienger brake anchored at the top of a hill with an endless cable running through a set of wheels and a friction clamp. It was hitched to a sleigh to brake it down an icy hill.

Crosscut saw Reciprocal saw, five feet long or more, to fell and buck trees. Most were two-man saws although smaller one-man saws were used in the early pulpwood days before the bucksaw. Swedish fiddle. (Quebec: *godendart*.)

Cross-haul Loading logs by passing a chain — decking line or parbuckle — under and back over a log and causing the log to roll when the line was pulled by a horse; the area cleared out to allow the horse room to work.

Crown Top foliage of a tree. When fire sweeps the dry branches at high speed, it is a crown fire.

Cruiser A company or government expert who walked, or "cruised," the forest to find and map the timber and estimate its value.

Cull Defective log rejected by the culler, or scaler, who measured logs after they were cut and stacked.

Cut A season's log production.

Davis raft Cigar-shaped raft of logs devised by G. G. Davis of B.C. before World War One to haul logs by tug for long distances through rough seas.

Deacon seat Split log, level side up, which ran along the ends of the bunks in 19th century shanties.

Deals Boards three inches thick or more; the first sawed wood ever shipped to Britain.

Decking line Chain run through block and tackle and, with hook on one end, snagged into a log so a horse could haul it on top of a skidway pile or sleigh load.

Depot Headquarters for a string of lumber camps.

Dog Iron hook with sharp point, used for hauling a "turn" of several logs down B.C. skidways. Also used to boom logs in water.

Donkey Steam engine geared to capstan or drum to haul or skid logs from the B.C. woods. So called from the days when, used on ships, it had less power than one horse.

Drive Annual spring flush of logs downstream. (Quebec: *la drave.*)

Feller Axeman or sawyer who cut down trees; called a faller on the west coast.

Filer Specialist who sharpened crosscut saws.

Fitter In a square timber gang he notched a pine for felling and marked it into lengths for bucking.

Floating camp Built on rafts in the steep inlets of British Columbia where level ground was scarce.

Flume Wooden troughs for sluicing logs down hills.

Flunkey West coast cook's assistant. Cookee.

Gabriel horn Long tin horn blown by cookee to signal meals.

Gin pole Primitive hoisting gear for loading logs.

Go-back road Diversion for empty sleighs returning to the hills so that they would not block loaded sleighs coming down.

Go-devil Crotch of a hardwood tree with bar fashioned across the open end to drag one end of a log free of the ground. A rough sled.

Ground lead logging The first phase of B.C. steam logging when donkey engines with capstans hauled logs out of the bush across the ground.

Gut hammer Iron triangle which the cookee hit at mealtimes.

Gyppo outfit Independent west coast logging contractor who often moved around like a gypsy.

Handspike Hardwood pole for prying logs before the use of cant-hook and peavey.

Hand logging Early B.C. loggers, working without horses or machinery, rolled logs down the mountainsides into the sea using hand jacks.

Haul-back Wire rope which hauled a heavy cable back into the bush in B.C. donkey engine logging.

Hay wire The binding from bales of hay, used to mend broken equipment.

Hay-wire camp An ill-equipped operation.

Head spar A tall, living Douglas fir topped off and stripped of branches and guyed up for high lead and skyline logging.

Headworks Rafts mounted with capstans pushed by men or horses to warp booms of logs across a lake.

Hewer The broad-axe man who hewed tree trunks into masts, square timber, and railway ties.

High ball High speed west coast logging whose expert practitioners called themselves "high ballers."

High rigger The dare-devil who climbed a 200-foot Douglas fir to trim the top and dress it as a spar tree.

High lead logging Replaced B.C. ground lead logging by rigging pulleys and cables on a spar tree and hauling one end of a log high over the ground to clear stumps and underbrush.

Hogger The engineer who drove a Shay or Climax "locie" on a logging railway.

Hook tender The strawboss of a B.C. skidding, or yarding, crew, or "side," hauling logs out of the bush with ground lead, high lead, or skyline.

Hot logging When an outfit failed to fill its quota late in the season, logs were cut and hauled direct from stump to river or mill without intermediate handling.

Hovel Stable for camp horses.

Jam Caused when logs snagged and piled up on the river drive and had to be pried or dynamited loose.

Jammer Block and tackle on a 20-foot A-frame to hoist logs.

Jobber A contractor who cut wood, using his own crew of men, for a logging company. To work "by the bushel, by the inch, by the mile" was jobbers' slang for measuring out piece-work on a job.

Kerf   The slit in a tree trunk made by a saw.

Key log   The log that river drivers had to pry or blast free to loosen a log jam.

Landing   Site by lake or river where the sleighs dumped logs for the spring drive. Often logs were dumped right onto the ice.

Lidgerwood Skidder   Best known of the powerful skidding engines; developed from the donkey engine. Some had three sets of engines, half a dozen drums, and weighed 200 tons.

Logger   Generic name for bush workers anywhere but applied specifically to west coast timber workers.

Logger's smallpox   Scars caused by fights between loggers wearing calked boots.

Logging chance   An area laid out for a season's logging operation.

Logging sleigh   Two sleds attached one behind the other and topped with timber "bunks" for hauling logs from skidways to the river.

Logging wheel   Two 10-foot wheels with an axle between them, used for dragging logs. Sulky. Arch.

Lumberer   Early 19th century name for logger.

Lumberjack   Any worker in an eastern lumber or pulpwood camp.

Lumberman   Owner of a logging business. (Quebec: *bourgeois*.)

Mackinaw   Heavy woollen cloth used for loggers' shirts, jackets, and pants, first made by Hudson's Bay Company in 1812.

Main road   Cut from the bush with double-bitted axes and grub-hoes and used by logging sleighs once snow and ice had made it firm and smooth.

Muzzle loader   Old-fashioned bunk whose only entrance was a narrow opening at the end.

Peavey   Invented in 1858 by Joseph Peavey of Maine, it had a swinging hook, like one-half of a pair of ice tongs, attached to a long stock with a spike in the end. Similar to a cant-hook, which had a blunt toe instead of a spike.

Pigsfoot   Iron, claw-like hook attached to a "bull rope" to steady a log being loaded.

Pike pole   Twelve- to sixteen-foot pole with a pike or a gaff on the end for prodding logs in the water. A shorter four-foot version for pulpwood was the picaroon.

Pointer   Light, sharp-ended rowboat on river drives.

Poll axe   Single-bitted felling axe with flat poll, or head.

Pulaski tool   Combined axe and hoe for fighting fires, named in 1910 for Edward C. Pulaski, an Idaho fire ranger.

Pulp hook   Short hook shaped like a sharpened question mark, with hand grip for handling four-foot pulpwood.

Raftsmen   Shantymen who crewed square timber rafts down the Ottawa and the St. Lawrence to the market at Quebec City in the 1800s.

Rigging slinger   Chief of the chokermen who hooked logs to the west coast power logging systems.

Robertson raft   The first successful raft for towing large quantities of logs, devised by Hugh Robertson of Saint John, New Brunswick, in the 1880s.

Rolling dam   Used to raise water and store it for use on the log drive. It had a low threshold so that logs could be rolled over it.

Rosser   The square timber man who peeled bark from a trunk before a tree was marked out for squaring.

Run   To "tough the run," or "route," meant staying on the job from autumn to spring, formerly the time period of logging in the east. B.C. loggers tended to work all year around as do loggers in modern eastern camps.

Sand hill   Hilly sections of a log haul road spread with sand to brake heavy sleighs.

Sawlog   Generally 12 to 18 feet long, cut for a lumber mill.

Scaler   The man who measured, for government or company, the volume of cut, merchantable wood. Culler.

Scorer   Square timber maker who notched out rough dimensions of a log so that the hewer could square it.

Sender   One of the loading crew who guided logs up the skidway pile.

Shacker   In Ontario a small sub-contractor, often Finnish or Swedish.

Shantyman   Nineteenth century lumberjack who lived in a shanty camp of logs, with cambuse fire in the middle of the floor for cooking and heating. The cambuse was replaced by stoves in the late 1800s.

Shoepack   Cowhide boots with moccasin soles worn by early loggers before the appearance of spiked boots and, later, lumbermen's rubbers. Larrigans. (Quebec: *bottes sauvages*.)

Skidder   Powerful version of the early donkey engine, sometimes weighing 200 tons and used for hauling wood from the bush in B.C.. The Lidgerwood was the best known.

Skidding   Hauling logs for short distances with oxen, horses, or mechanical means. Yarding.

Skidway   Logs piled beside the main haul road during the eastern cutting season to await the winter sleigh haul.

Skid road   A bush trail embedded with logs, like a railway without rails, over which heavy logs were hauled by oxen, horses, and steam donkey engines into B.C. mills. Since such roads led right into west coast towns the areas where loggers congregated became known as skid roads. Corduroy road in the east.

Skyline   The most spectacular system of B.C. power logging, with cable rigged like a giant's clothes-line from spar tree to spar tree to hoist great timber out of the bush and whizz it into a pile at 20 miles an hour.

Slash   Branches, bark, and chips lying in the woods after logging.

Snoose   Damp Copenhagen snuff for chewing. "To give her snoose" in B.C. meant to increase power.

Snye   Backwater or side channel on a stream or river.

Splash dam   It stored water during the spring run-off for use in washing logs down shallow streams.

Springboard   Iron-tipped board, wedged into the notch cut in a big tree in B.C., which served as a platform for the cutters.

Square timber   Long logs, usually of white or red pine or oak, hewed square with the broad-axe in the 19th century for export to Britain where it was sawed into planks or used as "dimension," or construction timber. A "ton," or "load," of square timber was a "stick" hewed roughly 12 inches square and 40 feet long.

Stick   A piece of square timber.

Strip   An area, usually 22 yards wide, marked out by foreman or strip boss, where a piece-work cutter felled and stacked his pile, or cord cradle, of pulpwood.

Swage set   Used by a professional saw filer to cause the teeth of a crosscut saw to flare out so that the saw made a cut somewhat wider than the width of the back of the blade. This kept the saw from binding.

Swamper   Unskilled lumberjack who cut, or swamped, hauling roads and skidding trails.

Sweep   To follow a log drive downstream in a pointer boat, salvaging logs snagged on the banks after the main drive had passed.

Timberbeast   A name loggers sometimes called themselves.

Timber mark   Registered symbol stamped with a hammer into the end of a log to identify the owner.

Tin pants Waterproof pants worn with similar coats and hats in the B.C. rain forests.

Tote road Rough bush trail for portaging supplies to camp.

Traîneau Quebec sleigh hauled by one horse.

Turkey Home-made duffle bag, often an old flour sack, containing a lumberjack's belongings. (Quebec: *poche de butin.*)

Turn Several logs chained together on B.C. skid roads.

Van Rudimentary store which dispensed clothing, tobacco, and odds and ends to men in camp. *Wangan.*

Walking Boss Superintendent in charge of several camps which he usually visited on foot. Bull of the Woods. "Agent" on the Ottawa.

Waney timber Similar to square timber but edges left rounded in natural curve or wane.

Wangan From an Algonquin word for "container of odds and ends." In lumber camps a wooden chest or, later, shelves from which the camp clerk sold clothes and tobacco and liniment. On river drives the *wangan* boat was the cook boat. Van.

Water tender Rough plank tank mounted on a sleigh for spraying the roads to form an ice surface for the logging sleighs.

Whiskey Jack The crestless Canada Jay, also called Lumberjack because it was believed to be the soul of a dead logger.

Whistle punk He transmitted signals from the hook tender or rigging slinger in the bush to the operator of the donkey engine.

White water man River driver who guided logs down rapids and broke jams.

Widow-maker Broken limb hanging loose in a tree.

Yarding Hauling logs short distances from stump to log pile. Skidding.

REFERENCES

Andrews, Ralph W. *Glory Days of Logging*. Seattle: Superior, 1956.

Bapti, Sue. *First Growth, The Story of British Columbia Forest Products, Ltd.* Vancouver: J. J. Douglas Ltd., 1975.

Beck, Earl Clifton. *Lore of the Lumber Camps*. University of Michigan Press, 1948.

Bell, Dr. Robert. *Geographical Distribution of Forest Trees in Canada*. Toronto, 1897.

Bergren, Myrtle. *Tough Timber*. Toronto: Progress Books, 1966.

Bigsby, John J. *The Shoe and the Canoe*. London, 1850.

Bradwin, Edmund W. *The Bunkhouse Man: A Study of Work and Pay in the Camps of Canada, 1903-04*. New York: Columbia University Press, 1928.

Brennan, Terence. *Lumbering in the Ottawa Valley*. Ottawa: National Museum of Man, 1974.

Bryant, Ralph Clement. *Logging*. New York: John Wiley and Sons, 1913.

Calvin, Delano Dexter. *A Saga of the St. Lawrence*. Toronto: Ryerson, 1945.

Canada Lumberman. Toronto, 1880– . (Now published as *Canadian Forest Industries Magazine*.)

Cape Breton's Magazine. Wreck Cove, Nova Scotia.

Connor, Ralph. *The Man from Glengarry*. Toronto: Revel, 1901.

Cooney, Robert. *A Comprehensive History of the Northern Part of the Province of New Brunswick*. Halifax, 1832.

Cross, Michael S. "The Shiner's War," *Canadian Historical Review*, Vol. 54, March 1973.

Davidson, W. H. *Historical Studies*. Saint John: New Brunswick Museum, 1947.

Defebaugh, James E. *History of the Lumber Industry of America*. 2 vols. Chicago: American Lumberman, 1907.

Dixon, L. B. "Birth of the Lumber Industry in British Columbia." *British Columbia Lumberman*, Nov.-Dec. 1955, Jan.-Sept. 1956.

Doerflinger, William. *Shantymen and Shantyboys*. New York: Macmillan, 1951.

Dupin, Pierre (Télesphore Giroux). *Les Anciens Chantiers du St. Maurice*. Trois-Rivières: Bien Public, 1953.

Fowke, Edith. *Lumber Songs from the North Woods*. Austin: University of Texas Press, 1970.

Fraser, Joshua. *Shanty, Forest and River Life in the Backwoods of Canada*. Montreal: J. Lovell and Sons, 1883.

Fraser, W. *The Emigrant's Guide*, or *Sketches of Canada*. 1867.

Gillis, Sandra J. *The Timber Trade in the Ottawa Valley, 1806-54*. MS Report 153. Ottawa: National Historic Parks and Sites.

Grainger, M. Allerdale. *Woodsmen of the West*. 1908. Reprint. Toronto: McClelland and Stewart, 1964.

Grant, G. M. *Picturesque Canada*. 2 vols. Toronto: Belden Bros., 1879.

Hughson, John W., and Bond, C. J. *Hurling Down the Pine*. Old Chelsea, Quebec: Historical Society of the Gatineau, 1964.

I.W.A. in British Columbia. Issued at Vancouver by Western Regional Council No. 1, International Woodworkers of America, 1971.

Journal of Forest History. Quarterly. Santa Cruz, California.

Kauffmann, Carl. *Logging Days in Blind River*. Blind River, Ont., 1970. (Published by the author.)

Keefer, Thomas C. *The Ottawa*. Montreal: J. Lovell, 1854.

Koroleff, Alexander. 1941. *Pulpwood Cutting.*

———. 1943a. *Pulpwood Hauling with Horse and Sleigh.*

———. 1943b. *Pulpwood Skidding with Horses.*

———. 1946. *River Drive of Pulpwood.* Montreal: Woodlands Section, Canadian Pulp and Paper Association.

Lafleur, Normand. *La Drave en Mauricie.* Trois-Rivières: Editions du Bien Public, 1970.

Lambert, R. S., and Pross, P. *Renewing Nature's Wealth.* Toronto: Dept. of Lands and Forests, 1967.

Langton, John. *Early Days in Upper Canada.* Toronto: Macmillan, 1926.

Laughead, W. B. *The Marvelous Exploits of Paul Bunyan.* Minneapolis: The Red River Lumber Co., 1922.

Le Moine, Sir James M. *Annals of the Port of Quebec.* Quebec, 1901.

Lower, A. R. M. *The North American Assault on the Canadian Forest.* Toronto: Ryerson, 1938.

———. *Great Britain's Woodyard, British America and the Timber Trade 1763-1867.* Montreal: McGill-Queen's University Press, 1973.

MacDonald, J. E. *Shantymen and Sodbusters.* Thessalon, Ont., 1966. (Published by the author.)

Manny, Louise, and Wilson, James Reginald. *Songs of Miramichi.* Fredericton: Brunswick Press, 1970.

McGregor, John. *British America.* 2 vols. Edinburgh: W. Blackwood, 1832.

MacTaggart, John. *Three Years in Canada, 1826-7-8.* 2 vols. London: Colborn, 1829.

Montpetit, A. N. *Nos Hommes Forts.* Quebec, 1884.

Picken, Andrew. *The Canadas.* London: Wilson, 1836.

Pulp and Paper Magazine of Canada. Montreal, 1903– .

Springer, John S. *Forest Life and Forest Trees, Lumbering on the various rivers of Maine and New Brunswick.* New York: Harper and Bros., 1851.

Strickland, Samuel. *Twenty-five years in Canada West.* 2 vols. London: R. Bently, 1852.

Sulte, Benjamin. *Histoire de Jos. Montferrand: Mélange Historique.* Montreal, 1912.

Swanson, R. E. *A History of Railroad Logging.* Victoria: Queen's Printer, 1960.

Taché, J. C. *Forestiers et voyageurs.* Montreal, 1863. Fides, 1946.

Tessier, Albert. *Jean Crête et la Mauricie.* Trois-Rivières: Bien Public, 1956.

Thompson, Capt. George S. *Up to Date, or the Life of a Lumberman.* Peterborough, Ont., 1895.

Thomson, J. W. *Lumbering on the Rivière du Lièvre, A saga of Maclaren's and Buckingham.* Ottawa: privately, 1973.

Trower, Peter. *Between the Sky and the Splinters.* B.C.: Harbour Publishing, 1974.

Whitton, Charlotte. *A Hundred Years A-Fellin', The Story of the Gillies on the Ottawa.* Ottawa: Runge, 1943.

Withrow, H. W. *Our Country, Scenic and Descriptive.* Toronto, 1899.

INDEX

315

ABOUT THE AUTHOR

Donald MacKay spent twenty-five years as a journalist in Canada, Europe and Asia, before returning to full-time authorship in 1975. Since then he has had ten books published, including:

The Lumberjacks (1978) McGraw-Hill,
Anticosti, The Untamed Island (in English and French 1979) McGraw-Hill,
Scotland Farewell (1980) McGraw-Hill; (1996) 2nd printing Natural Heritage Books; (1998) 3rd printing Natural Heritage Books,
Empire of Wood (1982) Douglas & McIntyre,
Heritage Lost, The Crisis in Canada's Forests (English and French 1983) MacMillan,
The Asian Dream (1986) Douglas & McIntyre,
The Square Mile, Merchant Princes of Montreal (1987) Douglas & McIntyre,
Flight from Famine, The Coming of the Irish to Canada (1990) McClelland & Stewart,
The People's Railway, a History of Canadian National (English and French 1992) Douglas & McIntyre,
Train Country (1993) Douglas & McIntyre.

Flight from Famine was winner of the QSPELL award (Quebec Society for the Promotion of English Language Literature).
The Lumberjacks was a Book-of-the-Month Club selection and, like *Scotland Farewell*, runnerup for the Governor General's award.